A SOURCEBOOK ON
NATURALIST THEATRE

A Sourcebook on Naturalist Theatre provides essential primary sources which document one of the key movements in modern theatre. Christopher Innes has selected three writers to exemplify the movement, and six plays in particular:

- Henrik Ibsen – *A Doll's House* and *Hedda Gabler*
- Anton Chekhov – *The Seagull* and *The Cherry Orchard*
- George Bernard Shaw – *Mrs Warren's Profession* and *Heartbreak House*

Innes' illuminating introduction provides a fascinating overview of naturalist theatre. Key themes include:

- the representation of women
- significant contemporary issues
- the links between theory, playwriting and stage practice
- the use of ideas as the basis for action and character.

The primary sources explore many aspects of Naturalism, among them:

- the dramatists' aims
- the first staging of each play
- public reception.

This is a must-have volume for all students studying theatre.

Christopher Innes is Distinguished Research Professor at York University, Toronto. Among his recent books are *Modern British Drama: 1890–1990* and *Avant Garde Theatre: 1892–1992*.

A SOURCEBOOK ON NATURALIST THEATRE

Edited and introduced by
Christopher Innes

London and New York

First published 2000 by Routledge
2 Park Square, Milton Park, Abingdon, Oxon OX14 4RN

Simultaneously published in the USA and Canada
by Routledge
270 Madison Ave, New York, NY 10016

Routledge is an imprint of the Taylor & Francis Group

Transferred to Digital Printing 2005

Typeset in Baskerville by RefineCatch Limited, Bungay, Suffolk

British Library Cataloguing in Publication Data
A catalogue record for this book is available from the British Library

Library of Congress Cataloging in Publication Data
Innes, C. D.
A sourcebook on naturalist theatre / Christopher Innes.
p.   cm.
Includes bibliographical references and index.
1. Drama—19th century—History and criticism.   2. Naturalism in
literature.   3. Ibsen, Henrik, 1828–1906—Sources.   4. Chekhov,
Anton Pavlovich, 1860–1904—Sources.   5. Shaw, Bernard, 1856–1950—
Sources.   I. Title.
PN1851.I56   2000
809.2'912—dc21   99–39133
CIP

ISBN 0–415–15228–3 (Hbk)
ISBN 0–415–15229–1 (Pbk)

Printed and bound by Antony Rowe Ltd, Eastbourne

CONTENTS

ILLUSTRATIONS

ACKNOWLEDGEMENTS

I am most grateful to the following publishers for permission to reprint extracts from the works cited below. I should also like to express particular gratitude to the authors who have allowed me to use their work – Albert Bermel, Bernard Dukore, Susan Mason, Anne-Lise Seip, Evert Sprinchorn – and to the family of Laurence Kitchin.

All extracts from the writings of Bernard Shaw are reproduced by permission of The Society of Authors.

Charles Archer, *William Archer*, Allen & Unwin, an imprint of HarperCollins.

Georg Brandes, *Inaugural Lecture*, trans. Evert Sprinchorn. Originally published in *The Theory of the Modern Stage* (ed. Eric Bentley), Penguin, 1968.

Basil Dmytryshyn, *Imperial Russia: A Sourcebook 1700–1917*, Holt, Reinhart, and Winston, 1967, currently being reissued by Academic International Press.

Bernard Dukore, *Bernard Shaw: Director*, Allen & Unwin, 1971.

Elizabeth Hapgood, ed. "Stanislavki's Letters," *Stanislavski's Legacy*, Theatre Arts Books, 1943.

Michael Heim, trans. "Letters of Anton Chekhov," *Anton Chekhov's Life and Thought*, (ed. Simon Karlinsky), Northwestern University Press. Originally published by Harper and Row, 1973.

B.J. Hovde, *The Scandinavian Countries, 1720–1865*, Kennikat Press. Originally published by Cornell University Press, 1943.

Henrik Ibsen, *Ibsen Letters and Speeches*, trans. Evert Sprinchorn, Hill and Wang, 1964.

Henrik Ibsen, "Notes for Hedda Gabler," trans. Evert Sprinchorn, originally published in *Playwrights on Playwriting*, Hill and Wang, 1961.

Laurence Kitchin, *Mid-Century Drama*, Faber and Faber, 1960.

Susan Mason, *Ibsen's Women: The Acting in Early Norwegian Productions*, unpublished Ph.D dissertation, University of Oregon, 1980.

Vsevolod Meyerhold, "Letter," trans. Nora Beeson, *Tulane Drama Review* (25, vol. 9, no. 1).

Anne-Lise Seip, "Culture in the Norwegian Nation-State in the Nineteenth Century," *Scandinavian Journal of History* (1995, vol. 20, no. 1).

ACKNOWLEDGEMENTS

Konstantin Stanislavsky, *My Life in Art*, trans. J.J. Robbins, Penguin, 1967.
Konstantin Stanislavsky, *An Actor Prepares*, trans. Elizabeth Hapgood, Theatre Arts
   Books, 1936.
Émile Zola, *Naturalism in the Theatre*, trans. Albert Bermel. Originally published in
   Theory of the Modern Stage (ed. Eric Bentley), Penguin, 1968.

Photographs come from the collection of John Styan, and from the Raymond
Mander and Joe Mitchenson Theatre Collection – to both of whom I am deeply
grateful. I should also like to thank Allana Lindgren, who acted as my research
assistant on this project.
   The following works are either out of copyright, or could not be tracked down:

Andre Antoine, "Commentary on la mise en scene," trans. Joseph M. Bernstein,
   Directors on Directing. (eds Toby Cole and Helen Chinoy), Bobbs-Merrill, 1953.
S.D. Balukhaty, ed. *The Seagull Produced by Stanislavsky*, trans. David Magarshack,
   Dennis Dobson, 1952.
Constance Garnett, *Chekhov's Letters to Olga Knipper*, Chatto and Windus, 1925.
Emma Goldman, *The Traffic in Women*, Mother Earth Publishing, 1917.
Henrik Ibsen, *The Letters of Henrik Ibsen*, trans. Mary Morrison, Hodder &
   Stoughton, 1905.
Henrik Ibsen, "Notes for a Doll's House," *From Ibsen's Workshop, The Works of
   Henrik Ibsen*, Charles Scribner, 1912.
Vladimir Nemirovich-Denchenko, *My Life in the Russian Theatre*, trans. John
   Cournos, Little Brown & Co, 1936.
Elizabeth Robins, *Ibsen and the Actress*, Hogarth Press, 1928.
Michel St Denis, *Theatre: The Rediscovery of Style*, Heinemann, 1960.
Henri Troyat, *Daily Life in Russia*, trans. Malcolm Barnes, Allen & Unwin, 1961.

1

INTRODUCTION

The aim of this sourcebook is to provide documentation on one of the key movements in modern theatre. Naturalism is not only a historical style, which reached the stage in the last decades of the nineteenth century. It forms the basis for mainstream plays and performances throughout the modern period, and is still the dominant theatrical form today. Indeed, Naturalism introduced a quintessentially modern approach, and defined the qualities of modern drama. Revolutionary in its own time, it has become the standard against which all subsequent stylistic experiments have measured themselves, and therefore deserves particular attention.

One characteristic of modern theatrical movements is a close link between theory, play writing, and stage practice. Theatrical Naturalism, developed from earlier naturalistic novels and preceded by theoretical essays, initiated this trend. Other crucial elements are the serious dramatic treatment of significant contemporary social issues, and the use of ideas as the basis for action and character. Again, both these elements were introduced by Naturalism. In addition, naturalist drama is particularly important in the way it represents women, setting a strikingly contemporary tone.

As a public art, the theatre is even more closely connected to the events and social concerns of its time than other artistic forms. It also reflects technological advances in the mechanics of staging. These general qualities – very much emphasized in theatre throughout the twentieth century – became particularly central to Naturalism, and are highlighted in the documentation. Since all artistic or literary movements are defined by individual works that incorporate their principles, key plays by three of the most important and influential writers have been selected to exemplify naturalist drama. To give a sense of development, two plays have been chosen from each writer's work: his first major naturalistic play, and one from later in his career. This enables us to see the parameters of the movement, as well as exploring specific theatrical events in depth. The documentation focuses on the dramatist's aims with respect to each play, its first staging, and the public reception – as well as illustrating the background, the theoretical basis, and (where relevant) the work of directors or theatre companies closely identified with each.

Unlike other published collections of documents, which are either limited to a single playwright, or reprint statements by a wide range of writers, the focus on three representative playwrights facilitates comparison, while also providing detailed material on individual works. It allows wider stylistic issues to be addressed, and sets the plays in their theatrical and cultural context. The selection of playwrights is also designed to challenge preconceptions.

NOTE ON DOCUMENTATION

This sourcebook contains a wide variety of different kinds of document. There are the theoretical writings and statements of principle. There is the material surrounding the composition, original production, and reception of each play – both written and visual. There are political and social documents from the period. In addition some contemporary sociological or critical analyses have been included, to provide factual material not readily accessible in historical documents.

Like all historical data, the writings themselves vary in documentary status. At one end of the scale are what might be called primary documents: for instance essays that influenced the naturalistic writers, establishing the principles of the movement; political manifestoes; working notes made by a dramatist in composing a play; or promptbooks recording a specific production. However, even these should not be read as wholly objective evidence – promptbooks, for instance, present a single, personal interpretation of a play; and although this itself may have documentary significance (as in the case of Stanislavsky) it might still not correspond to the playwright's concept. Similarly a playwright's letters can clarify authorial intention, but a play may well signify more than its author's concept and change its meaning depending on the context brought to it by spectator or reader. At the other end of the scale are reviews of performances, by definition subjective and seldom representing the general response of the audience – which still have documentary importance to the degree that they mould public opinion. In addition, an element of subjective judgement has necessarily been introduced in editing these documents to bring out the essential points of their authors as clearly as possible.

A further issue that should be taken into account is the nature of translation. Since the roots of the naturalistic movement were in France and Scandinavia, spreading to Germany and Russia, as well as England and America, a large percentage of the documents included were originally written in languages other than English. Even the best translator is likely to miss or substitute nuances. Then too, the longer the time between the original document and the translation, the more the overall tone is likely to have been updated; in general, where a choice of translations exist, the earliest has been preferred.

The nature of the visual documentation is equally variable. Visual documentation from the end of the nineteenth century and the early decades of the twentieth century lacks the degree of authenticity assumed for modern photography. It was not until the mid-1920s that camera speeds were fast enough to record actors in performance, the first example being Basil Dean's spectacular *Hassan* in 1924. Until then actors were required to hold a pose, motionless, for a period – in the 1880s and 1890s – of over a minute. In addition the technical quality of stage lighting made it hard to achieve sharply defined images on film which led in some cases to outlines being inked in on a photograph.

As a result, any photographs relating to early productions of Ibsen's plays are extremely rare. The one of *A Doll's House* is an exception, demonstrating the immediate impact and public importance of the play. More often at this time the only photographs are studio pictures, recording the actor in costume – as with Elizabeth Robins as Hedda Gabler – while visual evidence of the staging is limited to impressionistic (and often highly inaccurate) artists' sketches published in illustrated journals. The increased number of photos available for productions of Chekhov, or for Shaw's *Heartbreak House*, as camera technology advanced is directly reflected here. However, being posed, even the images from 1920 or 1921 cannot necessarily be taken as an accurate representation of acting style. What they do clearly document is blocking (e.g. the notorious bench across the front of stage in *The Seagull*), relationships between the characters/actors, costumes and setting.

THEORETICAL APPROACHES

Definitions

The terms "Naturalism" and "Realism" are particularly ambiguous. As critical labels they are also applied both to a broad category of art in general, and to specific movements in the novel and in drama that may be related, but are by no means identical. In addition, each term tends to be used more imprecisely than other literary or artistic designations, and both have been defined in various competing, even mutually exclusive ways.

In part this is due to their derivation from common words that have themselves gathered a wide set of meanings over time. Indeed, each has one of the longer entries in dictionaries. For instance, (in English, at least) the word "natural" originally related to justice, which was "based upon innate moral feeling; instinctively felt to be right" and evolved into "operating in accordance with the ordinary course of nature". This then acquired connotations of "in a state of nature, without spiritual enlightenment . . . physical existence, as opposed to what is spiritual, intellectual or fictitious . . . formed by nature, not artificial. . . ." (*The Shorter Oxford English Dictionary*, 1973). Thus the word "nature" itself is a variable and highly loaded concept that carries a strong moralistic charge – one that was intensified by the nineteenth-century evolutionary theory of nature established by Darwin.

The focus on external physical existence, as opposed to internal or spiritual experience, is associated with scientific observation, as opposed to a poetic or visionary view. That is to say, the word "nature" – or its derivative, "Naturalism" – inherently expresses a philosophy of existence, and sets up normative assumptions.

"Naturalism" and "Realism" are frequently interpreted in the broadest sense as synonyms, referring to an objective portrayal of daily life that appears true to the spectator or reader's actual experience. The commonly accepted criteria for a realistic work are that it deals with contemporary subjects, presented in a recognizable social context and stressing ordinary details that accurately reflect the way people of the time actually live, without editorializing or external commentary. But, like the common adjectives on which "Naturalism" and "Realism" are based, even this apparently simple formulation is inherently problematic.

The whole notion of "objectivity" in literature is questionable. It implies a statement that is impersonal, therefore generally valid, and factual. Yet all art (even communally produced art) is an individual, frequently very individualistic expression – and to the degree that artists are products of their age, expressing standards set by their social environment, their work is less likely to appear "objective" in a later period. Indeed the benchmark for "truth" – that the depiction corresponds with a public perception of what is "real" – is in fact a conditional and continually changing criterion, a point illustrated (inadvertently) by a critic of the "well-made play":

> In drama as in prose fiction, realism is wanted. Every man judges what is laid before him by his own experience. Resemblance to what he is acquainted with is the measure of excellence.
>
> (*The Era*, 1871)

Qualities seen as "realistic" are also determined by conventions of communication or representation – and these too evolve. As Gordon Craig pointed out, in their own day leading actors such as the Kembles, followed by Edmund Kean, Macready, then Henry Irving, and Antoine, had each successively been hailed as "natural", only for each to be dismissed in turn as "artificial" by the supporters of their successors. This led him to conclude that all were "examples of a new artificiality – the artificiality of naturalism" [*The Art of the Theatre*, 1909]. Alternatively a depiction may be "neutral" in the sense of non-judgmental (another connotation of "objective"), but this is almost always little more than a rhetorical strategy in pursuit of some specific agenda – as with an emphasis on "daily life", which automatically challenges hierarchical views of society privileging the actions of governments and rulers (almost exclusively men).

One method of bypassing such confusions and imprecision is to substitute a more technical word, which escapes the ideological weighting of common usage, as Erich Auerbach has done in borrowing "Mimesis" to describe his study of Realism in Western literature (1946). In his argument, the whole thrust of

European prose writing from the Old Testament to Edmond and Jules de Goncourt, and to Virginia Woolf, is mimetic – even if the concept of "reality" itself takes different forms in successive periods. But, however useful this term "mimesis" may be for categorizing literary types on the widest level, in terms of theatre it is unhelpful. On the stage the physical presence of actors in fictive situations automatically simulates human and social interactions, and by definition acting is imitative. Thus all theatre is "mimetic" to some degree – but what Shakespeare understood by the requirement (voiced through Hamlet) that the stage "Hold the mirror up to Nature" is very different from the aims of nineteenth-century naturalistic playwrights.

More narrowly, the terms "Naturalism" and "Realism" refer to a specific literary and theatrical movement. This emerged in the latter half of the nineteenth century, reaching its high point in the 1880s and 1890s, and was overtaken by other forms in the 1920s – although the general qualities it introduced are still reflected in the dominant mode of drama today. However, even when used in this specific sense there is still a wide divergence in meanings given to the two words. Generally critics attempt to distinguish between Naturalism and Realism, using each as a label for various qualities. For instance:

> Although naturalism in the arts shares the mimetic mode with realism, it takes more explicit cognizance of environment, not merely as a setting but as an element of the action of drama. In an essay on English naturalism [*English Drama: Forms and Development*, 1977] Raymond Williams summarizes: 'In high naturalism the lives of the characters have soaked into their environment . . . Moreover, the environment has soaked into the lives' . . . If the key play of realism is Ibsen's *Ghosts*, that of naturalism is Tolstoi's peasant *Power of Darkness*, forbidden in Russia but played in Paris in 1886.
>
> (*The Cambridge Guide to Theatre*, 1992)

> At one extreme, Zola and his fellow naturalists saw in the teachings of science license to emphasize the sordid and mechanistic aspects of life to the exclusion of all else. Their thinking was shadowed by a somber view of life, which threw a blighting chill of determinism on all human conduct. At the opposite extreme, realists of the Spencer-Fiske persuasion saw in science a buoyantly optimistic assurance of the perfectibility of mankind.
>
> (Theodore W. Hatlen, *Orientation to the Theater*, 1972)

Thus in one standard reference work Ibsen's *Ghosts* is labeled a defining example of Realism – presumably because heredity is the crucial factor – in contrast to the environmental stress in Tolstoi's *Power of Darkness*, which is seen as the essential quality of Naturalism. In the other the distinction is between pessimism and optimism, so that *Ghosts* is classified along with Tolstoi's *Power of Darkness* as a classic instance of Naturalism.

Leaving aside the contradictions, the effect is to subdivide a broad movement, emphasizing a single quality at the expense of other elements. It would seem more helpful – as well as being truer to the historical facts – to understand both "Naturalism" and "Realism" as applying to the movement as a whole. At the same time, taking advantage of the subtle distinction between the two words for greater critical precision, it would be logical to use "Naturalism" to refer to the theoretical basis shared by all the dramatists who formed the movement, and their approach to representing the world. "Realism" could then apply to the intended effect, and the stage techniques associated with it. Thus the same play might be both naturalistic and realistic, with each term describing a different aspect of the work.

The historical context

The primary influences on the naturalistic movement were Darwin's evolutionary theories of biology (*On the Origin of Species*, 1859), Claude Bernard's scientific observation of human physiology (*Introduction à l'étude de la médecine expérimentale*, 1865) and Karl Marx's economic analysis of society (*Das Kapital*, 1867) – plus, somewhat later, Sigmund Freud's work on psychology (*On the Psychical Mechanism of Hysterical Phenomena*, with Charcot, 1893; *The Interpretation of Dreams*, 1900). It also reflected the emergence of materialistic capitalism and the rise of middle-class democracy. There is general agreement that the crucial factors inspiring Naturalism were the perceptions that all life, human as well as animal, is in a process of continual evolution, and that human behavior can be explained through scientific analysis. These new ideas led to the assumption that peoples' character and personality are formed by a combination of heredity and their social environment, plus the value placed on the individual. This meant that ordinary citizens, including workers and the poor (who had traditionally played at best supporting or comic roles in literature, particularly drama) became the protagonists, and attention focussed on the family. Perhaps even more significant though less widely noted, naturalistic drama – which established itself in the 1880s and 1890s – coincided with the early women's movement, the struggle for legal equality and voting rights. It also coincided with a new sense of national identity in Scandinavia, and with the liberation of the serfs in Russia. All this was directly reflected in naturalistic plays.

Although this democratization of literary subject in itself was not new, Naturalism represented a significant change in treatment. From its first development, the novel had dealt with characters drawn from the common population: e.g. Defoe's *Moll Flanders*, Fielding's *Joseph Andrews*, Richardson's *Pamela*. There had also been isolated examples on the eighteenth-century stage – George Lillo's *The London Merchant* (1731), or in Germany Gotthold Lessing's *Miss Sara Sampson* (1755) and in France Denis Diderot's *The Natural Son* (1757, first performed 1771). But the characters in these earlier works are either picaresque (Defoe's prostitute–protagonist; Fielding's virtuous servant, who turns out to be nobly born), sentimental idealizations (Richardson's virginal heroine) and moral exemplars (the "domestic tragedy" of Lillo, Lessing, or Diderot). By contrast, the naturalistic approach is overtly scientific, presenting characters as case studies in human behavior or social problems.

These precursors were followed by others in the first half of the nineteenth century, who gradually built up the technical basis for naturalist drama. Diderot's theories in particular remained influential throughout the period. Attacking the rigid neo-classical division between tragedy and comedy, he called for a "serious genre", which would mix tears and laughter and deal with the conditions of ordinary life. Situations and characters with which the audience could identify would touch their sentiments, creating a moral effect. On a practical level, the development of the "well-made play" by Eugène Scribe was equally significant. His structural principles for introducing and developing interlinked dramatic situations, with a denouement that leads into the next situation, until all strands of the plot are neatly resolved in the conclusion, created an impression of logical coherence. Theatrically effective, this structuring rapidly became codified. It allowed Scribe to produce over 350 plays between 1813 and his death in 1861 – ranging from one-act *vaudevilles* to a new form of historical/political comedy. This explored the idea that great events can be the result of the most trivial incidents, which had the effect of bringing major social issues down to a human scale. Such a perspective was realistic, at least in intention, and his structure offered a basis for early naturalistic dramaturgy.

> The story usually turned upon some secret, of which the audience was aware, but of which the hero knew nothing until the truth was conveniently revealed at the critical moment (not unlike the Greek *anagnorisis* or *recognition*). In the judgement of the critic Francisque Sarcey, this was the *scène à faire*, or *obligatory scene* . . . Indeed, in his preface to *La Haine* [*Hatred*] Sardou confessed that he invented the *scène à faire* first, and then worked out his plot backwards. It is little wonder that characters and situations looked much the same from play to play. Yet it was an immensely successful arrangement, and well into the twentieth century the aspiring playwright could still have found rules for writing a well-made play as laid down by William Archer in his *Play-Making: A Manual of Craftsmanship* (1912) or, in America, by George Pierce Baker, director of the famous workshop at Harvard, in his *Dramatic Technique* (1919).
>
> (J. L. Styan, *Modern Drama in Theory and Practice I*, 1981)

Scribe's "well-made" techniques were widely imitated during the mid-nineteenth century. His plays were staged – and copied – throughout Europe, from England to Norway, where Ibsen staged several Scribean pieces during his early career as artistic director of the Norwegian Theatre in Christiana. The result was to substitute technique for substance. As one contemporary observer commented, describing the most popularly successful play on the French stage in 1875, *Ferréol* by Victorien Sardou, Scribe's most direct successor:

The charm with M. Sardou is not of a very high quality; he makes a play very much as he would a pudding; he has his well-tested recipes and his little stores of sugar and spice, from which he extracts with an unimpassioned hand exactly the proper quantity of each. The pudding is capital, but I can think of no writer of equal talent who puts so little of himself into his writing. Search M. Sardou's plays through and you will not find a trace of personal conviction, of a moral emotion, of an intellectual temperament, of anything that makes the 'atmosphere' of a work. They seem to have been produced in a moral vacuum.

(Henry James, "The Parisian Stage", *New York Tribune*, 29 January 1876)

Two years before Ibsen's first naturalistic play, *The Pillars of Society*, this standardized fare epitomizes the style of drama that the naturalists were reacting against. Indeed, on one level Naturalism was as much an aesthetic revolt as a moral or social revolution. In the words of the most influential naturalistic director, Konstantin Stanislavsky:

The founding of our new Moscow Art and Popular Theatre was in the nature of a revolution. We protested against the customary manner of acting, against theatricality, against bathos, against overacting, against the bad manner of production, against the habitual scenery, against the star system which spoiled the ensemble, against the light and farcical repertoire which was being cultivated on the Russian stage at that time.

(*My Life in Art*, 1926)

However, even among Scribe's followers in France, there were some who also paved the way for change. The most significant of these were Emile Augier, whose exposure of bourgeois hypocrisy and the false moral values of French society in the middle decades of the century was grounded in an extremely detailed depiction of social minutiae; and Dumas *fils*, who focussed on the *Demi-Monde*: the title for one of his plays produced in 1855. Augier wrote his final play – a condemnation of marriages arranged for monetary reasons – in 1878, while Dumas' last important play – which explored marital infidelity – appeared in 1876. Each added elements that were picked up in naturalistic drama, specifically the method of building up a social context for the characters, and the use of social outcasts to condemn a moralistic Establishment.

In addition, in 1873 Émile Zola's play *Thérèse Raquin* (an adaptation of his novel) reached the stage. It traces the adulterous passion of a housewife, which drives her to drown her invalid husband – then, consumed by guilt for the murder, she persuades her lover to join her in a suicide pact. Thérèse is presented as a victim of her background: trapped not only by an unsatisfying, repressive marriage and an impoverished lower middle-class existence, but also by her physical desires and rigid moral principles. However, structurally it still follows the mechanics of the well-made play; and the characters' emotions are portrayed melodramatically, as in the stage direction describing Thérèse's paroxysm of self-accusation for being a murderess:

> She is seized by spasms, totters towards the bed, tries to drag herself up by one of the curtains which she tears away, and comes to rest momentarily leaning against the wall, gasping and dreadful.

Despite these stylistic flaws – which were exacerbated by exaggerated traditional acting of the original performance – *Thérèse Raquin* served as a model for naturalistic playwrights. The play failed on the stage. But its focus on a woman who destroys herself under the pressures of society, and its detailed treatment of psychological struggle become standard features of plays by Ibsen, Strindberg, or Brieux.

In terms of stage presentation a further element was contributed by an English playwright, who had served a long apprenticeship as actor and stage manager: T. W. Robertson. Though in structure his work was also influenced by Scribe, Robertson's own productions of his plays provided meticulously detailed reproductions of Victorian social habits, which won them the label of "cup-and-saucer drama". The most significant of these were *Society* in 1865 and *Caste* in 1867 – titles that embody his characteristic subject, the class system, as well as indicating a proto-naturalistic emphasis on the social group rather than a single protagonist. Robertson's choice of the most ordinary details as dramatic material, in place of overtly theatrical action and the grand gestures of Romantic acting, also helped to lay the groundwork for naturalism. It is well illustrated in the closing act of *Caste*, where the stage directions show precisely why such plays were designated "cup-and-saucer drama":

> POLLY sets tea things . . .
> SAM motions approbation to POLLY, not wanting HAWTREE to remain . . .
> SAM cuts enormous slice of bread, and hands it on point of knife to HAWTREE. Cuts small lump of butter, and hands it on point of knife to HAWTREE, who looks at it through eye-glass, then takes it. SAM then helps himself. POLLY meantime has poured out tea in two cups, and one saucer for SAM, sugars them, and then hands cup and saucer to HAWTREE, who has both hands full. He takes it awkwardly, and places it on table. POLLY, having only one spoon, tastes SAM'S tea, then stirs HAWTREE'S, attracting his attention by doing so. He looks into his tea cup. POLLY stirs her own tea, and drops spoon into HAWTREE's cup, causing it to spurt in his eye. He drops eye-glass and wipes his eyes . . .
> SAM takes tea and sits facing fire.

In addition, over the course of the nineteenth century stage scenery gradually developed from the painted backcloths of Restoration drama to three-dimensional reproductions of interiors and elaborate impressions of natural effects. Initially these were used purely for spectacle: as in Philip de Louther-bourg's staging of a naval review for *Alfred* in 1773, or his transformation scenes and exotic light effects to represent romantic panoramas for *Wonders of Derbyshire* (1779). The first box set was introduced in London around 1830; and by the time of Robertson such scenic possibilities had become sufficiently familiar not to attract exclusive attention to themselves, and were being used to create a credible physical context for dramatic characters.

The next step was taken by the court theatre of the small German state of Saxe-Meiningen, under the artistic direction of its duke whose enthusiasm for Charles Kean's historically accurate stagings of Shakespeare in the 1850s led him to develop an ensemble dedicated to archeologically authentic productions. To reinforce the detailed reproduction of real places – classical Rome for *Julius Caesar* (with the assassination moved from Shakespeare's setting of the Capitol to its actual historic location at the Curia of Pompey); Domrémy for Schiller's *The Maid of Orleans* – any symmetry was avoided in the placing of his actors, and all supernumeraries in crowd scenes were individualized. Each production was pre-pared in meticulous detail and extensively rehearsed (in costume and with full sets in order to make the performers so familiar with their dramatic environment that they would appear to "live" in it); and the Meiningen Company gained an instant reputation with its first German tour in 1874. They also toured widely through Europe up to 1890, creating new standards of authenticity for the stage – even if this was largely limited to pictorial effect. Their productions were seen by Ibsen in Berlin – when they performed his early heroic play *The Pretenders* in 1876 – and by Shaw in London in 1881. Antoine was deeply impressed by the Meiningen hand-ling of crowd scenes and rehearsal techniques, spending time with the Company in Brussels in 1888. Stanislavsky saw their productions in St. Petersburg in 1885 and Moscow in 1890, trained with the Company for a year, and was particularly influenced by their archeological accuracy in staging historical plays.

Over the same period stage lighting, which had been limited solely to candles and oil lamps since the earliest indoor theatres, changed radically – from gas lights (demonstrated in 1803, and first introduced in Philadelphia in 1816 and in London in 1817), to limelight (invented in 1826, and initially used for a Covent Garden pantomime in 1837), and then electric lighting in 1881. With gas light, as with candles, the lighting was general, although it could to some extent be focussed by reflectors, most effectively in footlights along the front edge of the stage. But with gas the light was whiter, approximating more closely to natural daylight, and could be regulated for gradations of brightness. Limelight – using a block of quicklime heated by an oxygen flame – created an intense source of brightness that made it possible to use as a spotlight, and allowed differently colored light to be produced by shining it through a transparent colored plate. In place of the unnatural shadows thrown by lighting from floor level with foot-lights, light could now be projected from above and used to represent different times of day, or even seasons, as well as the passage of time. Henry Irving, who took control of the London Lyceum Theatre in 1878, was one of the earliest to

10

experiment with contrasts of light and shade – as one anecdote illustrates. Running through the duel scene in a rehearsal for *The Corsican Brothers* (one of the standard Lyceum melodramas), the actor fighting Irving found himself in deep shadow, while Irving's figure was brightly lit, and complained "Don't you think, Guv'nor, a few rays of the moon might fall on me? It shines equally on the just and the unjust" – and in this instance Irving agreed to share the limelight a little. Although these effects were primarily devoted to productions of Shakespeare or melodrama, Irving's lighting deeply impressed André Antoine, who introduced the works of Ibsen into France.

It is worth noting that Henrik Ibsen's first significant naturalistic play, *A Doll's House*, appeared in 1879, six years after Zola's *Thérèse Raquin* and just one year after Augier ceased writing for the stage. It was also twelve years after Robertson's *Caste*, and less than a year after Irving took over the Lyceum. Living at that point in Rome, in 1879 Ibsen would hardly have been aware of Irving's work. But having been stage director at the Bergen Theatre, and from 1857 to 1862 manager of the Norwegian Theatre in Christiana (now Oslo), where Scribe's were among the plays produced, he had practical experience of both the changes in dramatic construction and the new scenic and lighting techniques. In addition Ibsen's involvement with the Meiningen Company in 1876 had exposed him to the possibilities for using authentic detail in the setting. All these inform the sequence of plays initiated by *A Doll's House*. It is hardly coincidental that Ibsen's turn to Naturalism coincided with a significant change in stage practices – a difference that can be measured by the contrast in preparation for two early productions of his naturalistic plays. Following the standard practice for Romantic or Scribean drama, the Royal Theatre in Stockholm allowed just two rehearsals for blocking, eight general rehearsals and one dress rehearsal for *A Doll's House* in 1879. Four years later, in 1883 at the same theatre, *An Enemy of the People* was given a total of 32 rehearsals, twelve of which (reflecting Meiningen practice) were devoted solely to the crowd scene in Act IV.

Acting and character

For Ibsen's naturalistic plays to achieve their full dimension on stage, a new form of acting was required, as well as the integration of all these technical elements into a unified aesthetic. For most of the nineteenth century – particularly in continental Europe – the standard style of acting was histrionic, using codified gestures to display heightened emotion; and the naturalistic rejection of this traditional stage-expression is well-represented by Stanislavky:

> Some of these established cliches have become traditional, and are passed down from generation to generation; as for instance spreading your hand over your heart to express love, or opening your mouth wide to give the idea of death . . .
>
> There are special ways of reciting a role, methods of diction and speech.

11

(For instance, exaggeratedly high or low tones at critical moments in the role, done with specifically theatrical 'tremolo', or with special declamatory vocal embellishments.) There are also methods of physical movement (mechanical actors do not walk, they 'progress' on the stage), for gestures and for action, for plastic motion. There are methods for expressing all human feelings and passions (showing your teeth and rolling your eyes when you are jealous, or covering up the eyes and face with the hands instead of weeping; tearing your hair when in despair) . . .

According to the mechanical actor the object of theatrical speech and plastic movements – as exaggerated sweetness in lyric moments, dull monotone in reading epic poetry, hissing sounds to express hatred, false tears in the voice to represent grief – is to enhance voice, diction and movements, to make actors more beautiful and give more power to their theatrical effectiveness.

Unfortunately . . . in place of nobility a sort of showiness has been created, prettiness in place of beauty, theatrical effect in place of expressiveness.

(*An Actor Prepares*, 1926)

However suited to the Romantic drama of Victor Hugo or Schiller, this was incongruous for naturalistic plays representing the common lives of ordinary people expressed in deliberately unrhetorical dialogue against a detailed and recognizable contemporary background mirroring the middle-class homes of the audience. Indeed, it was the traditional staging and conventional Romantic acting that caused the failure of one early naturalistic piece, Henry Becque's strongly socialistic *Les Corbeaux* (*The Crows*, 1882), and may have contributed to the failure of Zola's *Thérèse Raquin*.

As August Strindberg pointed out in his well-known preface to *Miss Julie*, the way in which the new dramatists perceived people was the opposite of the type of figure expressed in traditional acting:

In real life an action – this, by the way, is a somewhat new discovery – is generally caused by a whole series of motives . . . I see Miss Julie's tragic fate to be the result of many circumstances . . .

I have made my people somewhat 'characterless' for the following reason. In the course of time the word character has assumed manifold meanings. It must have originally signified the dominating trait of the soul complex, and this was confused with temperament. Later it became the middle-class term for the automaton, one whose nature had become fixed or who had adapted himself to a particular role in life . . . while one continuing to develop was called characterless, in a derogatory sense, of course, because he was so hard to catch, classify and keep track of . . .

Because they are modern characters, living in a period of transition more feverishly hysterical than its predecessor at least, I have drawn my figures vacillating, disintegrated, a blend of old and new.

(1888)

Where plot was the dominant element in both melodrama and the well-made plays (which Strindberg and Zola intended to supersede), characterization is the basis of Naturalism – and the ambiguity of motive asserted by Strindberg is also in deliberate contrast to the singular passionate temperament of the earlier Romantic protagonists. This ambiguity is combined with a complex treatment of central figures. Although naturalistic drama may contain explicit moral messages (for instance, Brieux's plays campaigning for birth control, or dealing with the evils of prostitution) and strong social criticism (as in several of Ibsen's plays, including *A Doll's House* or *Ghosts*), the way the characters are portrayed precludes moral judgements. Strindberg is thus typical in describing his theme as "neither exclusively physiological nor psychological. I have not put the blame wholly on the inheritance from her mother, nor on her physical condition at the time, nor on immorality. I have not even preached a moral sermon. . . ." [Preface, *Miss Julie*, 1888].

In fact the primacy of character is one of the defining aspects of Naturalism. From the initial concept to the focus of the audience, naturalistic drama centres on highly individualized and completely realized people. As Ibsen stated:

Before I write a single word, I have to have each character in mind through and through. I must penetrate into the last wrinkle of his soul. I always proceed from the individual; everything else – the stage setting, the dramatic ensemble – comes naturally and does not cause me any worry, as soon as I am certain of the individual in every aspect of his humanity. But I also have to have his exterior in mind down to the last button: how he stands and walks, how he behaves, what his voice sounds like. Then I do not let him go until his fate is fulfilled.

(cit. Rudolph Lothar, *Henrik Ibsen*, 1902)

It was André Antoine, the founder of the Théâtre Libre (Free Theatre) in 1887, who created a theatrical context for such characters, by turning all the earlier scenic developments into the basis for naturalistic staging. Although Antoine was an eclectic director, who also experimented with commedia dell'arte and symbolism, in his first piece he set the tone that was to become identified with Naturalism. This was an adaptation of a short story by Zola, *Jacques Damour*. The (at the time) striking elements of his production were a deliberate simplicity in scenery and, like Robertson, a careful attention to props such as coffee cups and wineglasses. The furniture – borrowed for this first production from his mother's house – was worn with use and solid. This became a guiding principle for his subsequent productions: to transport real-life surroundings onto the stage that would create a recognizable and accurately reproduced environment, as a literal embodiment for the deterministic effect of environment on character. The effect of actuality was enhanced by the intimacy of the tiny theatres in which Antoine staged his Théâtre Libre productions. With an audience right on top of the actors there could be no exaggeration or gloss. Anything conventionally "theatrical" struck false.

13

Initially this scenic simplicity was the result of Antoine's lack of funding. But it became a model for the whole Independent Theatre movement (so-called because a subscription audience freed these theatres to produce "unpopular" or "scandalous" plays) which became the platform for the new naturalistic drama. The Théâtre Libre was followed in Germany by Otto Brahm's Freie Bühne (an exact translation of Antoine's Free Theatre), and in Sweden by August Strindberg's Scandinavian Experimental Theatre, both founded in 1889; John Grein's Independent Theatre in Britain, which opened in 1891 and performed Shaw's first plays; the Irish Literary Theatre (1897) and the Irish Players in Dublin; and Konstantin Stanislavsky's Moscow Art Theatre. It was also the model for the Little Theatre movement in America, which began around 1909, and included the Provincetown Players (1914) associated with Eugene O'Neill's early naturalistic plays. The output of the Théâtre Libre and its successor, the Théâtre Antoine, from 1897 to 1906 was typical of the Little Theatre movement as a whole. It included productions of Ibsen's *Ghosts* (1890) and *The Wild Duck* (1891), Strindberg's *Miss Julie* and Gerhart Hauptmann's *The Weavers* (both 1893) – all of which remained in Antoine's repertoire until 1908 – as well as Tolstoi's *Power of Darkness* (produced in 1878), plays by Eugène Brieux (such as *Maternité*, banned in 1901), and adaptations of Zola, such as *La Terre* (1902).

It is no accident that Antoine's repertory included adaptations of works by Zola and other French novelists, such as the Goncourts. These nineteenth-century developments in the democratization of character, dramatic structuring, and representational staging, were accompanied by advances in the novel that influenced the thematic approach taken by naturalistic playwrights. Just as eighteenth-century novels predated theatre in extending the range of literature to the common people, so Balzac, Flaubert, the Goncourt brothers, and in particular Zola first developed the principles of Naturalism in their novels. Zola also began to develop the theoretical basis for the theatrical movement, through his reviews as a drama critic from 1876–1880. Zola's writings directly influenced Antoine. Zola's reviews were published as two volumes in 1881, with the first being titled *Naturalism in the Theatre*; and it is no coincidence that just over a year later Ibsen wrote renouncing poetic drama in favor of "the straightforward, plain language spoken in real life":

The stage is for dramatic art alone; and declamation is not a dramatic art . . .
Verse has been most injurious to the art of the drama. A true artist of the stage, whose repertoire is the contemporary drama, should not be willing to let a single verse cross her lips. It is improbable that that verse will be employed to any extent worth mentioning in the drama of the future since the aims of the dramatists of the future are almost certain to be incompatible with it. Consequently it is doomed. For art forms become extinct, just as the preposterous animal forms of prehistoric time became extinct when their day was over. . . .

(Letter to Lucie Wolf, 1883)

Conventions and perspectives

The above discussion raises important questions of dramatic convention, and historical perspective. These have to be taken into account in order to evaluate naturalistic drama effectively. It also brings in gender-based issues, which are still more significant because it is here that Naturalism was most revolutionary.

As Ibsen's typically naturalistic evolutionary metaphor in his letter to Lucie Wolf implies, stylistic norms can change radically between one literary period and the next. All art, of course, is based on conventions: rules for representing one thing in terms of another, which are imaginatively accepted by the spectator or reader. For instance an observed landscape or person may be rendered in colored pigment on a flat canvas; and the painting will then be translated by a viewer back into something approximating its original. In general the more mimetic the painting, the closer the shared experience between artist and audience will be – although then any non-mimetic element in the representation is likely to detract from identification, whereas in a more stylized or abstract work subjective distortion is expected and adds to the effect. In other words, the rules vary depending on the artist's aims and choice of style, but the essential quality in any style is internal consistency. However the correspondence between concept and reception is never exact, depending as it does on the individual experience of the spectator.

At the same time, these rules governing representation are continually changing, generally in response to technological or social changes – a classic example being the introduction of perspective in painting during the late Middle Ages. This replaced hierarchical values expressed in making socially or religiously important figures larger in scale, whatever their position within the pictorial frame. However "unnatural" to a later viewer, trained to accept perspective principles, this would have appeared "realistic" to medieval eyes.

Theatrical performance, in which the basis of representation is the human body, has always been to a large degree mimetic. Yet it is still highly conventionalized. At its most fundamental level performance relies on an unstated contract, where the flat and strictly limited area of the stage (with or without visual aids such as scenic backdrops and furnishings) is accepted as an expandable imaginative space standing for a variety of physical locations, and the actors are credited as being people other than themselves. Even such fundamental conventions are culturally specific, and learned – not universal – as Peter Brook discovered when he toured Africa with a group of actors in the 1970s, performing to tribes that had no exposure to Western theatre. Superimposed on these, are other conventions of a stylistic kind. These might include the use of masks, specific types of gesture and facial expression to express the emotional state or moral nature of a character, and (as Ibsen emphasized) dialogue in verse or prose. In each case, however apparently artificial the conventions employed, the key factor is that they are unnoticed by the audience. As techniques of communication, to the extent they draw attention to themselves they distract from what is being communicated, and highlight the artifice of performance. This occurs particularly when the values embodied in particular conventions appear outdated – as with the use of verse, expressing an elevated and idealistic conception of life, which was clearly at odds with the scientific and materialist views of the naturalists.

It becomes easy to see the conventionalized nature of plays from the past. Classical Greek theatre is so clearly stylized that, even in comedy, it is difficult to identify the characters with ordinary people. Shakespeare's drama now appears far more overtly theatrical than it would have done to his Elizabethan audience. By contrast, since Naturalism is still the dominant mode of staging today its conventions are accepted as norms. There are, of course, other contrasting styles that have become common in twentieth-century theatre – most notably Expressionism and the epic theatre pioneered by Bertolt Brecht – which emphasize the artifice of performance. But these gain at least part of their effect from challenging Naturalism. As a norm, naturalistic conventions are in practice invisible. Yet indeed Naturalism is no less "conventional" than any other form of theatre. However close to everyday conversation it may sound, "the straightforward, plain language spoken in real life" is highly structured in any dramatic dialogue. The more closely a stage setting replicates a real place, the more it becomes a fake – and the further it moves away from the actual nature of theatrical performance. Even the most ordinary chair, borrowed from the home of people in exactly the same socioeconomic group as the characters (like the furniture in Antoine's early Théâtre Libre productions), automatically acquires a different signification on the stage, becoming emblematic in being a focus of attention. The familiar irony of the phrase "the illusion of reality" is particularly applicable to naturalistic theatre, since the nearer it approximates reality the more illusory it in fact is.

Theatrical conventions are perhaps less changeable than those of other art forms, because of the economics of performance, which generally require a mass audience and so exert a normative pressure. To some extent this may explain the continued presence of Naturalism on the stage, despite the rapidity of political and technological change in the last decades. However, the lifestyle and social concerns represented in the defining works of Naturalism – the plays of Ibsen and Chekhov, or Shaw – are now almost as distant from us in time as Restoration comedy was for the early naturalists. This presents the issue of historical perspective in an acute, but frequently unrecognized way.

From today's perspective, the key plays of Naturalism are in almost every sense historical. Social circumstances are no longer the same as those they reflect. The burning legal or moral topics that preoccupy their characters have little in common with current concerns. The fashions of clothing they wear are strongly associated with the past – yet, unlike plays from most other eras, they are hardly ever performed in modern-dress productions. In a very real sense, while many have been adapted by modern playwrights or completely rewritten as contemporary versions – for instance *Nora Helmer*, a television version of *A Doll's House* (Werner Fassbinder, 1974), or the film of *Vanya on 42nd Street* (adapted by David Mamet and directed by Louis Malle, 1994) – naturalistic plays do not seem to offer suitable material for updating. This is largely due to the central importance of the relationship between characters and their environment, together with the highly specific details of that social context built into the action. These plays not only have the status of modern classics, they are literally period pieces.

At the same time they are specifically modern in their approach and tone. The language their characters speak (albeit for most naturalist plays in translation) is still so close to contemporary usage that it sounds "normal". The way their dramatic action is structured continues to be used, particularly by Broadway and West End playwrights. While we may perhaps not share the characters' specific concerns, the general subjects explored in many of the plays – such as the position of women in the family, social inequality and economic exploitation, the destructive effect of rigid morality – are still being debated, even if in different terms. The mainly nineteenth-century or Edwardian society and its attitudes, depicted by the naturalists, may appear archaic; but the people who inhabit it are recognizably our near relatives. And this sense of familiarity is heightened by the fact that the plays of Ibsen, Chekhov and Shaw are still being staged today, almost as frequently as Shakespeare's plays.

It is this double vision through which turn-of-the-century Naturalists are perceived – as simultaneously anachronistic and contemporary – that creates problems of historical evaluation. To the extent that these plays are indeed based on accurate observation of society at the time, they can be treated as historical documents. However, there is a fundamental difference between them and the type of "documentary drama" developed by the German director Erwin Piscator and others from the late 1920s to the 1950s. Dealing directly with recent events, docu-drama relies on an impression of total factuality in the material presented, combining filmed scenes with stage action, and actors made up to resemble precisely well-known political figures (as in Piscator's 1927 *Rasputin, the Romanoffs, the War and the People, Who Rose Up Against Them*), or uses unaltered transcripts for dramatic scripts (as with *The Investigation* by Peter Weiss in 1965). Docu-drama is a derivative of Naturalism, extending its environmental principles to make society itself or historical processes the active agent, and reducing individuals to cyphers. By contrast, in naturalistic plays the focus is on a conflict between an individual and his or – more frequently – her environment. And as with the main figures of *A Doll's House* or Shaw's *Mrs Warren's Profession*, these individuals have at least a chance of emerging from this conflict with a conditional victory, liberating themselves from some destructive aspects of their environment. The level of factual reference is equally different. Clearly by the standard of docu-drama both the characters and plots of Ibsen or Chekhov are invented – although some of Shaw's figures are loosely based on composites of real people (as with the "merchant of death", Undershaft, in *Major Barbara*, who contains aspects of the leading arms manufacturers and salesmen in 1905: Nobel, Zaharoff and Krupp). Indeed, both Ibsen and Chekhov emphasized the existence of an underlying poetic vision in their naturalistic plays, while Shaw referred to the "mystic" qualities of *Heartbreak House* – qualities which are the antithesis of docu-drama.

Key themes

What gives naturalistic plays historical status is, in fact, their position in the history of ideas; and paradoxically, it is on this level that they are most contemporary. The challenge to social orthodoxies, which naturalistic playwrights introduced into the theatre, is a characteristic feature of much twentieth-century art and thought. The avoidance of stereotype characters and moral categories – as Shaw put it, "The conflict is not between clear right and wrong; in fact the question which makes [modern drama] interesting is which is the villain and which the hero" – corresponds with the relativistic morality of today. In particular the treatment of women in their plays strikes a modern chord.

From *Thérèse Raquin* on, the number of naturalistic plays with women as their title figures or central characters is striking. These include, most notably: Nora in *A Doll's House*, the title figures of *Hedda Gabler*, Strindberg's *Miss Julie*, and Chekhov's *The Three Sisters*, Nina who identifies herself with *The Seagull*, Blanche in Shaw's *Widowers' Houses*, Mrs. Warren and her daughter, as well as *Candida* and *Major Barbara*, the daughters and fashion models of Granville Barker's *The Madras House* – also Becque's *La Parisienne*, Brieux's *Blanchette*, *The Three Daughters of M. Dupont* and *Maternity*, plus D.H. Lawrence's *The Widowing of Mrs Holroyd* and *The Daughter-in-Law*. The theatrical franchise also extends to female children: Hedvig, the young girl who is the most obvious analogue to *The Wild Duck*, or Galsworthy's teenage title character in *Joy*. Of course there are examples of major female characters in classical and pre-naturalistic drama, from Medea to Lady Macbeth, or Racine's *Andromaque*, *Bérénice* and *Phèdre*, even Scribe's *L'Héritière (The Heiress)* or *Adrienne Lecouvreur*, up to Pinero's *The Second Mrs. Tanqueray* and *The Notorious Mrs. Ebbsmith*. However, these are a distinct minority, and are almost all presented as evil, immoral, or as tragic victims – implicitly condemned, or punished for playing an active male role or for achieving a prominence at odds with the traditional ideals of submissive and self-effacing women. An exception is Restoration comedy (Wycherley's *The Country Wife*, or the three contrasting wives of Edward Ravenscroft's *The London Cuckolds* – but even there the female figures are all (apart from Hellena in Aphra Behn's *The Rover*) type-characters. The naturalistic emphasis on women is something decisively new in theatre. Indeed, it could be seen as even more crucial than the other elements, such as the focus on environment and heredity, or the objective techniques, which Naturalism introduced.

The factor that makes this new is not the number, or even the centrality of female characters, but the way female experience is presented. Their views are given equal weight to those of the men in the plays. Indeed, since in general the women assert themselves in opposition to the male-dominated society ranked against them, their voice predominates. This is doubly significant, given that all the major plays in the naturalist movement were written by men. There are only a bare handful of plays by women over the whole period: *Alan's Wife* (1893) by Florence Bell and Elizabeth Robins, an actress particularly associated with Ibsen's plays including *Hedda Gabler*, which she performed in 1891; Constance Fletcher's

Mrs Lessingham (1894); Dorothy Leighton's *Thyrza Fleming* (also 1894); *Mrs Daintree's Daughter* (1895) by Janet Achurch, the actress who first performed *A Doll's House* in England; Elizabeth Robins' *Votes for Women!* (1906) – and these, mainly unpublished and forgotten, are never revived on the stage. The fact that it was largely male playwrights who voiced female concerns and created the figure of the "new woman" not only reflects the reality of gender inequity in the period, even ironically as an illustration that men felt it right to speak for and define women. It also indicates the intrinsic connection between Naturalism and the movement for female emancipation.

This was obvious to critics at the time, since the outcry when naturalistic drama (particularly Ibsen) first appeared on the stage was as much directed against the "new woman" as against the attack on established morality (of which, indeed, women were the primary victims) . However, the significance, and even the new-ness of this treatment of gender has subsequently become all too easy to overlook. The specific causes for which the playwrights fought and their female characters suffered have been long won. Indeed the first steps predated *A Doll's House.* In Norway, for example, laws had already been passed giving women equal inherit-ance rights (1854) and – for unmarried women – independence from male guard-ians (1863), and the right to work in any trade or profession (1866). It was only much later, after naturalist drama had become the standard form of mainstream theatre, that women were granted the right to vote: 1913 in Norway, 1918 in England. To put this in context it is necessary to remember that until shortly before this working-class men too had been denied voting rights, and that general male suffrage (for men over the age of 25) had only been introduced in Norway in 1898. The five-year gap between Norway and England can also perhaps be seen as a measure of literary influence – with *A Doll's House* only reaching the English stage in 1889, ten years after its first performance in Norway. It is now over 70 years since women gained full legal emancipation in England (1928); and with the battles having moved on to other areas of sexual and economic equality, the naturalist treatment of gender may now seem dated.

However, the 1890s image of the new woman has striking similarities with contemporary feminist concepts. As a recent commentary sums it up:

> She was not so much a person, or even group of people, as a constructed category which expressed metonymically some of the historic challenges being brought to bear in the 1890s on traditional ideas of women, in particu-lar, and gender as a whole. Individuals did not often identify themselves as New Women; and when they were so identified by others, the term seems usually to have been freighted with disparaging meanings, although these meanings were different, or contradictory, even while cohering as a symbol of 'disorder and rebellion' . . . One version of the New Woman defied traditional codes of female beauty, smoking cigarettes and dressing in simple and 'manly' fashion which seemed to complement her discontented mouth and a nose 'too large for feminine beauty' but indicative of intelligence [H. S. Scott

and E. Hall, *Cornhill*, 1894]. New Women were often perceived to be masculine in other ways too, sometimes devoting themselves to a profession or business in preference to the bearing and bringing up of children. This abrogation of a woman's supposed highest duty was perhaps the chief illustration of what one writer described as the New Woman's 'restlessness and discontent with the existing order of things' [H. M. Stutfield, *Blackwoods*, 1895]. Sometimes the New Woman was perceived to be freer in her dealings with men than custom allowed, and at other times a cold and 'apparently sexless' creature who rejected out of hand all relations with men [Stutfield, *Blackwoods*, 1897].

(Kerry Powell, in *The Cambridge Companion to George Bernard Shaw*, 1998)

This figure of the new woman was particularly promoted on the stage, although she also appeared in the novels of Sarah Grand and others. The challenge to gender stereotypes, as well as provocative statements on women's rights, and attacks on sexual inequality are a fundamental basis of theatrical Naturalism. Indeed, the defining moment of naturalistic drama is the slamming of the door, as Nora leaves her husband at the end of *A Doll's House*.

The naturalistic movement

The literary "canon" usually refers to "great works". These have usually gained such a designation through custom (in the sense that they have retained their appeal to a broad readership or audience over the generations), or because they are held to be superior in vision or technique. A work might also enter the canon because it represents a historical period particularly well, or if it epitomizes a specific style. In all cases canonization reflects critical opinion, which has become entrenched through educational practice. Plays or novels designated as great works are selected for studying, which in turn confirms their importance; and the effect is to obscure other works outside the canon. It is a normative process, which in the past has tended to marginalize writing by women or expressing non-European sensibilities. And since most of the critics who set the criteria have been European males, this has recently led to attacks on the canon and the process of canon formation – in particular by feminists and Black American writers. Battle has been joined in the cause of "multiplicity" and "inclusiveness" versus "aesthetic quality" and "standards". Right or wrong, the challenge is useful in forcing us to question conventional criteria and re-evaluate our approach to literature.

The same process of selection also occurs on a more specialized level. Critical labels (such as Naturalism, Symbolism, Expressionism) refer to ways of seeing the world, or styles of representing what is seen; and literary movements are defined and delimited by the correspondence of particular works to the way these labels have been interpreted. These too then become a canon against which other works are measured, and canon formation is intrinsically exclusive. No matter whether the artist might have seen his own work as part of a movement, if it does not appear to fit the way a category has subsequently become defined, then it is omitted. At the same time, where works that are indeed considered part of the movement contain other elements, then these tend to be ignored. The effect is doubly distorting. It both narrows down the usage of a critical label, and obscures the real nature of the works it is used to describe.

This is as true of theatrical Naturalism as it is of the overarching literary canon. Ibsen's plays from *The Pillars of Society* in 1887 and *A Doll's House* in 1879 through *Ghosts* and *An Enemy of the People* to *The Wild Duck* in 1884 and *Rosmersholm* in 1886 are accepted as major texts of Naturalism (with some critical reservations about the last two). However, his later drama – sometimes including *Hedda Gabler* – is excluded due to its perceived "non-naturalistic" elements. Just two of Strindberg's plays are held to qualify: *The Father* and *Miss Julie* (1881 and 1888). Similarly only Chekhov's last four plays, from *The Seagull* (1896) to *The Cherry Orchard* (1904) are generally seen as true examples of Naturalism – a perspective largely determined by their interpretation in Stanislavsky's productions. The other major figure in the canon of Naturalism is the German dramatist Gerhart Hauptmann. A number of Hauptmann's plays from *Before Dawn* (his first play in 1889) to *Rose Bernd* in 1903 are clearly influenced by Zola's theoretical writings and follow directly in Ibsen's footsteps – although much of his work is eclectic, including neo-Romantic allegory and poetic fantasy. Other single plays by various dramatists are also generally identified with Naturalism. These include Zola's proto-naturalistic *Thérèse Raquin* (1873), Tolstoi's *The Power of Darkness* (written in 1886, and banned in Russia until 1895), Maksim Gorky's *The Lower Depths* (1902), and D.H. Lawrence's working-class plays (1906–12, though none were performed until 20 years later), as well as O'Neill's early, semi-autobiographical sea-plays such as *Bound East for Cardiff* (1915–18). The dates of such plays, covering 45 years over the turn of the century, are usually taken as the limits of the movement proper, with its high point between 1881 and 1904 – although there are numerous later examples indicating the continuing influence of Naturalism, for instance O'Neill's *Long Day's Journey into Night* (1939–41).

One of the best ways of defining a literary movement is through shared sources and influences; and these are particularly clear with Naturalism. In addition to the directors and actors who (as already mentioned) were influenced by Antoine, connections among the dramatists are equally direct, leading back to Zola, whose writings also determined Antoine's theatrical approach, and to Ibsen. Chekhov's major connections were through naturalistic novelists such as Flaubert and Maupassant. However, he was certainly aware of Zola's theories, and one of his letters refers to *Thérèse Raquin* as "not a bad play", while one of his later letters paid distinctive tribute to Ibsen:

As I am soon coming to Moscow, please keep a ticket for me for 'The Pillars of Society'. I want to see the marvellous Norwegian acting, and I will even pay for my seat. You know Ibsen is my favorite writer. . . .

(7 November 1903)

Indeed the new approach pioneered by Ibsen directly influenced the change in Chekhov's drama marked by *The Seagull* (which was initially attacked for its "Ibsenism"), and having read Strindberg's *Miss Julie* some years earlier, he enthusiastically sent a new Russian translation of the play to Gorky in 1899. Strindberg, who specifically claimed to be following Zola, wrote his naturalistic plays in conscious opposition to Ibsen; and it was O'Neill's reading of Strindberg that (as he stated in his Nobel Prize acceptance speech) "first gave me the vision of what modern drama could be, and first inspired me to write for the theatre myself". In addition O'Neill's late play, *The Iceman Cometh* (1939) is an obvious rewriting of Gorky's *The Lower Depths* (1902), which in turn derived from one of Chekhov's early censored one-act plays, *On the High Road* (1885). Shaw too was explicitly influenced by Ibsen, following the dramatic principles he had analyzed in *The Quintessence of Ibsenism* (1890 and 1891), while Hauptman's *Lonely Lives* (1891) is obviously inspired by Ibsen's *Rosmersholm*.

The connections are equally clear in the work of directors associated with Naturalism. It was Otto Brahm's enthusiasm for Ibsen's plays that led him to found the Freie Bühne in Berlin, where his repertoire between 1899 and 1904 focussed specifically on Ibsen and Hauptmann, as well as including plays by Shaw. Over exactly the same five-year period Stanislavsky focussed on productions of Ibsen, as well as Chekhov and Gorky – who corresponded with Chekhov and used his plays as a model – and both Chekhov and Gorky remained in the Moscow Art Theatre repertoire until 1917.

However, limiting Naturalism to the era before 1920 gives an inaccurate picture. Naturalism is not simply an historical phenomenon. Although today there are competing forms of theatre (as indeed there were during the period from 1873 to 1906 when melodrama continued to hold the stage, and the Symbolist movement was also at its height with poetic mood plays by Maeterlinck, Hofmannsthal and W.B. Yeats), on a more general level the influence of Naturalism still pervades Western theatre. Arthur Miller, for instance, modeled his first play, *All My Sons* (1947), on Ibsen, and adapted *An Enemy of the People* (1950) as part of the preparatory work for *The Crucible*. Ibsen's techniques of dramatic construction, together with naturalistic settings that reproduce a physical environment in careful detail form the standard for mainstream plays and productions. And perhaps the most dominant theory of acting is still Stanislavsky's system, which he expounded in *An Actor Prepares* (first translated into English, 1936). This was promoted in particular by the Actor's Studio in New York under Lee Strasberg, who joined the Studio in 1949 and as its artistic director from 1951 to 1982 directly influenced several generations of leading actors. The Stanislavsky system gave rise to the whole school of "Method acting", epitomized by Marlon Brando, which has been called the quintessential American style.

Questioning the canon

If the generally accepted historical boundaries of the naturalistic movement are questionable, the usual canonical selection of playwrights is no less tendentious. The playwrights whose work is presented as representative of Naturalism are primarily the trio of Ibsen, Strindberg and Chekhov. Yet only a small fraction of Strindberg's work is in any way naturalistic: just two plays; and those rely heavily on non-naturalistic elements. Conversely, although one of his early plays, *Mrs Warren's Profession*, may be occasionally listed as "naturalistic", Bernard Shaw – the other major playwright of the period – is always excluded. Rather than being taken as evidence that Shaw is in the same camp as Ibsen, *The Quintessence of Ibsenism* tends to be seen as idiosyncratic (though in fact it is far less so than Strindberg's interpretation of Zola) to the point that it revises Ibsen into the basis for a very different form of – specifically Shavian – drama. At the same time Shaw's characteristic comic tone seems, according to conventional definitions of Naturalism, the antithesis of the naturalistic approach. So too does the intellectual articulacy and musical structure of his dialogue, as well as his use of paradox, and his preference for emphatic acting, all of which have overtones of artificiality. In addition, Shaw's output – like Hauptmann's – is eclectic. It would certainly be difficult to classify his 1903 *Man and Superman* as naturalistic, with its central act being a dream sequence set in Hell and involving symbolic figures; and after 1920 his later work alternates between historical chronicles and fantasy.

Yet Shaw was directly involved in the naturalistic movement. Together with the critic William Archer (who collaborated on Shaw's first play, *Widowers' Houses*) he was instrumental in introducing Ibsen to the English stage. Like Zola, in his profession as a drama reviewer during the 1890s Shaw promoted the new naturalistic plays, and attacked traditional drama for its romantic idealization and conventionalized morality. He admired Brieux, and wrote a preface for a collection of Brieux's plays. He subtitled one of his plays, *Heartbreak House*, as "in the Russian manner" – in other words, following Chekhov. In fact his expanded lecture on *The Quintessence of Ibsenism* offers remarkably acute insights into Ibsen's dramatic methods: the substitution of discussion for a traditionally melodramatic climax; the successive undercutting of false moral positions within a play; the social radicalism and the presence of a "definite thesis" in Ibsens' work. It is certainly true that in this extended essay Shaw is also highlighting qualities that became his own dramatic principles – but the very extent to which this is so underlines that his aims were essentially naturalistic. It is easy to find passages in his writings where he seems to reject some of the defining qualities of Naturalism. For instance:

> For [William Archer] there is illusion in the theatre: for me there is none. I can make imaginary assumptions readily enough; but for me the play is not the thing, but its thought, its purpose, its feeling and its execution . . . In these criticisms by Mr Archer . . . he still makes the congruity of the artist's performance with the illusion of the story his criterion of excellence in the acting . . . To

him acting, like scene-painting, is merely a means to an end, that end being to enable him to make believe. To me a play is only the means, the end being the expression of feeling by the arts of the actor, the poet, the musician.

(*Our Theatres in the Nineties*, 1895)

Or his rejection of verisimilitude (the accurate reproduction of actual social conditions) in favor of veracity (philosophical truth):

It is the business of the stage to make its figures more intelligible to themselves than they would be in real life; for by no other means can they be made intelligible to the audience . . . All I claim is that by this inevitable sacrifice of verisimilitude I have secured in the only possible way sufficient veracity to justify me in claiming that as far as I can gather from the available documentation, and from such powers of divination as I possess, the things I represent these . . . exponents of the drama as saying are the things they actually would have said if they had known what they were really doing.

(Preface to *Saint Joan*, 1924)

Yet over half the full-length plays Shaw wrote between 1892 and 1919 – 14 out of 25 – were placed in recognizable contemporary settings, while others set in the past were historically accurate. Indeed Stanislavsky, generally considered an epitome of Naturalism, made exactly the same distinction between authenticity and verisimilitude:

Like all revolutionaries we broke the old and exaggerated the value of the new . . .
    Those who think that we sought for naturalism on the stage are mistaken. We never leaned towards such a principle. Always, then as well as now, we sought for inner truth, for the truth of feeling and experience, but as spiritual technique was only in its embryo stage among the actors of our company, we . . . fell now and then into an outward and coarse naturalism.

(*My Life in Art*, 1926)

Shaw's plays do indeed have an overtly theatrical quality. They frequently build on the most conventional types of nineteenth-century drama, such as the military melodrama (*Arms and the Man; Caesar and Cleopatra*) or domestic and romantic comedy (*Candida; Pygmalion*), although they reverse the model in order to discredit its underlying assumptions about human behavior. His emphasis is indeed comic, which means that the action is structured by literary, rather than realistic needs. There is a clearly discernible thesis in his plays, which of course means that his approach cannot be completely neutral or objective. The underpinning – and even, in *Heartbreak House*, the surface tone – is usually symbolic.

None of these qualities (at least in theory) are "naturalistic". However, ruling

24

them out has effectively distorted Naturalism. In addition to imposing arbitrary limits on the movement, it disguises central elements in the plays that are assigned to the naturalistic canon.

Like Shaw, some of Ibsen's plays copy traditional dramatic models to reject them – most obviously *A Doll's House*, which incorporates clear elements of Scribean domestic melodrama. Chekhov specifically subtitled both *The Seagull* and *The Cherry Orchard* as "comedy"; and there are extensively comic, even farcical, sequences in both these and his other plays – although (as Chekhov complained) Stanislavsky's strictly limited view of Naturalism turned them into tragic expressions of "blank despondency". There are clearly discernable theses about society and sexual relations in Strindberg's naturalistic plays (as well as in Ibsen). In addition, almost all naturalistic dramatists in fact use symbolic elements as key devices to communicate wider meanings.

Given its poetic basis, implying an idealized and interior depiction of human activity, symbolism is generally seen as the opposite of Naturalism. However – more obviously even than in Shaw – the major plays of the naturalistic canon are structured around symbols, and their central importance is demonstrated by the frequency with which these controlling symbols appear in the titles. Examples are Ibsen's *A Doll's House*, which also includes a highly symbolic dance, the tarantella; *The Wild Duck*, in which extreme near-sightedness also becomes deeply symbolic; and *Ghosts*, with its symbolic use of light (the burning orphanage, dawn) and darkness – or Chekhov's *The Seagull*; and *The Cherry Orchard*, which also introduces heavily symbolic sounds (a breaking string, the thud of axes). Symbolism is equally prominent, even plays where the title is naturalistically neutral, referring to the name of the major character. Ibsen's *Hedda Gabler* and Strindberg's *Miss Julie* both revolve around heavily loaded objects, which take on symbolic significance: for instance, the General's portrait and pistols, the Count's boots and razor. Chekhov's *Uncle Vanya* includes a Helen of Troy figure and a "wood demon" (the title for an earlier version of the play).

At best, viewing these plays through the lens of strict naturalistic theory downplays such elements. At worst, it distorts the plays by ignoring them. The way the theory of Naturalism has been generally applied creates equal difficulties for more sensitive commentators, who recognize the presence of these elements but are unable to categorize them. In these cases even key plays in the canon tend to be excluded from the movement; and the reception of Chekhov is a particularly good example:

> W.H. Bruford defined the Chekhovian method as 'psychological naturalism' [*Anton Chekhov*: Yale, 1957]. Francis Fergusson, however, came to a different conclusion; analyzing *The Cherry Orchard* he said that 'Chekhov's poetry . . . is behind the naturalistic surfaces; but the form of the play as a whole is "nothing but" poetry in the widest sense. . . .' [*The Idea of a Theatre*: Doubleday, 1949] . . . Maurice Valency diverged even further. He saw *The Three Sisters* as 'the flower of impressionism in the drama' [*The Breaking String*:

Oxford, 1966]. Even earlier a synthesis of sorts that lumped together symbol-ism, realism and naturalism was attempted by John Gassner; yet his state-ment that 'if Maeterlinck's plays are mood pieces, so are the plays of Chek-hov, who is considered a supreme realist or naturalist' [*Directions in Modern Theatre and Drama*: Holt, Reinhart, 1966], was also readily disputed by N. Efros who categorically proclaimed that 'Chekhov is an artistic realist; no other definition can be applied to him' [in *Literary and Theatrical Reminiscences*, ed. S.S. Koteliansky: New York, 1927].

(Nicholas Moravcevich, in *Comparative Drama*, 1970)

Clearly the theory of Naturalism, and the canon created to exemplify it need revision.

Even for theatre artists of the time who explicitly labeled themselves as part of the movement, "Naturalism" was understood very differently in terms of practice. For instance there were clear divergences in the concept of naturalistic acting – although the style of performing might seem fundamental to portraying natural-istically conceived characters. Thus Antoine's actors physically "lived" their roles, reproducing mannerism and gesture based on close observation of the type or class of person represented, and moving with a sense of spontaneity. But a letter by Frank Fay, the lead actor of the Irish Players and an admirer of Antoine, reveals a widely divergent view.

I saw Antoine twice and was somewhat disappointed. Curiously Archer's comments in this week's *World* agree with mine. He says Antoine had no facial expression, of that I could not judge being too far away. I could not see any-thing vitally different in his method for the others, except that once or twice he spoke more quietly than the others with little or no regard for the necessities of a theatre and though the effect was very 'natural' in an everyday sense it was, I think, the sort of naturalness that, like the Duse's Italian company is of doubtful value. His intonation (a vital thing after all) did not strike me, whereas I think Réjane's tones would strike anyone from anywhere as being absolutely real. Antoine is very restless, moves about and fidgets with his tie and collar.

(Letter to Maire Garvey, 30 June 1904)

Shaw made a similar comment on seeing Antoine's production of *The Wild Duck*.

The garret scene was admirable; but there would not be room for it at the Court. It was played at great speed and raced to the end of every act to get to a curtain. Gregers described by Relling as an expectorator of phrases, went full steam ahead all through. There was no character in Gina or old Ekdal [acted by Antoine] – indeed there was no character in the acting at all as we understand it, but it was a bustling piece of work . . . Stage management ad lib.; Gregers and his father walked ten miles in the first act if they walked a foot.

(Letter to Granville Barker, 7 May 1906)

To some extent (as both commentaries acknowledge) this critical reaction may have been due to the size of theatre in which Antoine was now staging his productions, compared to the small-scale intimacy of the early Théâtre Libre. However, the unanimity of these responses indicates a significant contrast between the style of acting Antoine had developed, and the type of performance seen as naturalistic in Britain that took the intrinsic artificiality of theatre into account. This emphasized achieving a convincingly realistic effect translated through orchestrated and histrionic means, while in France actors and directors focussed on transferring real-life behavior directly to the stage.

Both should be seen as aspects of the same movement, marking two extremes in a spectrum of Naturalism. Expanding the concept of Naturalism in this way includes Shaw as one of the major examples. It also makes it easier to recognize the true qualities of playwrights previously established in the canon, such as Ibsen and Chekhov.

2

THE CONTEXT OF NATURALIST THEATRE: A CHRONOLOGY

	Theatre	Art and society	Politics
1830	Victor Hugo: *Hernani.*	First box set is introduced on a stage in London.	Poland revolts against Russian rule (1830–1831)
1833	Victor Hugo: *Lucrèce Borgia* and *Marie Tudor.*	Edmund Kean (1789–1833) dies; K.F. Gauss and Wilhelm E. Weber invent the electromagnetic telegraph.	British Factory Act is enacted, regulating some of the abuses against workers.
1834			Abolition of slavery in the British Empire.
1835	Georg Büchner: *Danton's Death.*	Hans Christian Andersen publishes the first four of his 168 tales for children.	
1836	Nikolai Gogol: *The Inspector General.*	Caroline Norton: poetry, *A Voice from the Factories.*	The People's Charter marks the first national working-class movement in Great Britain.
1837	Robert Browning: *Strafford.*	Limelight is used for a Covent Garden pantomine.	Victoria succeeds William IV to become the queen of England; reforms affecting state-owned serfs in Russia are introduced (1837–1841).
1838	Victor Hugo: *Ruy Blas.*		London Working Men's Association adopts the People's Charter, the main document of the Chartist movement.
1841	Johan Ludvig Heiberg: *A Soul After Death.*	Asbjørnsen and Moe publish *Norwegian Folk Tales.*	
1844	Friedrich Hebbel: *Mary Magdalen.*	John Stuart Mill: *Essays on Some Unsettled Questions of Political Economy.*	Karl Marx meets Friedrich Engels in Paris.
1845	Anna Cora Mowatt: *Fashion; or, Life in New York.*	Margaret Fuller: *Woman in the Nineteenth Century* – a call for women's equality; Friedrich Engels: *The Condition of the Working Class in England.* Published in Leipzig.	British defeat Sikhs in the Punjab, in the First Sikh War (1845–1846).

	Theatre	Art and society	Politics
1848	Emile Augier: *L'Aventurière.*	Karl Marx and Friedrich Engels: *The Communist Manifesto.*	The Thrane movement for reform in Norway (1848–1851); the Year of Revolutions in Europe.
1849	Eugène Scribe: *Adrienne Lecouvreur.*	Johan August Strindberg is born; Dostoyevsky is sentenced to four years in a labor camp at Omsk; Richard Wagner participates in Dresden revolt and is forced to flee to Zurich.	
1850	Henrik Ibsen: *The Burial Mound*; *Catiline*; Ivan Turgenev: *A Month in the Country.*		Prussia and Denmark sign the Peace of Berlin on Schleswig-Holstein.
1851	Henrik Ibsen: *Norma, or a Politician's Love.*	Anon.: *On the Enfranchisement of Women* (attributed to Harriet Taylor).	
1852	Charles Kean stages *Macbeth.*		
1853	Henrik Ibsen: *St. John's Night.*		
1854	Dumas *fils: Le Demi-Monde*; Henrik Ibsen: *Lady Inger.*	Heinrich Geobel, German watchmaker, invents first form of the electric light bulb.	Law passed to give women equal inheritance rights in Norway; Crimean War (1854–1856).
1855		David E. Hughes invents the printing telegraph.	Czar Nicholas I of Russia dies and is succeeded by Alexander II.
1856	Henrik Ibsen: *The Banquet at Solhaug.*	Bernard Shaw is born.	Britain annexes Oudh, India, and establishes Natal as a Crown colony.
1857	Henrik Ibsen: *Olaf Liljekrans.*		Alexander II appoints Secret Committee to plan the abolishment of serfdom in Russia.
1858	Henrik Ibsen: *The Vikings at Helgeland.*		

	Theatre	Art and society	Politics
1859		Charles Darwin: *On the Origin of Species by Means of Natural Selection*; Karl Marx: *Critique of Political Economy*; John Stuart Mill: *Essay on Liberty*.	King Oscar I of Sweden dies and is succeeded by Charles XV.
1860	Dion Boucicault: *The Colleen Bawn*; Alexander Ostrovski: *The Storm*.	Anton Chekhov is born; Christopher L. Sholes invents an early form of the typewriter.	
1861		Eugène Scribe: (1791–1861) dies; Vladimir Dahl: *Dictionary of the Living Russian Tongue* (1861–1866).	Manifesto on emancipation of serfs published in Russia; peasant and student unrest in Russia (1861–1862).
1862	Sarah Bernhardt débuts at the Comédie Française in Racine's *Iphigénie en Aulide*; Henrik Ibsen: *Love's Comedy*.		Activity of secret revolutionary organization *Zemlia I Volia* (Land and Freedom) in Russia (1862–1863).
1863	Henrik Ibsen: *The Pretenders*.	John Stuart Mill: *Utilitarianism*.	Law passed in Norway to give unmarried women independence from male guardians; Frederick VII, King of Denmark, dies and is succeeded by Christian IX.
1864		Louis Pasteur invents pasteurization.	
1865	David Belasco (aged 12): *Jim Black, or The Regulator's Revenge*; T.W. Robertson: *Society*; Emile Zola: *Madeleine*.	Richard Wagner: *Tristan und Isolde*; Claude Bernard: *Introduction à l'étude de la médecine expérimentale*.	Russian conquest of Central Asia (1865–1885).
1866	Henrik Ibsen: *Brand*.	Fydor Mikhailovich Dostoyevsky: *Crime and Punishment*; Henry Irving makes his London début; Alfred Nobel invents dynamite; Robert Whitehead invents underwater torpedo; "Black Friday" on the London Stock Exchange.	Law created in Norway to allow women the right to work in any trade or profession; attempt on Alexander II's life in Russia by Karakozov; Prussia annexes Schleswig-Holstein from Denmark.

	Theatre	Art and society	Politics
1867	Henrik Ibsen: *Peer Gynt*; T.W. Robertson: *Caste*.	Karl Marx: *Das Kapital*; John Stuart Mill: *Admission of Women to Electorial Franchise*; Émile Zola: *Thérèse Raquin* (novel).	Russia sells Alaska and the Aleutian Islands to the United States for $7,200,000.
1868		Georg Brandes: *Aesthetic Studies*; Fydor Mikhailovich Dostoyevsky: *The Idiot*; Elizabeth Cady and Susan B. Anthony found the women's rights periodical, *The Revolution*.	
1869	Henrik Ibsen: *The League of Youth*.	John Stuart Mill: *On the Subjection of Women*.	
1870	The **Saxe-Meiningen Players** produce William Shakespeare's *Julius Caesar*.		Married Women's Property Act in Britain allows married women to keep £200 of their own earnings; Education Act in Britain provides elementary education for girls as well as boys; Franco-Prussian War (1870–1871).
1871	Alexander Ostrovski: *The Forest*; August Strindberg: *The Outlaw*.	**Georg Brandes: *Inaugural Lecture*.**	
1872	Eleonora Duse (age 14) makes her début in Verona as Juliet; Henry Irving stages *The Bells*.	First Russian translation of Karl Marx's *Das Kapital*.	Ballot Act in Britain legislates voting by secret ballot.
1873	**Émile Zola: *Thérèse Raquin***; Henrik Ibsen: *Emperor and Galilean*.		
1874	The **Saxe-Meiningen Players'** first tour of Germany; Victorien Sardou: *La Haine*.	First Impressionist Salon; Paris Opéra opens.	
1875	Victorien Sardou: *Ferréol*.	London Medical School for Women is founded.	

	Theatre	Art and society	Politics
1876	The **Saxe-Meiningen Players** perform Ibsen's *The Pretenders* in Berlin; Wagner's theatre, Bayreuth Festspielhaus, opens and performs *The Ring*.	Alexander Graham Bell invents the telephone.	"Land and Freedom" populist secret society established in Russia.
1877	**Henrik Ibsen: *The Pillars of Society*.**	Thomas Edison invents the phonograph; Émile Zola: *L'Assommoir*.	Russo-Turkish War (1877–1878); Queen Victoria becomes Empress of India.
1878	Emile Augier: *Les Fourchambeault*; Anton Chekhov: *Platonov*.	Henry Irving takes control of the Lyceum Theatre in London.	
1879	**Henrik Ibsen: *A Doll's House*.**	Jules Bastien-Lepage paints "Portrait of Sarah Bernhardt"; Friedrich Nietzsche: *Birth of Tragedy*; Thomas Edison invents electric light; August Strindberg: *The Red Room*.	"Land and Freedom" split into "People's Will" and "Black Partition" in Russia.
1880	Henry Irving stages *The Corsican Brothers*.	Fydor Mikhailovich Dostevsky: *The Brothers Karamozov*; **Émile Zola: *Naturalism in the Theatre*.**	
1881	August Strindberg: *Master Olaf*.	Electric lighting introduced in British theatres; Émile Zola's theatre reviews are published in two volumes.	Alexander II assassinated in Russia.
1882	**Henrik Ibsen: *Ghosts*; Henry Becque: *The Crows*;** Victorien Sardou: *Fédora*.	The Peasant Bank is founded in Russia.	Married Women's Property Act in Britain is expanded to enable women the right to own and administer their own property.
1883	**Henrik Ibsen: *An Enemy of the People*** at the Royal Theatre in Stockholm; August Strindberg: *Lucky Peter's Travels*.	Deutsches Theater, Berlin, is founded.	

	Theatre	Art and society	Politics
1884	**Henrik Ibsen: *The Wild Duck*;** Anton Chekhov: *On the Highroad.*	Bernard Shaw becomes a founding member of Britain's Socialist Fabian Society.	Married Women's Property Act in Britain deems that women are no longer "chattel" but are autonomous people.
1885		Émile Zola: *Germinal.*	
1886	Henrik Ibsen: *Rosmersholm;* **Henrik Ibsen: *Ghosts* staged by The Saxe-Meiningen Players** in Germany; Anton Chekhov: *The Swan Song;* **Lev Tolstoi:** *Power of Darkness* (banned in Russia until 1895).	Émile Zola: *L'Œuvre;* Bernard Shaw: *Cashel Byron's Profession.*	
1887	**Henrik Ibsen: *The Pillars of Society;* August Strindberg: *The Father;*** Victorien Sardou: *La Tosca* (written for Sarah Bernhardt); **Anton Chekhov:** *Ivanov.*	Émile Zola: *La Terre;* **André Antoine founds the Théâtre Libre** in Paris.	"Bloody Sunday" in Britain; Social Democratic Federation meeting in Trafalgar Square is quashed by police and military troops in London.
1888	**André Antoine** with the **Saxe-Meiningen Players; Henrik Ibsen:** *The Lady from the Sea;* **August Strindberg: *Miss Julie.***	Émile Zola: *La Rêve;* "Jack the Ripper" murders six women in London; Anton Chekhov is awarded the Pushkin Prize.	
1889	**Henrik Ibsen:** First English production of *A Doll's House;* **Freie Bühne** is founded in Berlin by Otto Brahm and stages **Gerhart Hauptmann's *Before Dawn*;** August Strindberg's Scandinavian Experimental Theatre is founded; **Anton Chekhov: *The Wood Demon.***	Bernard Shaw: *Fabian Essays;* Théâtres Moderne, Independent, Libre Ancien and d'Applic are founded in Paris.	London Dock strike.

	Theatre	Art and society	Politics
1890	**Henrik Ibsen: Ghosts** staged by Théâtre Libre; Henrik Ibsen: *Hedda Gabler.*	Bernard Shaw: *Quintessence of Ibsenism;* **Le Théâtre Libre** manifesto; The **Saxe-Meiningen Players** tour through Europe.	William II and Alexander III meet at Narva.
1891	**Henrik Ibsen: Wild Duck** staged by **Théâtre Libre**; Victorien Sardou: *Thermidor;* The Symbolist Théâtre d'Art produces Maeterlinck's *Intruder* and *The Blind.*	W.L. Judson invents the clothing zipper (not in common use until 1919); work on the Trans-Siberian railway begins; John T. Grein founds the **Independent Theatre Club** in London.	British military takes Nyasaland; winter famine in Russia.
1892	Henrik Ibsen: *The Master Builder;* Maurice Maeterlinck: *Pelléas and Mélisande;* **Gerhart Hauptmann: The Weavers** staged by Freie Bühne; **Bernard Shaw: Widowers' Houses** staged by the **Independent Theatre Club.**	William Morris: *News from Nowhere.*	Strikes and massacres of workers in Russia.
1893	**Bernard Shaw: Mrs Warren's Profession** (first produced by **The Stage Society** in 1902); **Florence Bell: Alan's Wife;** Oscar Wilde: *A Woman of No Importance;* Arthur Pinero: *The Second Mrs. Tanqueray;* **Gerhart Hauptmann: The Weavers** staged by **Théâtre Libre;** **August Strindberg: Miss Julie** staged by **Théâtre Libre.**	Sigmund Freud (with Charcot): *On the Psychical Mechanism of Hysterical Phenomena;* Théâtre d'Œuvre founded in France.	Britain's Independent Labour party is founded.
1894	Bernard Shaw: *Arms and the Man;* August Strindberg: *Father* is staged by Théâtre d'Œuvre; **Constance Fletcher: Mrs Lessingham; Dorothy Leighton: Thyrza Fleming.**	Thomas Edison opens his Kinetoscope Parlour in New York; Benoit-Constant Coquelin: *L'Art du comédien* is published.	Local Government Act in Britain: women are eligible to vote for parochial councils; Nicholas II becomes Czar in Russia.

	Theatre	Art and society	Politics
1895	**Janet Achurch: *Mrs Daintree's Daughter*;** Oscar Wilde: *An Ideal Husband*; Oscar Wilde: *The Importance of Being Earnest*; Henrik Ibsen: *Little Eyolf* opens in Berlin; **Bernard Shaw: picture *Candida*.**	Oscar Wilde: unsuccessful libel action against Marquis of Queensberry and in a sensational trial found guilty of homosexuality; Auguste and Louis Lumière invent a motion-picture camera; Wilhelm Röntgen discovers x-rays; Adolphe Appia: *Mise-en-scène in Wagnerian Drama* is published.	Vladimir Illich Lenin becomes an active member of the Russian Social Democratic party and is exiled to Siberia (1895–1900).
1896	**Anton Chekhov: *The Seagull*;** Alfred Jarry: *Ubu Roi* is staged by Théâtre d'Œuvre.	Olympic Games are reestablished and hosted by Athens.	
1897	Bernard Shaw: *The Devil's Disciple*; **Bernard Shaw: *You Never Can Tell*;** Henrik Ibsen: *John Gabriel Borkman*.	August Strindberg; autobiography, *Inferno*; **Théâtre Antoine**, the successor to **Théâtre Libre** is founded; The Irish Literary Theatre is founded; **Moscow Art Theatre** is founded.	Winter famine in Russia.
1898	**Moscow Art Theatre**'s first production (A. Tolstoi's *Tsar Fyodor Ioanovich*); **Moscow Art Theatre** produces *The Seagull*.	Émile Zola publishes open letter to the President of France, "J'accuse", and is imprisoned.	Manhood suffrage in Norway.
1899	**Anton Chekhov: *Uncle Vanya*** is produced by the **Moscow Art Theatre**; Bernard Shaw: *Caesar and Cleopatra* staged by Mrs Patrick Campbell; **The Stage Society** is founded and produces **Bernard Shaw's *You Never Can Tell*;** August Strindberg: *Gustav Vasa;* August Strindberg: *Erik XIV.*	Adolphe Appia: *Music and Stage Scenery.*	The Boer War (1899–1902).
1900	George Bernard Shaw: *Captain Brassbound's Conversion*; August Strindberg: *To Damascus.*	Sigmund Freud: *The Interpretation of Dreams.*	Britain's Independent Labour party becomes the Labour Representation Committee.

	Theatre	Art and society	Politics
1901	Eugène Brieux: *Maternité* is banned; **Anton Chekhov: *The Three Sisters* is** produced by the **Moscow Art Theatre**; August Strindberg: *The Dance of Death*.	Nobel Prize established.	Queen Victoria dies and is succeeded by Edward VII; women's suffrage in local elections in Norway.
1902	Harley Granville Barker: *The Marrying of Ann Leete*; **Maksim Gorki: *The Lower Depths***; Émile Zola: *La Terre* staged by **Théâtre Antoine**; August Strindberg: *A Dream Play*; Maurice Maeterlinck: *Monna Vanna*; W.B. Yeats: *Cathleen Ni Houlihan*	Vladimir Illich Lenin: *What Is to Be Done?*; Leon Trotsky escapes from a Siberian prison and settles in London; Kleines Theater is founded by Max Reinhardt in Berlin; Otodziro Kawakami's Japanese theatre company tours to Moscow.	Socialist Revolutionary party is formed to protest peasant interests in Russia.
1903	**Gerhart Hauptmann: *Rose Bernd***; Bernard Shaw: *Man and Superman*; August Strindberg: *Queen Christina*; Victorien Sardou: *Dante* (written for Henry Irving).	Orville and Wilbur Wright successfully fly an engine-powered airplane; Bjørnsterne Bjørnson wins the Nobel Prize for Literature; Women's Social and Political Union is started in Britain by Emmeline Pankhurst and her daughters Christabel and Sylvia. Their agenda is to champion ardently for women's suffrage ('suffragettes').	Russian Social Democratic party splits into *Bolshevik* and *Menshevik* sects.
1904	James Barrie: *Peter Pan*; **Bernard Shaw: *John Bull's Other Island*; Anton Chekhov: *The Cherry Orchard*** is produced at the **Moscow Art Theatre**.	Georg Fuchs: *The Stage of the Future*; Anton Chekhov (1860–1904) dies; Abbey Theatre is founded; Dublin English Stage Society founded.	Russo-Japanese war (first use of trenches); Britain and France form the Entente Cordiale, settling some disputes over colonial land.
1905	David Belasco: *Girl of the Golden West*; **Harley Granville Barker: *The Voysey Inheritance***; Maurice Maeterlinck: *The Blue Bird*; **Bernard Shaw: *Major Barbara***.	Gordon Craig: *The Art of the Theatre*; Henry Irving (1838–1905) dies; Albert Einstein formulates his Special Theory of Relativity; Sigmund Freud: *Three Contributions to the Theory of Sex*; Vsevolod Meyerhold founds the Moscow Art Studio Theatre.	Union between Norway and Sweden is dissolved; Bloody Sunday in Russia; October Manifesto in Russia establishes reforms; The crew of the battleship *Potemkin* mutiny.

	Theatre	Art and society	Politics
1906	**Henrik Ibsen: *Ghosts*** is staged by **André Antoine; Elizabeth Robins: *Votes for Women!***	The Symbolist journal *The Golden Fleece* appears in Russia; Henrik Ibsen (1828–1906) dies; Max Reinhardt founds the Kammerspielhaus in Berlin.	Britain's Labour Representation Committee becomes the Labour party.
1907	**Harley Granville Barker: *Waste*;** August Strindberg: *The Ghost Sonata*; **John Synge: *The Playboy of the Western World*;** The first "Ziegfeld Follies" is staged in New York.	First Symbolist exhibition, *Blue Rose*, is held in Moscow; August Strindberg founds the Intimate Theatre in Stockholm; first cubist exhibition is held in Paris; Vladimir Illich Lenin: leaves Russia and starts the newspaper, *The Proletarian*; first English Repertory theatre founded in Manchester.	Female suffrage in Norway (1907–1913); Oscar II, King of Sweden, dies and is succeeded by Gustavus V.
1908	**Bernard Shaw: *Getting Married*.**	Actresses' Franchise League is founded in Britain.	
1909	**Harley Granville Barker: *The Madras House*; John Galsworthy: *Strife*; D.H. Lawrence: *A Collier's Friday Night*** (first staged in 1968).	Diaghilev's first season of the Ballets Russes in Paris.	
1910	Max Reinhardt directs Sophocles' *Oedipus Rex*; **Bernard Shaw: *Misalliance*; John Galsworthy: *Justice*.**	Workers' Theatre Movement is founded in Britain.	Violence in the women's suffrage movement in Britain including demonstrations, arson attacks and picture slashing. The government asserts that it will only deal with women's suffrage as part of a wider extension of the franchise. Prisoners mount hunger strikes; King Edward VII dies and is succeeded by George V.

	Theatre	Art and society	Politics
1911	Max Reinhardt directs *Everyman* in Berlin; Konstantin Stanislavsky directs *Hamlet* at the Moscow Art Theatre in a production designed by Gordon Craig; Bernard Shaw: *Fanny's First Play*; **D.H. Lawrence: *The Widowing of Mrs Holroyd*** (staged by **The Stage Society** in 1926).	Vasily Kandinsky and Franz Marc found "Blue Rider" in Munich, Germany; first manifesto of the Futurists in Italy; Maurice Maeterlinck wins the Nobel Prize for Literature; Emile Jacques-Dalcroze establishes his institute for the teaching of eurthythmics at Hellerau, Germany.	
1912	Somerset Maugham: *The Land of Promise*; Bernard Shaw: *Androcles and the Lion* opens in Berlin; **Bernard Shaw: *Overruled.***	August Strindberg (1849–1912) dies; William Archer: *Play-Making: A Manual of Craftsmanship*; Vaslav Nijinsky choreographs and directs *L'Après-midi d'un faune* in Paris, the score is composed by Debussy; Vsevolod Meyerhold: *On Theatre*; Gerhart Hauptmann wins the Nobel Prize for Literature; C.G. Jung: *The Theory of Psychoanalysis*; The S.S. Titanic sinks.	First issue of *Pravda*, the Bolshevik paper, appears in Russia; Balkan Wars begin.
1913	**Bernard Shaw: *Pygmalion*;** Georg Büchner: *Woyzeck* (written 1837).	Postimpressionism and Cubism introduced in New York at the "Armory Show"; Jacques Copeau founds Vieux-Colombier (Old Dovecote).	Women are granted the right to vote in Norway.
1914	Elmer Rice: *On Trial* (the first play to use flashbacks); **Bernard Shaw: *Androcles and the Lion***	Margaret Sanger coins the term "birth control"; Bernard Shaw: *Commonsense About the War;* **Provincetown Players** founded.	World War I (1914–1918); Britain declares war on Germany, Austria, and Turkey; suffragette riots in London; the Panama Canal opens.
1916	Luigi Pirandello: *It Is So . . .*; William Butler Yeats: *At the Hawk's Well;* **Eugene O'Neill: *Bound East for Cardiff*** staged by **The Provincetown Players.**	Cabaret Voltaire opens in Zurich; Tristan Tzara publishes first "Dada" manifesto.	Easter Rising in Dublin is suppressed; the Russian Czar abdicates.

	Theatre	Art and society	Politics
1917	Erik Satie: *Parade*. Surrealist sets and costumes designed by Pablo Picasso; **Somerset Maugham: *Our Betters*.**	Sarah Bernhardt (age 72) begins her last tour of the United States; C.G. Jung: *Psychology of the Unconscious.*	October (Bolshevik) Revolution in Russia; Soviet power is established.
1918	Bertolt Brecht: *Baal*; James Joyce: *Exiles.*	Theater Guild of New York is founded by Lawrence Langer.	Representation of the People Act in Britain allows women over thirty to vote. Rights to vote given in local elections on similar terms; women entitled to become MPs in Britain; Turkey surrenders; Allies grant armistice to Austria, and then to Germany; German revolution begins; Kaiser abdicates.
1919	**Bernard Shaw: *Heartbreak House*.**	The film *The Cabinet of Dr. Caligari* is made in Germany; Vsevolod Meyerhold sentenced to death; he escapes and joins the Red Army; George Pierce Baker: *Dramatic Technique*; Max Reinhardt founds Grosses Schauspielhaus in Berlin.	Sex Disqualification Removal Act in Britain opens all professions to women with the exception of the Church; Lady Astor becomes the first woman MP in Britain to take her seat; Paris Peace Conference begins; Irish Free State is declared.
1920	**Bernard Shaw: *Heartbreak House*** staged by the Theatre Guild; Eugene O'Neill: *Beyond the Horizon* staged on Broadway; Eugene O'Neill: *The Emperor Jones.*	Vsevolod Meyerhold is appointed head of Theatre Section, Narkompros; Erwin Piscator founds the Proletarian Theatre in Berlin.	Irish Civil War; Treaty of Versailles; League of Nations is established; Poland invades Russia.

3

CONTEMPORARY THEORIES OF NATURALISM

The documentation in this section focuses on the theoretical basis for Naturalism in dramatic writing and on the stage. It traces the development of each of the major playwrights, covering both the intellectual and political impetus expressed in the movement, as well as aspects of performance and theatrical presentation.

1 GEORG BRANDES AND HENRIK IBSEN

Georg Brandes' polemic 1871 lecture emphasized the need for social relevance in contemporary literature. Demanding political involvement – and citing Ibsen's *Brand* as an example of the abstract idealism to be avoided – it acted as a clarion call for the new naturalistic drama. The opening lecture in a series delivered at the University of Copenhagen, which aroused violent controversy, it was published a year later in the first of his influential six-volume study of *Main Currents in Nineteenth-Century Literature*. This made him a dominant figure in the intellectual world of the time, even if it was almost 30 years before he gained a university appointment. Although focussed almost entirely on Danish writing, given the political (and linguistic) history of Scandinavia, Brandes' arguments were equally applicable to the other countries, particularly Norway. And while dealing with literature in general rather than drama, this in itself foreshadowed the link between drama and the novel, which was one of the most productive aspects of the naturalistic movement.

To a significant degree, this inaugural lecture forms part of an ongoing argument between Brandes and Ibsen, who was already in the habit of sending his scripts to Brandes for commentary, and had been following Brandes' lectures closely since 1866. Indeed some of the points are a rebuttal of a letter by Ibsen from ten months before, in which Ibsen had asserted his principle of individualism, dismissing Brandes' call for national independence:

As to liberty, I take it that our dispute is a mere dispute about words. I shall

43

never agree to making liberty synonymous with political liberty. What you call liberty, I call liberties; and what I call the struggle for liberty is nothing but the constant, living assimilation of the idea of freedom. He who possesses liberty otherwise than as a thing to be striven for, possesses it dead and soulless; for the idea of liberty has undoubtedly this characteristic, that it develops steadily during its assimilation. So that a man who stops in the midst of the struggle and says: 'Now I have it' – thereby shows he has lost it. It is, however, exactly this dead maintenance of a certain given standpoint of liberty that is characteristic of communities which go by the name of states – and this it is that I have called worthless. Yes, to be sure, it is a benefit to possess the franchise, the right of self-taxation, etc., but for whom is it a benefit? For the citizen, not for the individual. Now there is absolutely no reasonable necessity for the individual to be a citizen. On the contrary – the state is the curse of the individual . . . The state must be abolished! In that revolution I will take part.

(17 February 1871)

On publication Brandes' first volume was immediately read by Ibsen, who responded:

I must turn to what has lately been constantly in my thoughts and has even disturbed my sleep. I have read your Lectures.

No more dangerous book could fall into the hands of a pregnant poet. It is one of those works which place a yawning gulf between yesterday and today. After I had been in Italy, I could not understand how I had been able to exist before I had been there. In twenty years, one will not be able to comprehend how spiritual existence at home was possible before these lectures.

(4 April 1872)

It became one of the major factors leading to the sharp switch in Ibsen's work from his early poetic and philosophical plays (*The Vikings at Helgeland*, or *Emperor and Galilean*) to his first naturalistic play, *The Pillars of Society*, which was completed just five years later and staged in 1877.

3.1.1 Georg Brandes, *Inaugural Lecture*, November 1871 (Extracts)

Translated by Evert Sprinchorn

What keeps a literature alive in our days is that it submits problems to debate. Thus, for example, George Sand debates the problem of the relations between the sexes. Byron and Feuerbach religion, John Stuart Mill and Prudhon property, Turgenev, Spielhagen and Émile Augier social conditions. A literature that does not submit problems to debate loses all meaning. The people who produce such a literature may long believe that the redemption of the world will ensue, but they will eventually see their expectations disappointed. Such people have as little to do with development and progress as the fly that thought it was driving the wagon forward because it occasionally gave the four horses some harmless stings [. . .]

If such a society produces any kind of serious literature, one should not be very surprised if its essential aim is to cast scorn on the present and put it to shame. This literature will repeatedly call the people of its time miserable wretches, and one may even find that the works which are most highly praised and most widely sold (Ibsen's *Brand*, for example) are those in which the reader may discover first with horror and then with delight what a worm he is, how pitiful he is, and how cowardly! One may also notice that Will becomes the watchword of such people, and that everywhere plays about Will and philosophies of Will are being peddled. One demands what one does not possess. One calls for what one misses most bitterly. And one peddles what is most called for [. . .]

Higher and higher mounts the enthusiasm for asceticism and positive religion. One writer outdoes the other in piling up ideals, from the top of which pile reality appears only as a distant black dot.

Where does this current finally emerge? In such figures as Paludan-Müller's Kalanus [1854], who ecstatically commits himself to the stake, and Ibsen's Brand, whose moral principles if realized would cause half of mankind to starve to death for the sake of an ideal.

This is where we have ended. Nowhere in all of Europe can one find more exalted ideals and only on a few places a duller intellectual life. For one would be extremely naïve to believe that these heroes have their counterparts in our actual life. So strong has the current been that even a spirit as revolutionary as Ibsen's has been seized by it. Does Brand stand for revolution or reaction? I cannot tell, there is so much of both in it.

The main principles of the previous century were freedom of research in science and the unimpeded development of humanity in literature. Whatever does not hold with this current flows down into decadence and takes the way to Byzantium. For all other movements are Byzantine: in science, Byzantine scholasticism, and in poetry, bodies and soul that do not resemble bodies and souls, but are abstract and all alike [. . .]

Oehenschläger emancipated our poetry from the ethics of utilitarianism. Heiberg [banished from Denmark in 1799 for his republican views] freed criticism from the subjective school, gained for logic a position as honourable as that of creative literature, and won new territory for philosophy. Then came the first demands for political freedom. But the standard-bearers in literature asked, 'Why on earth do you want political freedom when the true freedom is the inner freedom of the Will? It is always permissible to gain this and, once gained, the other freedom is absolutely without significance [. . .]' But these arguments did not appease the public, and we won our political freedom.

Now if once again the slogan for further progress were, 'Freedom, the freedom of the spirit', I think a chorus of voices would cry out in unison, 'We mean freedom of thought and the freedom of mankind.' These voices would not be silenced by being asked, 'Why on earth call for freedom when you already have all you could wish for?' – political freedom being understood. The people would be satisfied with that. For it is not so much our laws that need changing as it is our whole conception of society. The younger generation must plough it up and replant it before a new literature can bloom and flourish. Their chief task will be to channel into our country those currents that have their origin in the revolution and in the belief in progress, and to halt the reaction at all points where its historic mission has been fulfilled.

2 ÉMILE ZOLA AND ANDRÉ ANTOINE

Written between 1875 and 1880 for *Le Bien Public* then *Le Voltaire*, Émile Zola's dramatic criticism was collected into two volumes in 1881. Together with the chapter on theatre in his book *The Experimental Novel* and his Preface to *Thérèse Raquin* these formed a manifesto for naturalistic drama. In addition to Zola's attack on artificial conventions and demand for realism, his crucial contribution (from the extract selected here) was to promote the integration of naturalistic plays with the revolutionary scientific approach that had emerged in the nineteenth century. The argument for moral experiment and scientific analysis, together with his practical awareness of the necessity for a coherent form of stage presentation appropriate to the new style of dramatic writing provided the basis for Naturalism in the theatre. His ideas directly influenced the French actor/ director, André Antoine, the founder of the Théâtre Libre, whose first production in 1887 was an adaptation of a short story by Zola. Zola's critical writings provided the theory; and the extent to which it was given concrete realization in Antoine's productions is indicated by his "Commentary on *mise en scène*" written for *La Revue de Paris* in 1903, shortly before he was appointed to head the Comedie Française.

The new dramatist Zola was calling for had already appeared in Ibsen, whose plays together with Strindberg's were introduced to France by André Antoine. Strindberg consciously followed Zola in plays written after 1887; and Chekhov also admired Zola, taking a close interest in his writings about the Dreyfus affair. In addition to spreading the example of Ibsen and Strindberg through his productions of their plays, the realistic style of staging Antoine evolved encouraged a new generation of young French dramatists. Antoine's wider influence was spread by both tours of the Théâtre Libre and by journal articles in England and elsewhere. For instance, an early description of Antoine's work by Marie Belloc covered his first performances, critical response and commentary by leading French writers (such as Edmond de Goncourt – "Antoine's valiant efforts in the cause of literary and dramatic truth . . . has profoundly modified the drama of today"). It pointed to Antoine's effect on French acting as well as the new type of realistic detail in settings of other theatres (including the Comédie Française), and emphasized that it is the younger French writers and foreign dramatists who owe a sincere debt of gratitude to the Théâtre Libre. To name but a few of the many who owe at least their first successes in literature to M. Antoine's venture are Henri Lavedan, Paul Marguerite, Henri Céard, Francois de Curel, Georges Ancey, Oscar Mètènier, Count Rzewuskei (Balzac's nephew), Paul Alexis and Michel Carré. Most of these have now taken a leading place among the French playwrights of today. . . .

(*The New Review*, 1894)

3.2.1 Émile Zola, *Naturalism in the Theatre*, 1881

Translated by Albert Bermel

1

Each winter at the beginning of the theatre season I fall prey to the same thoughts. A hope springs up in me, and I tell myself that before the first warmth of summer empties the playhouses, a dramatist of genius will be discovered. Our theatre desperately needs a new man who will scour the debased boards and bring about a rebirth in an art degraded by its practitioners to the simple-minded requirements of the crowd. Yes, it would take a powerful personality, an innovator's mind, to overthrow the accepted conventions and finally install the real human drama in place of the ridiculous untruths that are on display today. I picture this creator scorning the tricks of the clever hack, smashing the imposed patterns, remaking the stage until it is continuous with the auditorium, giving a shiver of life to the painted trees, letting in through the backcloth the great, free air of reality.

Unfortunately, this dream I have every October has not yet been fulfilled, and is not likely to be for some time. I wait in vain, I go from failure to failure. Is this, then, merely the naive wish of a poet? Are we trapped in today's dramatic art, which is so confining, like a cave that lacks air and light? Certainly, if dramatic art by its nature forbids this escape into less restricted forms, it would indeed be vain to delude ourselves and to expect a renaissance at any moment. But despite the stubborn assertions of certain critics who do not like to have their standards threatened, it is obvious that dramatic art, like all the arts, has before it an unlimited domain, without barriers of any kind to left or right.

[. . .]

2

It seems impossible that the movement of inquiry and analysis, which is precisely the movement of the nineteenth century, can have revolutionized all the sciences and arts and left dramatic art to one side, as if isolated. The natural sciences date from the end of the last century; chemistry and physics are less than a hundred years old; history and criticism have been renovated, virtually re-created since the Revolution; an entire world has arisen; it has sent us back to the study of documents, to experience, made us realize that to start afresh we must first take things back to the beginning, become familiar with man and nature, verify what is. Thenceforward, the great naturalistic school, which has spread secretly, irrevocably, often making its way in darkness but always advancing, can finally come out triumphantly into the light of day. To trace the history of this movement, with the misunderstandings that might have impeded it and the multiple causes that have thrust it forward or slowed it down, would be to trace the history of the century itself. An irresistible current carries our society towards the study of reality. In the novel Balzac has been the bold and mighty innovator who has replaced the observation of the scholar with the imagination of the poet. But in the theatre the evolution seems slower. No eminent writer has yet formulated the idea with any clarity.

[. . .]

Certain things have come to pass and I point them out. Can we believe that *L'Ami Fritz* would have been applauded at the Comédie-Française twenty years ago? Definitely not! This play, in which people eat all the time and the lover talks in such homely language, would have disgusted both the classicists and the romantics. To explain its success we must concede that as the years have gone by a secret fermentation has been at work. Lifelike paintings, which used to repel the public, today attract them. The majority has been won over and the stage is open to every experiment. This is the only conclusion to draw.

So that is where we stand. [. . .] I maintain that Romanticism in the theatre was an uncomplicated revolt, the invasion by a victorious group who took over the stage violently with drums beating and flags flying. In these early moments the combatants dreamed of making their imprint with a new form; to one rhetoric they opposed another: the Middle Ages to Antiquity, the exalting of passion to the exalting of duty. And that was all, for only the conventions were altered. The characters remained marionettes in new clothing. Only the exterior aspect and the language were modified. But for the period that was enough. Romanticism had taken possession of the theatre in the name of literary freedom and it carried out its revolutionary task with incomparable bravura. But who does not see today that its role could extend no farther than that? Does romanticism have anything whatever to say about our present society? Does it meet one of our requirements? Obviously not. It is as outmoded as a jargon we no longer follow. [. . .] It provided the occasion for a magnificent flowering of lyricism; that will be its eternal glory. Today, with the evolution accomplished, it is plain that romanticism was no more than the necessary link between classicism and naturalism. The struggle is over; now we must found a secure state. Naturalism flows out of classical art, just as our present society has arisen from the wreckage of the old society. Naturalism alone corresponds to our social needs; it alone has deep roots in the spirit of our times; and it alone can provide a living, durable formula for our art, because this formula will express the nature of our contemporary intelligence. There may be fashions and passing fantasies that exist outside naturalism but they will not survive for long. I say again, naturalism is the expression of our century and it will not die until a new upheaval transforms our democratic world.

Only one thing is needed now: men of genius who can fix the naturalistic formula. Balzac has done it for the novel and the novel is established. When will our Corneilles, Molières and Racines appear to establish our new theatre?

[. . .]

Take our present environment, then, and try to make men live in it: you will write great works. It will undoubtedly call for some effort; it means sifting out of the confusion of life the simple formula of naturalism. Therein lies the difficulty: to do great things with the subjects and characters that our eyes, accustomed to the spectacle of the daily round, have come to see as small. I am aware that it is more convenient to present a marionette to the public and name it Charlemagne and puff it up with such tirades that the public believes it is watching a colossus; it is more convenient than taking a bourgeois of our time, a grotesque, unsightly man, and drawing sublime poetry out of him, making him, for example, Père Goriot, the father who gives his guts for his daughters, a figure so gigantic with truth and love that no other literature can offer his equal.

[. . .]

The future is with naturalism. The formula will be found; it will be proved that there is more poetry in the little apartment of a bourgeois than in all the empty, worm-eaten palaces of history; in the end we will see that everything meets in the real: lovely fantasies that are free of capriciousness and whimsy, and idylls, and comedies, and dramas. Once the soil has been turned over, the task that seems alarming and unfeasible today will become easy.

I am not qualified to pronounce on the form that tomorrow's drama will take; that must be left to the voice of some genius to come. But I will allow myself to indicate the path I consider our theatre will follow.

First, the romantic drama must be abandoned. It would be disastrous for us to take over its outrageous acting, its rhetoric, its inherent thesis of action at the expense of character analysis. The finest models of the genre are, as has been said, mere operas with big effects. I believe, then, that we must go back to tragedy – not, heaven forbid, to borrow more of its rhetoric, its system of confidants, its declaiming, its endless speeches, but to return to its simplicity of action and its unique psychological and physiological study of the characters. Thus understood, the tragic framework is excellent; one deed unwinds in all its reality, and moves the characters to passions and feelings, the exact analysis of which constitutes the sole interest of the play – and in a contemporary environment, with the people who surround us.

My constant concern, my anxious vigil, has made me wonder which of us will have the strength to raise himself to the pitch of genius. If the naturalistic drama must come into being, only a genius can give birth to it. Corneille and Racine made tragedy. Victor Hugo made romantic drama. Where is the as-yet-unknown author who must make the naturalistic drama? In recent years experiments have not been wanting. But either because the public was not ready or because none of the beginners had the necessary staying-power, not one of these attempts has had decisive results.

[. . .]

The domain of the novel is crowded; the domain of the theatre is free. At this time in France an imperishable glory awaits the man of genius who takes up the work of Molière and finds in the reality of living comedy the full, true drama of modern society.

[. . .]

Costume, stage design, speech

Modern clothes make a poor spectacle. If we depart from bourgeois tragedy, shut in between its four walls, and wish to use the breadth of larger stages for crowd scenes we are embarrassed and constrained by the monotony and the uniformly funereal look of the extras. In this case, I think, we should take advantage of the variety of garb offered by the different classes and occupations. To elaborate: I can imagine an author setting one act in the main marketplace of les Halles in Paris. The setting would be superb, with its bustling life and bold possibilities. In this immense setting we could have a very picturesque ensemble by displaying the porters wearing their large hats, the saleswomen with their white aprons and vividly-coloured scarves, the customers dressed in silk or wool or cotton prints, from the ladies accompanied by their maids to the female beggars on the prowl for anything they can pick up off the street. For inspiration it would be enough to go to les Halles and look about. Nothing is gaudier or more interesting. All of Paris would enjoy seeing this set if it were realized with the necessary accuracy and amplitude.

And how many other settings for popular drama there are for the taking! Inside a factory, the interior of a mine, the gingerbread market, a railway station, flower stalls, a racetrack, and so on. All the activities of modern life can take place in them. It will be said that such sets have already been tried.

Unquestionably we have seen factories and railway stations in fantasy plays; but these were fantasy stations and factories. I mean, these sets were thrown together to create an illusion that was at best incomplete. What we need is detailed reproduction: costumes supplied by tradespeople, not sumptuous but adequate for the purposes of truth and for the interest of the scenes. Since everybody mourns the death of the drama our playwrights certainly ought to make a try at this type of popular, contemporary drama. At one stroke they could satisfy the public hunger for spectacle and the need for exact studies which grows more pressing every day. Let us hope, though, that the playwrights will show us real people and not those whining members of the working class who play such strange roles in boulevard melodrama.

As M. Adolphe Jullien* has said – and I will never be tired of repeating it – everything is interdependent in the theatre. Lifelike costumes look wrong if the sets, the diction, the plays themselves are not lifelike. They must all march in step along the naturalistic road. When costume becomes more accurate, so do sets; actors free themselves from bombastic declaiming; plays study reality more closely and their characters are more true to life. I could make the same observations about sets I have just made about costume. With them too, we may seem to have reached the highest possible degree of truth, but we still have long strides to take. Most of all we would need to intensify the illusion in reconstructing the environments, less for their picturesque quality than for dramatic utility. The environment must determine the character. When a set is planned so as to give the lively impression of a description by Balzac; when, as the curtain rises, one catches the first glimpse of the characters, their personalities and behaviour, if only to see the actual locale in which they move, the importance of exact reproduction in the decor will be appreciated. Obviously, that is the way we are going. Environment, the study of which has transformed science and literature, will have to take a large role in the theatre. And here I may mention again the question of metaphysical man, the abstraction who had to be satisfied with his three walls in tragedy – whereas the physiological man in our modern works is asking more and more compellingly to be determined by his setting, by the environment that produced him. We see then that the road to progress is still long, for sets as well as costume. We are coming upon the truth but we can hardly stammer it out.

Another very serious matter is diction. True, we have got away from the chanting, the plainsong, of the seventeenth century. But we now have a 'theatre voice', a false recitation that is very obtrusive and very annoying. Everything that is wrong with it comes from the fixed traditional code set up by the majority of critics.

[. . .]

* The book cited is *Histoire du Costume au Théâtre*, 1880.

Alas, yes, there is a 'theatre language'. It is the clichés, the resounding platitudes, the hollow words that roll about like empty barrels, all that intolerable rhetoric of our vaudevilles and dramas, which is beginning to make us smile. It would be very interesting to study the style of such talented authors as MM. Augier, Dumas and Sardou. I could find much to criticize, especially in the last two with their conventional language, a language of their own that they put into the mouths of all their characters, men, women, children, old folk, both sexes and all ages. This irritates me, for each character has his own language, and to create living people you must give them to the public not merely in accurate dress and in the environments that have made them what they are, but with their individual ways of thinking and expressing themselves. I repeat that that is the obvious aim of our theatre.

3.2.2 André Antoine, Commentary on *la mise en scène*

Translated by Joseph M. Bernstein

La Revue de Paris, April 1903

Modern directing must perform the same function in the theatre as descriptions in a novel. Directing should – as, in fact, is generally the case today – not only fit the action in its proper framework but also determine its true character and create its atmosphere.

This is an important task and one that is completely new – for which our classical French theatre has done little to prepare us. The result is that, despite the wealth of effort expended these past twenty years, we have not yet formulated any principles, laid down any foundations, established any teaching methods, trained any personnel [. . .]

The first time I had to direct a play, I saw quite clearly that the work was divided into two distinct parts: one was quite tangible, that is, finding the right *décor* for the action and the proper way of grouping the characters; the other was impalpable, that is, the interpretation and flow of the dialogue.

First of all, therefore, I found it useful, in fact indispensable, carefully to create the setting and the environment, without worrying at all about the events that were to occur on the stage. For it is the environment that determines the movements of the characters, not the movements of the characters that determine the environment.

This simple sentence does not seem to express anything very new; yet that is the whole secret of the impression of newness which came from the initial efforts of the Théâtre Libre [. . .]

For a stage set to be original, striking and authentic, it should first of all be built in accordance with something seen – whether a landscape or an interior. If it is an interior, it should be built with its four sides, its four walls, without worrying about the fourth wall, which will later disappear so as to enable the audience to see what is going on.

Next, the logical exits should be taken care of, with due regard for architectural accuracy; and, outside the set proper, the halls and rooms connecting with these exits should be plainly indicated and sketched. Those rooms that will only be partly seen, when a door opens slightly, should be furnished on paper. In short the whole house – and not just the part in which the action takes place – should be sketched [. . .]

In our interior sets, we must not be afraid of an abundance of little objects, of a wide variety of small props. Nothing makes an interior look more lived in. These are the imponderables which give a sense of intimacy and lend authentic character to the environment the director seeks to re-create.

Among so many objects, and with the complicated furnishings of our modern interiors, the performers' acting becomes, without their realizing it and almost in spite of themselves, more human, more intense, and more alive in attitude and gestures.

And now the lights!

[. . .] Light alone, intelligently handled, gives atmosphere and colour to a set, depth and perspective. Light acts physically on the audience: its magic accentuates, underlines, and marvellously accompanies the inner meaning of a dramatic work. To get excellent results from light, you must not be afraid to use and spread it unevenly.

The audience, though it is thrilled by a beautiful stage set skillfully lighted, is not yet at the point where it can forgo discerning clearly the face and slightest gestures of a favorite actor. We know your aversion for those carefully prepared effects in half darkness; yet far from spoiling your impression, these effects really safeguard it, without your suspecting it. So we directors must stand our ground and make no concessions in that respect. One day we shall be right: the broad public will finally realize or feel that, to create a stage picture, values and harmonies are needed which we cannot obtain without sacrificing certain parts. The audience will realize that it gains thereby a deeper and more artistic impression [. . .]

3 ANTON CHEKHOV AND KONSTANTIN STANISLAVSKY

Even if the founding of Antoine's Théâtre Libre predates the Moscow Art Theatre by a whole decade, it was Konstantin Stanislavsky who developed a specific theory of naturalistic acting. More than any other major naturalistic playwright, Anton Chekhov had the advantage of working with a theatre dedicated to his plays. Shaw only effectively achieved this in the 1904–07 Court Theatre seasons, Strindberg still more briefly for the single season of 1889 at his Scandinavian Experimental Theatre (modeled on the Théâtre Libre). Ibsen had already moved out of theatrical production and was in exile before he began writing his naturalistic plays. By contrast the MAT was associated from the beginning with Chekhov (*The Seagull* having marked its first season and provided the logo for its curtain). All his major plays were written specifically for Stanislavsky, and he was an active presence in rehearsals.

Chekhov wrote significantly less about his work than any of the other naturalists, and where extended comments occur in his letters these are generally concerned with fiction. However, a letter to Maria Kiselyova (written shortly after he had completed *The Seagull*) illuminates the naturalistic principles at the core of his drama. In particular his claim of a moral value for realism, objectivity, and the immediate connection between a writer and his/her time offers a clear statement of qualities central to all the naturalistic playwrights.

While Stanislavky's theatre also flirted with Symbolism, its significance was as an experimental proving-ground for his development of naturalistic staging and performance. In addition to Chekhov, whose plays remained in the repertoire for over half a century, up until the Russian Revolution, the MAT concentrated on plays by Maxim Gorki as well as standard works of Naturalism, which had also appeared on Antoine's programme (Ibsen, Hauptmann, Lev Tolstoi's *The Power of Darkness*). Stanislavsky's productions were reported in the press outside Russia, and seen in Europe on tours by the MAT in the 1920s. But it was his writings (first translated into English in the 1930s) that had the greatest impact. In addition to the concept of acting "truly", the practical correlative to Chekhov's aim of depicting life "as it really is", this extract outlines one of the most important keys to Stanislavsky's system: establishing objectives, which in terms of acting is the equivalent to the naturalists' focus on motivation. Dramatizing his theories in the form of workshop rehearsals, Stanislavsky projects his own voice into an imaginary alter-ego, the teacher Tortsov.

The most influential reports from Moscow followed this line in describing the rehearsal practices of the MAT. Severed from its roots in Chekhov and the spiritual aspect of Stanislavsky's acting, corresponding to the lyrical symbolic aspect of Chekhov and other naturalistic dramatists, his training rapidly became "the Method". This reduction to a series of acting exercises – which was one of the major factors that led to the widespread adoption of Stanislavsky in the American theatre – is well illustrated by a report by Norris Houghton, who listed the principles of the Moscow Art Theatre company as: (1) Physical development; (2) work with the actor's personal psychology involving self-control of the nervous system; (3) development of imagination and fantasy; (4) "offered circumstances" – learning to communicate the specific situations presented by an author; (5) naiveté – the actor "must believe in what he does and says"; (6) contact between the actors; (7) memorizing emotions; (8) rhythm; (9) developing the internal qualities of a character as well as its external form; (10) defining aim, or motivation. "The exercises based on this system of Stanislavsky's are practiced constantly" [*Moscow Rehearsals*, 1937].

3.3.1 Anton Chekhov, letter to Maria Kiselyova, January 1887

Translated by Michael Heim

"Letters of Anton Chekhov," *Anton Chekhov's Life and Thought*, Simon Karlinsky (ed.), Northwestern University Press. Originally published by Harper and Row, 1973

First of all, I have no more love for literature of the school we have been discussing [muck-raking realism] than you do. As a reader and man in the street I try to stay clear of it. But if you ask me my sincere and honest opinion about it, I must say that the issue of whether it has a right to exist or not is still open and unresolved by anyone, even though Olga Andreyevna thinks she has settled it. Neither you nor I nor all the critics in the world have any hard evidence in favor of denying this literature a right to exist. I don't know who is right: Homer, Shakespeare, Lope de Vega and the ancients as a group, who, while not afraid of digging around in the "manure pile," were morally much more stable than we are, or our contemporary writers, prudish on paper, but cold and cynical down deep and in life. I don't know who is in bad taste: the Greeks, who were not ashamed to celebrate love as it actually exists in all its natural beauty, or the readers of Gaboriau, Marlitt and Pierre Bobo [popular writers of pulp fiction]. Just like the problems of nonresistance to evil, free will and so on, this problem can only be settled in the future. All we can do is bring it up; any attempt at resolving it would involve us in spheres outside the realm of our competence. Your reference to the fact that Turgenev and Tolstoi avoid the "manure pile" throws no light on the matter. Their squeamishness proves nothing; after all, the generation of writers that came before them condemned the description of peasants and civil servants beneath the rank of titular councilor as filth, to say nothing of your "villains and villainesses." And anyway, one period, no matter how glorious it is, does not give us the right to draw conclusions in favor of one or another school. Your reference to the corrupting influence of the school under discussion does not solve the problem either. Everything in this world is relative and approximate. There are people who can be corrupted even by children's literature, who take special pleasure in reading all the little piquant passages in the Psalter and the Book of Proverbs. And there are people, who become purer and purer the more they come into contact with the filth of life. Journalists, lawyers and doctors, who are initiated into all the mysteries of human sin, are not known to be particularly immoral, and realist writers are more often than not of a higher moral caliber than Orthodox churchmen. And anyway no literature can outdo real life when it comes to cynicism. You're not going to get a person drunk with a jigger when he's just polished off a barrel.

2. Your statement that the world is "teeming with villains and villainesses" is true. Human nature is imperfect, so it would be odd to perceive none but the righteous. Requiring literature to dig up a "pearl" from the

pack of villains is tantamount to negating literature altogether. Literature is accepted as an art because it depicts life as it actually is. Its aim is the truth, unconditional and honest. Limiting its functions to as narrow a field as extracting "pearls" would be as deadly for art as requiring Levitan to draw a tree without any dirty bark or yellowed leaves. A "pearl" is a fine thing, I agree. But the writer is not a pastry chef, he is not a cosmetician and not an entertainer. He is a man bound by contract to his sense of duty and to his conscience. Once he undertakes this task, it is too late for excuses, and no matter how horrified, he must do battle with his squeamishness and sully his imagination with the grime of life. He is just like any ordinary reporter. What would you say if a newspaper reporter as a result of squeamishness or a desire to please his readers were to limit his descriptions to honest city fathers, high-minded ladies, and virtuous railroadmen?

To a chemist there is nothing impure on earth. The writer should be just as objective as the chemist; he should liberate himself from everyday subjectivity and acknowledge that manure piles play a highly respectable role in the landscape and that evil passions are every bit as much a part of life as good ones.

3. Writers are men of their time; and so, like the rest of the public, they must submit to the external conditions of life in society. There is therefore no question but what they must keep within the bounds of decency. That is all we have a right to demand of the realists. But since you have nothing to say against the execution or form of [the short story] "Mire," I must have remained within the bounds.

4. I must admit I rarely consult my conscience as I write. This is due to habit and the trivial nature of my work. Consequently, whenever I expound one or another view of literature, I always leave myself out of consideration.

3.3.2 Konstantin Stanislavsky, *An Actor Prepares*

Translated by Elizabeth Hapgood

' "You may play well or you may play badly; the important thing is that you should play truly," wrote Shchepkin to his pupil Shumski.

'To play truly means to be right, logical, coherent, to think, strive, feel and act in unison with your role.

'If you take all these internal processes, and adapt them to the spiritual and physical life of the person you are representing, we call that living the part. This is of supreme significance in creative work. Aside from the fact that it opens up avenues for inspiration, living the part helps the artist to carry out one of his main objectives. His job is not to present merely the external life of his character. He must fit his own human qualities to the life of this other person, and pour into it all of his own soul. The fundamental aim of our art is the creation of this inner life of a human spirit, and its expression in an artistic form.

'That is why we begin by thinking about the inner side of a role, and how to create its spiritual life through the help of the internal process of living the part. You must live it by actually experiencing feelings that are analogous to it, each and every time you repeat the process of creating it.'

[. . .]

'From what you have said I gather that to study our art we must assimilate a psychological technique of living a part, and that this will help us to accomplish our main object, which is to create the life of a human spirit,' Paul Shustov said.

'That is correct but not complete,' said Tortsov. 'Our aim is not only to create the life of a human spirit, but also to "express it in a beautiful, artistic form". An actor is under the obligation to live his part inwardly, and then to give to his experience an external embodiment. I ask you to note especially that the dependence of the body on the soul is particularly important in our school of art. *In order to express a most delicate and largely subconscious life it is necessary to have control of an unusually responsive, excellently prepared vocal and physical apparatus.* This apparatus must be ready instantly and exactly to reproduce most delicate and all but intangible feelings with great sensitiveness and directness. *That is why an actor of our type is obliged to work so much more than others*, both on his inner equipment, which creates the life of the part, and also on his outer physical apparatus, which should reproduce the results of the creative work of his emotions with precision.

'Even the externalizing of a role is greatly influenced by the subconscious. In fact no artificial, theatrical technique can even compare with the marvels that nature brings forth.'

[. . .]

'We find innumerable objectives on the stage and not all of them are either necessary or good; in fact, many are harmful. An actor must learn to recognize quality, to avoid the useless, and to choose essentially right objectives.'

'How can we know them?' I asked.

'I should define right objectives as follows,' said he:

'(1) They must be on our side of the footlights. They must be directed toward the other actors, and not toward the spectators.

'(2) They should be personal yet analogous to those of the character you are portraying.

'(3) They must be creative and artistic because their function should be to fulfil the main purpose of our art: to create the life of a human soul and render it in artistic form.

'(4) They should be real, live, and human, not dead, conventional or theatrical.

'(5) They should be truthful so that you yourself, the actors playing with you, and your audience can believe in them.

'(6) They should have the quality of attracting and moving you.

'(7) They must be clear cut and typical of the role you are playing. They must tolerate no vagueness. They must be distinctly woven into the fabric of your part.

'(8) They should have value and content, to correspond to the inner body of your part. They must not be shallow, or skim along the surface.

'(9) They should be active, to push your role ahead and not let it stagnate.

'Let me warn you against a dangerous form of objective, purely motor, which is prevalent in the theatre and leads to mechanical performance.

'We admit three types of objectives: the external or physical, the inner or psychological, and the rudimentary psychological type.'

[. . .]

'Dostoyevski was impelled to write *The Brothers Karamazov* by his lifelong *search for God*. Tolstoy spent all of his life struggling for *self-perfection*. Anton Chekhov wrestled with the *triviality* of bourgeois life and it became the leitmotive of the majority of his literary productions.

'Can you feel how these larger, vital purposes of great writers have the power to draw all of an actor's creative faculties to absorb all the details and smaller units of a play or part?

'In a play the whole stream of individual, minor objectives, all the imaginative thoughts, feelings and actions of an actor, should converge to carry out the *super-objective* of the plot. The common bond must be so strong that even the most insignificant detail, if it is not related to the *super-objective*, will stand out as superfluous or wrong.

'Also this impetus towards the super-objective must be continuous throughout the whole play. When its origin is *theatrical* or *perfunctory* it will give only an approximately correct direction to the play. If it is human and directed towards the accomplishment of the basic purpose of the play it will be like a main artery, providing nourishment and life to both it and the actors.

'Naturally, too, the greater the literary work, the greater the pull of its super-objective.'

[. . .]

'Perhaps it would be mote graphic if I made a drawing for you.'

This is what he drew:

THE THROUGH LINE OF ACTION

'All the minor lines are headed towards the same goal and fuse into one main current,' he explained.

'Let us take the case, however, of an actor who has not established his ultimate purpose, whose part is made up of smaller lines leading in varying directions. Then we have:

'If all the minor objectives in a part are aimed in different directions it is, of course, impossible to form a solid, unbroken line. Consequently the action is fragmentary, uncoordinated, unrelated to any whole. No matter how excellent each part may be in itself, it has no place in the play on that basis.

'Let me give you another case. We have agreed, have we not, that the main line of action and the main theme are organically part of the play and they cannot be disregarded without detriment to the play itself. But suppose we were to introduce an extraneous theme or put what you might call a tendency into the play. The other elements will remain the same but they will be turned aside, by this new addition. It can be expressed this way:

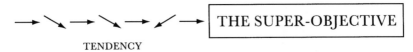

TENDENCY

'A play with that kind of deformed, broken backbone cannot live.'

4 BERNARD SHAW

Apart from short articles on individual plays (the first being Edmund Gosse's reviews of Ibsen's *Poems* followed by *Peer Gynt* in 1872), the earliest analysis in English of Ibsen's drama was Bernard Shaw's 1891 book, *The Quintessence of Ibsenism* (a collection of the lectures previously given to the Fabian Society). Widely read and hotly discussed, it made Ibsen a rallying point for progressive forces throughout the English-speaking world. It also provides a signal example of the impact of Ibsen's plays – even simply as dramatic texts: at the time none had yet been staged in England – in their effect on Shaw himself. His lectures on Ibsen marked Shaw's switch from novel-writing to drama. The Fabian origins of the *Quintessence* demonstrates the link between Naturalism and socialist politics; and the qualities Shaw highlighted in his discussion of each of Ibsen's plays (to that point) are precisely those that formed the basis of his own early plays. The extent of the parallel can be indicated by Shaw's defence of *Arms and the Man*, "A Dramatic Realist to his Critics":

Stage life is artificially simple and well understood by the masses; but it is very stale . . . Real life, on the other hand, is so ill understood, even by its clearest observers, that no sort of consistency is discoverable in it; there is no 'natural justice' corresponding to that simple and pleasant concept 'poetic justice'.

As a realist dramatist . . . it is my business to get outside these systems [the ethical systems to which the classifications of saint and sinner belong].

(*The New Review*, July 1894)

The extract from the *Quintessence* focuses on qualities perceived by Shaw in Ibsen's drama, that reappear in his own plays. These are the moral challenge inherent in the accurate and objective depiction of social life at the core of Naturalism, as well as picking out the attack on idealism as Ibsen's major theme – Ibsen's response to Brandes' 1871 lecture – and the naturalistic emphasis on women's experience.

The centrality of the political emphasis, posited by Shaw, in the wider reception of naturalistic drama is illustrated by a contemporary commentary from one of the earliest books to use the title "Modern Drama". This was by the American anarchist and feminist, Emma Goldman, whose view of naturalistic drama was heavily influenced by Shaw.

Art for art's sake presupposes an attitude of aloofness on the part of the artist toward the complex struggle of life: he must rise above the ebb and tide of life. He is to be merely an artistic conjurer of beautiful forms, a creator of pure fancy.

That is not the attitude of modern art, which is preeminently the reflex, the mirror of life. The artist being part of life cannot detach himself from the events and occurrences that pass panorama-like before his eyes, impressing themselves upon his emotional and intellectual vision.

The modern artist is, in the words of August Strindberg, 'a lay preacher popularizing the pressing questions of his time' . . . Ibsen, Strindberg, Hauptmann and a host of others mirror in their work as much of the spiritual as social revolt as is expressed by the most fiery speech of the propagandist. And more important still, they compel far greater attention. Their creative genius, imbued with the spirit of sincerity and truth, strikes root where the ordinary word often falls on barren soil . . .

Ibsen, Strindberg, Hauptmann, Tolstoy, Shaw, Galsworthy and the other dramatists contained in this volume represent the social iconoclasts of our time. They know that society has gone beyond the stage of patching up, and that man must throw off the dead weight of the past, with all its ghosts and spooks, if he is to go free of foot to meet the future.

This is the social significance which differentiates modern dramatic art from art for art's sake. It is the dynamite which undermines superstition, shakes the social pillars, and prepares men and women for the reconstruction.

(*The Social Significance of Modern Drama*, 1914)

3.4.1 Bernard Shaw, *The Quintessence of Ibsenism*, 1891

Ibsen had now written three immense dramas [*Brand, Peer Gynt, Emperor and Galilean*] all dealing with the effect of idealism on individual egotists of exceptional imaginative excitability. This he was able to do whilst his intellectual consciousness of his theme was yet incomplete, by simply portraying sides of himself. He has put himself into the skin of Brand, of Peer Gynt, and of Julian; and these figures have accordingly a certain direct vitality which belongs to none of his subsequent creations of the male sex. There are flashes of it in Relling, in Lövborg, in Ellida's stranger from the sea; but they are only flashes: henceforth all his really vivid and solar figures are women. For, having at last completed his intellectual analysis of idealism, he could now construct methodical illustrations of its social working, instead of, as before, blindly projecting imaginary personal experiences which he himself had not yet succeeded in interpreting. Further, now that he understood the matter, he could see plainly the effect of idealism as a social force on people quite unlike himself: that is to say, on everyday people in everyday life – on ship-builders, bank managers, parsons, and doctors, as well as on saints, romantic adventurers, and emperors. With his eyes thus opened, instances of the mischief of idealism crowded upon him so rapidly that he began deliberately to inculcate their moral by writing realistic prose plays of modern life, abandoning all production of art for art's sake. His skill as a playwright and his genius as an artist were thenceforth used only to secure attention and effectiveness for his detailed attack on idealism. No more verse, no more tragedy for the sake of tears or comedy for the sake of laughter

[. . .]

A typical Ibsen play is one in which the "leading lady" is an unwomanly woman, and the "villain" an idealist. It follows that the leading lady is not a heroine of the Drury Lane type; nor does the villain forge or assassinate, since he is a villain by virtue of his determination to do nothing wrong. Therefore readers of Ibsen – not playgoers – have sometimes so far misconceived him as to suppose that his villains are examples rather than warnings, and that the mischief and ruin which attend their actions are but the tribulations from which the soul comes out purified as gold from the furnace.

[. . .]

In following this sketch of the plays written by Ibsen to illustrate his thesis that the real slavery of to-day is slavery to ideals of virtue, it may be that readers who have conned Ibsen through idealist spectacles have wondered that I could so pervert the utterances of a great poet. Indeed I know already that many of those who are most fascinated by the poetry of the plays will plead for any explanation of them rather than that given by Ibsen himself in the plainest terms through the mouths of Mrs Alving, Relling, and the rest. No great writer uses his skill to conceal his meaning.

[. . .]

The statement that Ibsen's plays have an immoral tendency, is, in the sense in which it is used, quite true. Immorality does not necessarily imply mis-chievous conduct: it implies conduct, mischievous or not, which does not conform to current ideas. Since Ibsen has devoted himself almost entirely to shewing that the spirit or will of Man is constantly outgrowing his ideals, and that therefore conformity to them is constantly producing results no less tragic than those which follow the violation of ideals which are still valid, the main effect of his plays is to keep before the public the importance of being always prepared to act immorally to remind men that they ought to be as careful how they yield to a temptation to tell the truth as to a tempta-tion to hold their tongues, and to urge upon women that the desirability of their preserving their chastity depends just as much on circumstances as the desirability of taking a cab instead of walking. He protests against the ordinary assumption that there are certain supreme ends which justify all means used to attain them; and insists that every end shall be challenged to shew that it justifies the means. Our ideals, like the gods of old, are con-stantly demanding human sacrifices. Let none of them, says Ibsen, be placed above the obligation to prove that they are worth the sacrifices they demand; and let every one refuse to sacrifice himself and others from the moment he loses his faith in the reality of the ideal. Of course it will be said here by incorrigibly slipshod readers that this, so far from being immoral, is the highest morality; and so, in a sense, it is; but I really shall not waste any further explanation on those who will neither mean one thing or another by a word nor allow me to do so. In short, then, among those who are not ridden by current ideals no question as to the morality of Ibsen's plays will ever arise; and among those who are so ridden his plays will seem immoral, and cannot be defended against the accusation.

There can be no question as to the effect likely to be produced on an individual by his conversion from the ordinary acceptance of current ideals as safe standards of conduct, to the vigilant open-mindedness of Ibsen. It must at once greatly deepen the sense of moral responsibility.

[. . .]

I have a word or two to add as to the difficulties which Ibsen's philosophy places in the way of those who are called on to impersonate his characters on the stage in England. His idealist figures, at once higher and more mischievous than ordinary Philistines, puzzle by their dual aspect the con-ventional actor, who persists in assuming that if he is to be selfish on the stage he must be villainous; that if he is to be self-sacrificing and scrupulous

62

he must be a hero; and that if he is to satirize himself unconsciously he must be comic. He is constantly striving to get back to familiar ground by reducing his part to one of the stage types with which he is familiar, and which he has learnt to present by rule of thumb. The more experienced he is, the more certain is he to de-Ibsenize the play into a melodrama or a farcical comedy of the common sort. [. . .] If an actress of established reputation were asked to play Hedda Gabler, her first impulse would probably be not only turn Hedda into a Brinvilliers, or a Borgia, or a "Forget-me-not," but to suppress all the meaner callosities and odiousnesses which detract from Hedda's dignity as dignity is estimated on the stage. The result would be about as satisfactory to a skilled critic as that of the retouching which has made shop window photography the most worthless of the arts. The whole point of an Ibsen play lies in the exposure of the very conventions upon which are based those by which the actor is ridden. [. . .] He has not only made "lost" women lovable; but he has recognized and avowed that this is a vital justification for them, and has accordingly explicitly argued on their side and awarded them the sympathy which poetic justice grants only to the righteous. He has made the terms "lost" and "ruined" in this sense ridiculous by making women apply them to men with the most ludicrous effect. Hence Ibsen cannot be played from the conventional point of view: to make that practicable the plays would have to be rewritten. In the rewriting, the fascination of the parts would vanish, and with it their attraction for the performers. *A Doll's House* was adapted in this fashion, though not at the instigation of an actress; but the adaptation fortunately failed. Otherwise we might have to endure in Ibsen's case what we have already endured in that of Shakespear, many of whose plays were supplanted for centuries by incredibly debased versions, of which Cibber's *Richard III.* and Garrick's *Katharine and Petruchio* have lasted to our own time.

4

HENRIK IBSEN:
1828–1906

1 CONTEXT

Ibsen's development as a playwright can only be understood in terms of the cultural battle for Norwegian independence. Up until 1814 Norway had been ruled by Denmark, and even then remained in a union with Sweden, subordinated to a foreign King and unable to deal with foreign affairs. Ibsen himself puts emphasis on the libertarian effect of revolution elsewhere in Europe: as he remarked in the Preface to a reprinting of *Catiline* in 1875, his first play was written in "exciting and stormy times. The February Revolution of 1848, the revolutions in Hungary and elsewhere, the Prussian–Danish war over Schleswig and Holstein – all this had a powerful and formative effect on my development." But the struggle for a Norwegian culture was even more central. During the first half of the century Norwegian art and literature remained almost exclusively Danish, while (as in Ireland before the Irish Renaissance of the early twentieth century) the Norwegian language itself was largely restricted to the peasants.

It is only fairly recently that historians have analyzed the social and cultural aspect of national development, which forms the context for Ibsen's writing. Significantly, the areas considered crucial by historians are also integral elements in Ibsen's early plays: the recording of folklore and the historical glorification of the Vikings (which became the subject of several heroic tragedies), and the development of the Norwegian language (the first grammar being published when Ibsen was just 20 years old). From the first Ibsen was associated with cultural independence, being appointed as resident dramatist, then director at the first theatre to perform in Norwegian, the new Norske Theater in Bergen.

In choosing to write his poems and plays in Norwegian, Ibsen was making a political statement. At the same time, once he began writing naturalistic drama, he ensured that his plays were available for the world repertoire by having them immediately translated into German.

His early historical dramas may have had nationalistic themes, however his study of history (including *Emperor and Galilean*) also formed a basis for his naturalistic plays. As he commented just after completing *A Doll's House*: "An extensive knowledge of history is indispensable to an author; without it he is not in a position to understand the conditions of his own age, or to judge men, their motives and actions, except in the most incomplete and superficial manner" (Letter to John Paulsen, 20 September 1879). His letters, and later public speeches, also show that as he turned to naturalistic work, with its inherent criticism of society, he was less concerned with nationalism than individual freedom. One of his comments on the proposed new Norwegian flag is typical:

> It is said that Norway is an independent state, but I do not value much this liberty and independence so long as I know that the individuals are neither free nor independent. And they surely are not so with us. There do not exist in the whole country of Norway twenty-five free and independent personalities
> . . .
>
> Let the union sign remain, but take the monkhood sign out of the minds; take out the sign of prejudice, narrow-mindedness, wrong-headed notions, dependence and the belief in groundless authority – so that individuals may come to sail under their own flag. The one they are sailing under now is neither pure, nor their own.
>
> (Letter to Bjørnstjerne Bjørnson, July 1879)

Indeed Ibsen's dissatisfaction with Norwegian society had already led to self-imposed exile in 1864 (25 years before *A Doll's House*).

4.1.1 Anne-Lise Seip, *Cultural Nationalism in Norway*

The 1830s was a period in which a compromise was prepared. In three cultural fields important work was started which led to what has been labelled the "national breakthrough" in the 1840s. History became a science dedicated to the building up of an independent, national past. The first attempts at collecting folklore, folk-songs and folk-tales were made, and the possibility of creating a proper Norwegian language was discussed.

History became the handmaiden of nationalism. The historians Rudolf Keyser and Peter Andreas Munch established what was to be labelled by Danish colleagues "The Norwegian historical school". Keyser (1803–1864) was the theorist. In 1828 he gave his first lectures at the University, and maintained that Norway was populated from the north – an old idea, as we remember – while most of the Swedes and the Danes were "Goths", coming from the south and even being conquered by the northern race later on. He found his evidence in comparative linguistics. The quest for a separate "ethnic", in Anthony Smith's words, had started.

The instrumentality of the immigration theory in nation-building was clear. The Norwegians were seen as descendants of *one* race, with a common language, legal code and religion. From this "mother-race" the

Norwegians had developed into a people with its own "national character" and "an undiluted Norwegian spirit (*Volks-geist*)".

This theory, which by the way was contested also in Norway, was taken up by P. A. Munch, the greatest Norwegian historian of his time. It underpinned the Norwegian claim to be the true "owner" of the old Nordic language and culture, notably the sagas. The Norwegians fought hard for these and other historical treasures: "No right of property deserves more to be respected among nations than the right each has to its historical relics. To deprive a nation of these, is almost as unjust as to deprive it of part of its territory". And this generation indeed made an almost superhuman effort to secure these treasures for the nation.

Also, other treasures had survived into the present. Folk-tales, songs and fairy-tales had long been the object of scientific interest in other countries, including Denmark and Sweden. The first collection of folk legends was not published in Norway until 1833. It was an edition more in the tradition of the 18th century, exposing superstition in a dry language so as to expel it. In the years to come other important works were published: folk-songs collected by Jørgen Moe, M. B. Landstad and their informant Olea Crøger, daughter of a priest in Telemark and a great collector, and folk-tales by the same Jørgen Moe and P. C. Asbjørnsen.

[. . .]

The third field for cultural nation-building was in language. Here too, lines of demarcation were drawn in the 1830s. Henrik Wergeland wanted to enrich his prose and poetry with everyday expressions and words taken from the spoken language, which in many ways differed from the printed language, which was pure Danish. He met with fierce opposition from P. A. Munch. To create a genuine Norwegian language, he maintained, one had to go to those dialects which were less changed in the course of time, and which could bridge the gap with the old Norse language. This historical, etymological approach came to influence development immensely. Very soon a young genius took up the task of creating a Norwegian language. Ivar Aasen, son of a peasant on the west coast, started to collect samples of dialects in the vernacular, and also to prepare a grammar to create a common language. His motives were both national and social. Language was "the most distinctive mark of a nation", and Norway needed a language of its own. But the elements of such a language he found in his own social class, the rural population. He wanted to give it a language of its own. He was himself an autodidact, and declined to take his baccalaureate. In his personal conduct he underlined his peasant upbringing, never hanging his hat on the peg on the wall, but dropping it on the floor behind the door. His self-conceit was, however, mixed with true modesty, which perhaps explains why he gave up his own first plan to base a written Norwegian language on the existing dialects. He succumbed to the theories of P. A. Munch, who became his friend and mentor, and modelled his language after historical etymological principles, making it archaic and much less suited to the task he had set himself of creating a language that was easy to understand for the uneducated masses. Nevertheless, his Norwegian grammar, first published in 1848, as well as his dictionary of 1850 confirmed his theory that the vernacular was founded on the old Norse language, and was not, as hitherto believed, a distortion of Danish.

In the two decades from 1830 to 1850 the elements on which to build a Norwegian national identity had thus been established: a scientifically argued theory of a separate origin as a separate race, with its own territory and its own culture and institutions and "character", a documentation of a rich cultural heritage of music and orally transmitted literature hidden among the rural population, and a theory of a Norwegian language which had survived also among this population, going back to the Middle Ages, that distant but glorious time in history before the union with Denmark.

All this gave occasion for pride, and in the year 1849 the national enthusiasm exploded, so to speak, in the capital. In a series of so-called "tableaux", the daughters of Christiania acted as peasant girls against a background of curtains painted by Norwegian artists whom the revolutions of 1848 had forced back to Norway, while folk-music was played on the Hardanger fiddle and a choir of 100 men performed songs composed by musicians educated in Leipzig, but inspired by the "Norwegian tone" of the folk-songs.

These evening performances in 1849 were later on seen as the culmination of an epoch imprinted with national feeling.

> It was a time in the latter part of the 1840s when we, who were then young, so to speak realized that we – in the concrete and not only in the abstract – had a country (*Vaterland*), when we discovered that our people possessed a beautiful, big, common treasure of history, tales, songs, music, language, poetry and art, which all at once made it a cultured people (*Kulturvolk*) with a distinctive national stamp.

This was the verdict of an acute observer, the art historian Lorentz Dietrichson.

[. . .]

The 1860s saw the rise of a new wave of nationalism.

It started with a crisis in the relationship with Sweden. Toward the end of the 1850s the government decided to do away with one of the marks of inferiority which had been much resented, the provision that the king could place a Swedish governor in Norway. Nobody had occupied this post since the 1830s, and the abolishment of the office was considered in Norway to be uncontroversial, an impression which had been confirmed by the king himself. But the Swedish government said no. This created an intense national animosity, and once more a series of questions concerning the nature of the union were raised. [. . .]

This went together with other conflicts. Scandinavism was revitalized, but instead of uniting the elite, it divided it. In the wake of 1864, when Denmark was left to fight alone against Germany, some wanted to strengthen the bonds between Sweden and Norway, to protect the Scandinavian Peninsula. Others insisted on Denmark joining in. The split between "two-state Scandinavism" and "three-state Scandinavism" was seen as a conflict of nationalism. [. . .]

On this political background a nationalist revival took place. It centred around the same old questions: history and language.

Even though many of the theories of the Norwegian historical school had been abandoned, the problem of how to interpret the past was still there. The idea that the union with Denmark represented a "false soldering" between two parts of a broken golden ring – the Norwegian history – once put forward by Henrik Wergeland, was challenged by younger historians. "Who are our true ancestors?" asked the historian Mikael Birkeland in a speech to the Student Association in Christiania in 1866. Could it be denied that the economic development had been favourable during the union with Denmark? Was it not true that commerce and the cities had played a great part in this economic growth? Had not Norway benefited from the contact with other nations? Were our forefathers during those 400 years of civilizing development not our true fathers?

But this interpretation was not echoed by the new, radical intellectuals who gathered around the young historian Ernst Sars. The more "materialist" interpretations of conservative historians met with an idealist history-writing, which was for the rest of the century – and far into the next – to dominate the understanding of the past, stressing the link with the glorious Middle Ages through the mediation of the rural, peasant population. The bureaucracy was seen as "aliens" and "colonists". The task was to "demolish foreign elements and rebuild national unity."

The radical writers and publicists who gathered around Sars, also took up the cause of a national language. It was a cultural movement at first. Language societies were formed, uniting radical urbans and rural intellectuals, and a publishing house was established. In the course of the century the question was politicized. A series of laws strengthened the position of the "landsmål". In 1885 both languages became official.

*

Another crucial element in Ibsen's plays, which only became central once he turned to naturalistic subjects, was the position of women. Writing to Camilla Collett, one of the earliest and most influential advocates of women's rights through her novels *The Sheriff's Daughter* (*Amtmandens Dotre*, 1855) and *From the Camp of the Dumb* (*Fra de Stummes Lejr*, 1877), Ibsen recorded his "warm, complete sympathy with you and your life-task" and made a clear connection between literature and political change:

> The ideas and visions with which you have presented the world are not of the kind destined merely to lead a barren life in literature. Living reality will seize on them and build upon them. That this may happen soon, soon, I too wish with all my heart.
>
> (Letter to Camilla Collett, August 1881)

As the first historical survey below indicates, the situation of women in Scandinavia had already become a subject of debate by 1854 (the date when Norwegian daughters were given equal inheritance rights to sons). The way ideals of femininity frustrated self-expression and isolated women from public life forms the context for Ibsen's characters such as Hedda Gabler. Similarly, although male guardianship of unmarried women was abolished in Norway in 1863, and after 1866 women had the right to earn an independent living, the situation facing unmarried women was still bleak, giving added weight to both Mrs. Linde's attitude and Nora's decision in *A Doll's House*. In addition Norwegian nationalism itself contained a symbolic representation of gender, which denied equality. For instance, at the 17 May celebration of statehood in 1827 the procession carried paintings of Nora – a female symbol of the Norwegian nation – while the national anthem composed by Bjørnstjerne Bjørnson and first performed on 17 May 1864 (*Ja, vi elsker dette landet* – "Yes, we love this country") codified different roles for men and women. As a recent historical study argues,

> The song reflected the roles assigned to each gender in the construction of the national home: the strong father protecting his house, actively supported by his wife . . . Women, however, were given another activity as well: "all that the fathers have fought for, the mothers have wept for." Against this background, it seemed natural that men, as fathers and defenders of the nation, had the right to take part in political decisions. Men were obviously associated with the nation, whereas women had a more ambiguous role. As mothers they had their special function in the national home, but to take part in active combat did not comply with their femininity . . .
>
> This was clearly expressed, for example, in the debate in the Storting in 1890 about the first constitutional proposal for female suffrage. One argument cited against female suffrage was "the word 'public' – for how fine and ironic language often is – there is nothing to prevent us from saying that all of us, we are public men, but we know of course that if we linked the word public with the name of a woman, it would be the utmost disgrace . . . the veil is a garment that belongs to the woman, but never to the man, and whoever tears a woman's veil is guilty of a shameless deed" [Bishop J. C. Heuch]. The idea

that women had no place in the public sphere could scarcely have been expressed more clearly.

(Ida Blom, "Nation – Class – Gender," *Scandinavian Journal of History*, 1966)

The Norwegian Women's Rights League was founded in 1884, just five years after the first performance of *A Doll's House*, and from 1886 on published a biweekly woman's suffrage magazine, *Nylaende*. When they invited Ibsen to address their Festival in 1898, it was in recognition of the role his drama had played in fostering public awareness of the position of women in Norwegian society (as well as generally in Europe). That Festival marked the campaign for the first constitutional proposal to give women the vote, which reached parliament in 1890. But it was typical that his speech rejected any specific gender bias – just as he earlier denied the relevance of national liberation.

4.1.2 B.J. Hovde, The Position of Women in Scandinavia

The Scandinavian Countries 1720–1865: The Rise of the Middle Classes
(vol. II), Kennikat Press, 1972

The exploitation of Danish and Swedish wives, daughters, and servants by the men aroused the wholesouled anger of Mary Godwin, and the submissiveness of the women excited her contempt. But her description of the hardships of female servants was hardly as graphic as that of the Swedish economists Agardh and Ljungberg, written in 1854:

> The servant woman's duty is . . . to wait on every member of the household; to run every one's errands, and the language of her contract stipulates that, "she shall do all that is to be done." She must keep the rooms in order and tend the fires, carry wood up all the stairs, cook, bake, and brew; she must make, patch, and wash everyone's dirty clothes, often standing knee-deep in cold water; she must scrub the floors on hands and knees. She is expected to brush the men's clothing and clean their shoes. In the country districts she is sent out upon the fields in the heat, – and in several provinces only in her underwear – to work as strenuously as the men. Furthermore, she must make the beds for the master's family, and even for the male servants, conduct the masters to their bedrooms and there apply all her strength . . . to drag off their boots. Finally it became the lot of woman in Sweden to serve as odalisks at every inn and restaurant in order to attract customers. In short, woman in the North is the household beast of burden and the slave of man. We are so used to it that it does not arouse our shame.

Women of the middle classes although spared from drudgery, were even more cut off from really functional activity. They were either more intimate servants or decorative hothouse plants. If their fathers and husbands were rich enough to keep them in indolence, they might be given excellent formalistic educations, but they were separated from the world and from life by a Chinese wall of proprieties which usually served to frustrate any desires for active self expression. The wall was built of modesty, helplessness, delicacy, gratitude, and a chastity valued the more as it approached ignorance. The supreme virtue was obedience. As far as their means permitted, the men of the lower middle classes demanded of their women the same behavior. Never so much as then was home the woman's place; never did poets so ecstatically eulogize the "beautiful, weaker sex." [. . .]

If the lot of the daughter and the wife was drab, that of the unmarried woman was incredibly dreary. She was not even ornamental. Where she could perform some useful work in the house of her relatives she was able to maintain her self-respect and was often welcome. Otherwise she must become a burden, or seek refuge in some sort of foundation, or take employment as a servant. For women of the middle classes it was an almost insuperable degradation to become a servant. Refuges after the pattern of the Catholic convents – in Denmark they even continued to be called convents – were maintained by endowments, but were generally open only to members of the nobility and the bourgeoisie. The unmarried women of the common people had to shift for themselves. Agardh and Ljungberg estimated that Sweden had 270,000 of them in 1854, of whom about one fourth had given birth to illegitimate children.

> Very few of our readers have any conception of the extent of the misery and the consequent temptations, to which Swedish womanhood is at present exposed.

[. . .]

In Norway, Camilla Collett's book *Amtmandens dötre* (1855) marked the real beginning of the Norwegian feminist problem. Camilla Collett (1813–1895), the gifted daughter of Nicolai Wergeland and sister of Henrik Wergeland, measured her girl's wits with the best in Norway and held her own. No wonder she fretted under the conventional restraints. As early as 1833, she was clear in her own mind on the intellectual equality of woman with man, though neither her brother nor J. S. Welhaven, the man she loved, agreed. In her diary she recorded her sense of frustration.

> My life passes uselessly and without importance, suffocated by the eternal question whether this is really the kind of existence to which I am destined. It awakens me suddenly at night, I arise with it in the morning, and when I put on my night-cap in the evening and contemplate what I have done the whole day since I took it off I am saddened and ask myself why I dress at all, why I do not always wear it, for that would be most appropriate to such a night-cap life:

The experiences of her youth were interwoven with happiness and grief. Though freedom marked her father's liberal household, she could not escape the constraints of an illiberal society; she fell passionately in love with her brother's bitter rival, Welhaven, and, already torn between conflicting loyalties, lost her lover in part, at least, because her open adoration offended his sense of feminine propriety. Later Camilla Collett married the understanding and honorable professor of jurisprudence, John Collett, whom she could respect but never fully love. Hence, when she wrote *Amtmandens dötre*, she drew from her own experience the devastating realism with which she indicted the tyranny of convention over Norwegian women. Love and marriage was woman's career? Beautiful. But what woman was free to marry for love? In this and in her subsequent work the influence of George Sand is manifest. Though a bitter and disappointed woman, Camilla Collett made two important contributions to Norwegian culture: she inaugurated the woman's movement, and she ranks as the first pioneer in literary realism. *Amtmandens dötre* was at first denounced as an ugly book, even by Bjørnson, both for "feminine immodesty" and for its realism. But three of Norway's greatest literary artists have readily acknowledged their indebtedness to its authoress, namely Jonas Lie, Alexander Kielland, and Henrik Ibsen. In Ibsen's mind it planted the seed of *A Doll's House.*

Had it been left to the women to win their battles by their own pressure, nothing would have been won before 1865, for it is hardly possible to speak of a woman's *movement* until the early 1870's. But, as has been said, there were more fundamental forces at work which caused the men to begin reform before the women themselves became active. As early as 1825 the draft of the reformed Swedish legal code, due to the efforts of J. G. Richert, proposed to make women independent of guardianship at the age of twenty-five. Significantly, the two lower chambers supported it, but the nobility and the clergy successfully resisted adoption. As late as 1854, Swedish law classified unmarried women as minors along with children and the insane. Finally, in the session of 1856–58, the *riksdag* adopted the proposition, but only with reservations. Unmarried Danish women were made independent of guardians in 1857, Norwegian in 1863.

The adoption of equal rights in inheritance for women and men is, in each country, usually described as the true beginning of legal emancipation. It came first in Sweden (1845), then in Norway (1854), and finally also in Denmark (1857).

[. . .]

A famous proposal by the city physician of Copenhagen, Dr. Paul Scheel, in 1810, to combat prostitution by affording women opportunities to engage in trades and crafts was defeated by the gilds. After 1830, however, the problem became increasingly acute. On the one hand people realized that, "However much there may be conceded to the woman in thought, song, and speeches, she is denied practically everything as long as she is denied a personal life work." On the other, here were many who felt instinctively that ". . . the young woman who wants to earn a living represents an active social danger. She forecasts the twilight of many ancient gods. Beyond her lies a day when even the services of the wife do not belong to the husband but to herself." The pressure of surplus women and the triumphant course of the capitalistic motive of profit proved too strong to resist, however, especially when the growing complexity of life and increasing emigration created a demand for female labor. Hence it is not strange to find occupational freedom extended to unmarried women as part of the larger movement to establish occupational freedom. The Danish law of 1857, the Swedish of 1864, and the Norwegian ones of 1842 and 1866 established the right of the unmarried woman to earn her living in any craft or trade. But this concession only began the struggle for the economic equality of woman with man.

4.1.3 Henrik Ibsen, *Speech at the Festival of the Norwegian Women's Rights League*, Christiana, 26 May 1898

Translated by Evert Sprinchorn

I am not a member of the Women's Rights League. Whatever I have written has been without any conscious thought of making propaganda. I have been more the poet and less the social philosopher than people generally seem inclined to believe. I thank you for the toast, but must disclaim the honor of having consciously worked for the women's rights movement. I am not even quite clear as to just what this women's rights movement really is. To me it has seemed a problem of mankind in general. And if you read my books carefully you will understand this. True enough, it is desirable to solve the woman problem, along with all the others; but that has not been the whole purpose. My task has been the *description of humanity*. To be sure, whenever such a description is felt to be reasonably true, the reader will read his own feelings and sentiments into the work of the poet. These are then attributed to the poet; but incorrectly so. Every reader remolds the work beautifully and neatly, each according to his own personality. Not only those who write but also those who read are poets. They are collaborators. They are often more poetical than the poet himself.

With these reservations, let me thank you for the toast you have given me. I do indeed recognize that women have an important task to perform in the particular directions this club is working along. I will express my thanks by proposing a toast to the League for Women's Rights, wishing it progress and success.

The task always before my mind has been to advance our country and to give our people a higher standard. To achieve this, two factors are important. It is for the *mothers*, by strenuous and sustained labor, to awaken a conscious feeling of *culture* and *discipline*. This feeling must be awakened before it will be possible to lift the people to a higher plane. It is the women who shall solve the human problem. As mothers they shall solve it. And only in that capacity can they solve it. Here lies a great task for woman. My thanks! And success to the League for Women's Rights!

2 IBSEN'S NATURALISTIC DRAMA

Each of Ibsen's mature plays marks a new development. As he wrote in a tribute to Leopold Sacher-Masoch, "in these times every piece of creative writing should attempt to move the frontier markers" (1882). However, he repeatedly refers to the conceptual unity of his naturalistic plays – as in "I dare not go further than *Ghosts* . . . But *Ghosts* had to be written. After Nora, Mrs. Alving had to come" (Letter to Sophie Adlersparre, 24 June 1882). For Ibsen there was also an essential continuity, in the most general thematic terms, between his earlier heroic drama and his naturalistic work. Looking back on his first play, *Catiline* (completed in 1849), he commented: "Much that my later work concerns itself with – the conflict between one's aims and one's abilities, between what man purposes and what is actually possible, constituting at once both the tragedy and comedy of mankind and of the individual – is already vaguely intimated in this work" (Preface to *Cataline*, 1 February 1875). He had also adopted the stylistic principles associated with Naturalism while still engaged with heroic historical drama. Ibsen's statement in writing to his English translator, Edmund Gosse, in January 1874 is often cited as programmatic for naturalistic drama:

> The play is, as you must have observed, conceived in the most realistic style; the illusion I wished to produce was that of reality. I wished to produce the impression on the reader that what he was reading was something that had really happened. If I had employed verse, I should have counteracted my own intention and prevented the accomplishment of the task I had set myself. The many ordinary, insignificant characters whom I have intentionally introduced into the play would have become indistinct and indistinguishable from one another, if I had allowed them all to speak in the same rhythmical measure. We are no longer living in the days of Shakespeare. Among sculptors there is already talk of painting statues in the natural colours . . . I have no desire to see the Venus of Milo painted, but I would rather see the head of a negro executed in black than in white marble. Speaking generally the style must conform to the degree of ideality which pervades the representation. My new drama is no tragedy in the ancient acceptation; what I desired to depict were human beings, and therefore I would not let them talk the 'language of the Gods'.

The play referred to is in fact *Emperor and Galilean*, set in ancient Rome and dealing with highly philosophical and religious issues. However, the general principles outlined are those that Ibsen followed in his subsequent plays dealing with contemporary society: the stress on modernity, the individualization of even minor characters, and the use of everyday language. At the same time, it should be noted that he emphasizes both the illusory nature of the impression of reality, and a degree of symbolism – e.g. the relative abstraction of using "natural" material (unicolored marble) rather than detailed mimesis (representational painting). Writing to the director of *Ghosts* a decade later the same principles are restated. Ibsen insists that the "realism and ruthless honesty" in the "spirit and tone of the play" be rendered in the production, while the Swedish translation should make the dialogue "seem perfectly natural, and the manner of expression must differ from character to character . . . The effect of the play depends a great deal on making the spectator feel as if he were actually sitting, listening, and looking at events happening in real life" (Letter to August Lindberg, 1883). Responding to the "terrible uproar in the Scandinavian press" (Letter to Ludwig Passarge, 1881) Ibsen stressed the objectivity inherent in naturalistic presentation in an open letter:

> They [the critics] endeavour to make me responsible for the opinions expressed by some of the characters in the play. And yet there is not in the whole book a single opinion that can be laid to account of the author . . . The method in itself, the technique which determined the form of the work, entirely precluded the author's appearing in the speeches. My intention was to produce the impression in the mind of the reader that he was experiencing something real. Now nothing would more effectively prevent such an impression than the insertion of the author's private opinions in the dialogue . . .
>
> And they say that the book preaches nihilism. It does not. It preaches nothing at all. It merely points out that there is a ferment of nihilism under the surface, at home as elsewhere.
>
> (*Morgenbladet*, 14 January 1882)

However, this claim to objectivity was recognized as a "cowardly" evasion by Strindberg (in a letter to Edvard Brandes, 18 January 1882) and by Brandes. Like any other dramatist, a naturalistic playwright's opinions determine choice of subject and dramatic focus, and are expressed through structure and use of symbols.

As his letters show, Ibsen exercised control over the casting of his plays in Scandinavia (and to a lesser extent in Germany). He also advised directors on characterization and the way characters should be played, the setting and particularly the lighting, even the blocking of key scenes. So for *The Wild Duck* in 1884, he instructs Lindberg:

> I have supposed Hjalmar will be played by Reimers. This part must definitely not be rendered with any touch of parody nor with the faintest suggestion that

the actor is aware that there is anything funny about his remarks . . . His sentimentality is genuine, his melancholy charming in its way – not a bit of affectation . . .

The lighting too, has its significance; it differs from act to act and is calculated to correspond to the basic mood that characterizes each of the five acts . . . [in *A Doll's House* too Ibsen's lighting was keyed to the emotional tone of the action, with a gradual transition from brightness to deep darkness.] When Hedvig has shot herself, she should be placed on the couch in such a way that her feet are downstage, so that her right hand holding the pistol can hang down.

Similarly, for *Ghosts* in 1886 he describes the interior of a Norwegian country house to Duke Georg of Meiningen:

The living rooms of the oldest family house of this type are sometimes covered with coloured, dark wallpaper. Below the paper the walls are lined with simple wainscotting . . . The stoves are big and massive, generally of cast iron. The furniture is kept to the style of the First Empire; however, the colours are consistently darker.

And he also gives explicit instructions to individual actors, as for Sofie Reimers in the 1887 production of *Rosmersholm*:

. . . carefully observe what the other persons say about Rebecca. In earlier times our actors often committed the great mistake of studying their parts in isolation and without paying sufficient attention to the character's position in and connection with the work as a whole . . .

No declamation! No theatrical emphases! No pomposity at all! Give each mood credible, true to life expression. Do not ever think of this or that actress you may have seen.

Such comments display both the degree to which Ibsen's practical experience as a theatre-director informs the writing of his plays, and the way he intended his naturalistic principles to be carried through in the staging.

But his references to *Ghosts* as a "book" and to "readers" of the play are a recognition that the major influence of his work came through publication, rather than stage performance. His first naturalistic play, *The Pillars of Society*, was published in Norway a month before its first production, and had already sold 6,000 copies, with a second printing of 4,000 copies being required within two months. In the English-speaking countries the effect was even more marked. The first play by Ibsen to reach the London stage was *The Pillars of Society*, given a single matinee in 1880. By 1892 five other plays had been staged in England; *Ghosts* and *Rosmersholm* (two performances each), *The Lady from the Sea* (three performances), *Hedda Gabler* (ten matinees), plus *A Doll's House* (one week, but extended to 24 performances, in 1889) – though *A Doll's House* had also been presented in two short-lived adaptations, *Breaking a Butterfly* (1884) and *Nora* (1885). Up to 1893 fewer than 10,000 people in England can have seen staged performances of any play by Ibsen. By contrast, as William Archer pointed out,

> *The Pillars of Society, Ghosts* and *An Enemy of the People* were published in a shilling volume [in 1879] . . . up to the end of 1892 Mr. Walter Scott had sold 14,367 copies. In 1890 and 1891 the same publisher issued an authorized uniform edition of Ibsen's prose dramas in five volumes, at three, and six-pence each. Of these volumes up to the end of 1892, 16,834 copies had been sold. Thus, Mr. Walter Scott alone has issued (in round numbers) thirty-one thousand volumes . . . and each volume contains three plays. Thus we find that one publisher alone has placed in circulation ninety-three thousand plays by Ibsen. Other publishers have issued single-volume editions of *A Doll's House, Ghosts, Rosmersholm, The Lady from the Sea, Hedda Gabler* and *The Master Builder* . . . Thus, I think, we are well within the mark in estimating that one hundred thousand prose dramas by Ibsen have been bought by the English-speaking public in the course of the past four years. Is there a parallel in the history of publishing for such a result in the case of translated plays? Putting Shakespeare in Germany out of the question (and he has been selling, not for four years, but for a century), I doubt whether any translated dramas have ever sold in such quantities.
>
> ("The Mausoleum of Ibsen," *Fortnightly Review*, 1 July 1893)

The official view of Ibsen in England was still the one expressed by E.F.S. Piggott, the Examiner of Stage Plays, in 1892:

> I have studied Ibsen's plays pretty carefully, and all the characters seem to me to be morally deranged. All the heroines are dissatisfied spinsters who look on marriage as a monopoly, or dissatisfied married women in a chronic state of rebellion . . . as for the men, they are all rascals or imbeciles.
>
> (Testimony to the 1892 Select Committee on Censorship)

However, given such figures – and following Janet Achurch's success in the extended run of *A Doll's House* – it is perhaps not surprising that in 1893 there were successful productions of *The Master Builder*, Beerbohm Tree's *An Enemy of the People*, and an Ibsen "season" at the Opera Comique. From that point on, Ibsen's naturalistic plays became a standard feature of the English-speaking repertoire, as they had a decade earlier in Germany.

3 *A DOLL'S HOUSE*

As William Archer remarked, Ibsen's notes for *A Doll's House* "throw invaluable light upon the genesis of his ideas . . . Of *A Doll's House* we possess a first brief memorandum, a fairly detailed scenario, a complete draft in quite actable form, and a few detached fragments of dialogue" (Introduction, *From Ibsen's Workshop*, 1912). In particular the notes reveal the feminist critique of patriarchal society at the core of the play, and Ibsen's concept of the action as a tragedy for all the characters, and the ending as a "catastrophe" – not, even for Nora, a liberation.

The play

Henrik Ibsen, Notes for the modern tragedy

The Works of Henrik Ibsen, New York, 1912

Translated by A.G. Chater

There are two kinds of spiritual law, two kinds of conscience, one in man and another, altogether different, in woman. They do not understand each other; but in practical life the woman is judged by man's law, as though she were not a woman but a man.

The wife in the play ends by having no idea of what is right or wrong; natural feeling on the one hand and belief in authority on the other have altogether bewildered her.

A woman cannot be herself in the society of the present day, which is an exclusively masculine society, with laws framed by men and with a judicial system that judges feminine conduct from a masculine point of view.

She has committed forgery, and she is proud of it; for she did it out of love for her husband, to save his life. But this husband with his commonplace principles of honor is on the side of the law and looks at the question from the masculine point of view.

Spiritual conflicts. Oppressed and bewildered by the belief in authority, she loses faith in her moral right and ability to bring up her children. Bitterness. A mother in modern society, like certain insects who go away and die when she has done her duty in the propagation of the race. Love of life, of home, of husband and children and family. Now and then a womanly shaking off of her thoughts. Sudden return of anxiety and terror. She must bear it all alone. The catastrophe approaches, inexorably, inevitably. Despair, conflict, and destruction.

(Krogstad has acted dishonorably and thereby become well-to-do; now his prosperity does not help him, he cannot recover his honor.)

Scenario: first act

A room comfortably, but not showily, furnished. A door to the right in the back leads to the hall; another door to the left in the back leads to the room or office of the master of the house, which can be seen when the door is opened. A fire in the stove. Winter day.

She enters from the back, humming gaily; she is in outdoor dress and carries several parcels, has been shopping. As she opens the door, a porter is seen in the hall, carrying a Christmas tree. *She:* Put it down there for the present. (Taking out her purse) How much? *Porter:* Fifty öre. *She:* Here is a crown. No, keep the change. The porter thanks her and goes. She continues humming and smiling contentedly as she opens several of the parcels she has brought. Calls off to find out if he is home. Yes! At first, conversation through the closed door; then he opens it and goes on talking to her while continuing to work most of the time, standing at his desk. There is a ring at the hall door; he does not want to be disturbed; shuts himself in. The maid opens the door to her mistress's friend, just arrived in town. Happy surprise. Mutual explanation of the state of affairs. He has received the post of manager in the new joint-stock bank and is to begin at New Year's; all financial worries are at an end. The friend has come to town to look for some small employment in an office or whatever may present itself. Mrs. Stenborg encourges her, is certain that all will turn out well. The maid opens the front door to the debt collector. Mrs. Stenborg terrified; they exchange a few words; he is shown into the office. Mrs. Stenborg and her friend; the circumstances of the collector are touched upon. Stenborg enters in his overcoat; has sent the collector out the other way. Conversation about the friend's affairs; hesitation on his part. He and the friend go out; his wife follows them into the hall; the Nurse enters with the children. Mother and children play. The collector enters. Mrs. Stenborg sends the children out to the left. Big scene between her and him. He goes. Stenborg enters; has met him on the stairs; displeased; wants to know what he came back for? Her support? No intrigues. His wife cautiously tries to pump him. Strict legal answers. Exit to his room. *She:* (repeating her words when the collector went out) But that's impossible. Why, I did it from love!

Second act

The last day of the year. Midday. Nora and the old Nurse. Nora, driven by anxiety, is putting on her things to go out. Anxious random questions of one kind and another intimate that thoughts of death are in her mind. Tries to banish these thoughts, to make light of it, hopes that something or other may intervene. But what? The Nurse goes off to the left. Stenborg enters from his room. Short dialogue between him and Nora. The Nurse re-enters; looks for Nora; the youngest child is crying. Annoyance and questioning on Stenborg's part; exit the Nurse; Stenborg is going in to the children. Doctor enters. Scene between him and Stenborg. Nora soon re-enters; she has turned back; anxiety has driven her home again. Scene between her, the Doctor, and Stenborg. Stenborg goes into his room. Scene between Nora and the Doctor. The Doctor goes out. Nora alone. Mrs. Linde enters. Scene between her and Nora. Lawyer Krogstad enters. Short scene between him,

Mrs. Linde, and Nora. Mrs. Linde in to the children. Scene between Krogstad and Nora. She entreats and implores him for the sake of her little children; in vain. Krogstad goes out. The letter is seen to fall from outside into the letter box. Mrs. Linde re-enters after a short pause. Scene between her and Nora. Half confession. Mrs. Linde goes out. Nora alone. Stenborg enters. Scene between him and Nora. He wants to empty the letter box. Entreaties, jests, half-playful persuasion. He promises to let business wait till after New Year's Day; but at 12 o'clock midnight ...! Exit. Nora alone. *Nora*: (looking at the clock) It is five o'clock. Five; seven hours till midnight. Twenty-four hours till the next midnight. Twenty-four and seven – thirty-one. Thirty-one hours to live.

Third act

A muffled sound of dance music is heard from the floor above. A lighted lamp on the table. Mrs. Linde sits in an armchair and absently turns the pages of a book, tries to read, but seems unable to fix her attention; once or twice she looks at her watch. Nora comes down from the party; so disturbed she was compelled to leave; surprise at finding Mrs. Linde, who pretends that she wanted to see Nora in her costume. Helmer, displeased at her going away, comes to fetch her back. The Doctor also enters, to say good-by. Meanwhile Mrs. Linde has gone into the side room on the right. Scene between the Doctor, Helmer, and Nora. He is going to bed, he says, never to get up again; they are not to come and see him; there is ugliness about a deathbed. He goes out. Helmer goes upstairs again with Nora, after the latter has exchanged a few words of farewell with Mrs. Linde. Mrs. Linde alone. Then Krogstad. Scene and explanation between them. Both go out. Nora and the children. Then she alone. Then Helmer. He takes the letters out of the letter box. Short scene; good night; he goes into his room. Nora in despair prepares for the final step, is already at the door when Helmer enters with the open letter in his hand. Big scene. A ring. Letter to Nora from Krogstad. Final scene. Divorce. Nora leaves the house.

As this scenario indicates, although the names of some characters are different, the action of the play has been worked out in detail from its first conception. Apart from the broadening of focus – in the scenario everything is presented from Nora's viewpoint – the most significant change in the final text is the introduction of the tarantella. Off-stage in the scenario, the dance may have been brought in to capitalize on the abilities of Betty Hennings, the first actress to play the role (at the Copenhagen Royal Theatre, 1879) who had been a ballerina.

All Ibsen's naturalistic plays aroused protests, but *A Doll's House* was met with more vehement denunciation than any other, with the possible exception of *Ghosts* – and one recurring criticism was that "Nora has only shown herself as a little Nordic 'Frou-Frou' and as such she cannot be transformed in a flash to a Soren

Kierkegaard in skirts" (*Dagens Nyheder*, 22 December 1879). The notes make clear that Nora is confused by conflicting value systems; and as Archer was the first to point out, commenting on Eleonora Duse's performance:

> If she were really and essentially the empty-headed doll we hear so much about, the whole point of the play would be gone; so that there is not the least reason why we should demand from the actress a waxen, flaxen prettiness, on which experience has left no traces. The critics, in fact, sublimely unconscious of the way in which they thereby drive home the poet's irony, fall into the very same misunderstanding of Nora's character which makes Helmer a bye-word for masculine stupidity, and are no less flabbergasted than he when the doll puts off her masquerade dress and turns out to be a woman after all. And if Nora is not really childish, still less is she "neurotic".

(Theatrical World, 1893)

A Doll's House: chronology of major early performances

December 1879, *A Doll's House*, is published by Gyldendal, Copenhagen		
December 1879 Copenhagen	Royal Theatre	Nora: Betty Hennings
January 1880 Stockholm	Christiana Theatre	Nora: Johanne Juell
March 1880 Munich	Residenztheater	Nora: Marie Ramlo
1882 Warsaw	Imperial Theatre	Nora: Modjeska [Helene Modrzejewska]
June 1889 London	Novelty Theatre (later the Kingsway) Director: Charles Charrington	Nora: Janet Achurch
February 1891 Milan	Teatro di Filodrammatici	Nora: Eleonora Duse
April 1892 London	Avenue Theatre	Nora: Janet Achurch
March 1893 London	Royalty Theatre	Nora: Janet Achurch
October 1894 Berlin	Deutsches Theater Director: Otto Brahm	Nora: Agnes Sorma
May 1897 London	Globe Theatre	Nora: Janet Achurch
May 1905 New York	New Lyceum Theatre	Nora: Ethel Barrymore
December 1906 St. Petersburg	Komissarzhevskaya Theatre Director: Vsevolod Meyerhold	Nora: Vera Komissarzhevskaya
November 1917 Berlin	Kammerspiele Director: Max Reinhardt	Nora: Irene Triesch

April 1918	Plymouth Theatre	Nora: Alla Nazimova
New York		
June 1918	Workers' Club	
Petrograd	Director: Vsevolod	
	Meyerhold	
February 1933	Companie Pitoëf	Nora: Mme. Pitoëf
Paris		
December 1937	Morosco Theatre	Nora: Ruth Gordon
New York	Director and Producer:	
	Jed Harris	

Performance and reception

Apart from the initial performances in Scandinavia between 1879 and 1880, for the first decade, audiences saw adaptations of *A Doll's House* with a very different ending from the one Ibsen had written. This was initially due to Ibsen himself. Commenting later on the public reaction to *Ghosts*, he acknowledged "A writer dare not alienate himself so far from people that there is no longer any understanding between them and him" (Letter to Sophie Adlersparre, 1882). So when the Berlin actress Hedwig Niemann-Raabe, who was to play Nora in the first German production, declared she could never leave her children – and would be unable to play such an unnatural act convincingly – Ibsen revised the ending specifically for her.

Figure 4.1 A Doll's House, Royal Theatre, Copenhagen: 1879. The 'tarantella' scene in Act II with Betty Hennings

At the same time in an open letter Ibsen protested against the change. Despite the growing acceptance of his work, he was forced to continue defending the integrity of the original ending by theatre managers who wished to stage the play in a form more acceptable to their audiences. His correspondence indicates the extent to which bourgeois society felt threatened by *A Doll's House*, even over a decade after it first appeared.

Ibsen's revised ending – with its sentimental appeal, restoration of the sexual status quo, and evasion of the moral issues raised in the preceding discussion – was preferred by such leading dramaturges as Heinrich Laube in Vienna and Maurice in Hamburg. It became the standard ending for European productions between 1880 and 1882, and formed the basis for further adaptations – as in Helene Modjeska's *Thora*, first performed in St. Petersburg in 1881 then toured across America in 1883 – though even critics who objected to the original ending found the revision inconsistent:

> A brilliant audience crowded Macaulay's Theater last evening, the occasion being the first presentation in America of 'Thora', a Norwegian drama by Henrik Ibsen . . .
>
> The drama opens promisingly . . . The third and last act, however, does not fulfill the promise of the first and second. It begins dramatically, but ends turgidly . . . finally through the medium of the children and some indefinite talk about 'religion' there is a reunion, a rushing together and a falling curtain on a happy family tableau. The principal inconsistency of the play is at this point. A woman cherishing as high an ideal of her husband as *Thora* did, and finding him as unworthy of it as *Helmer* was, cannot mount him again on his pinnacle through any such superficial means as here employed. In the original drama, *Thora* carries out the logic of the situation by leaving her husband. Probably after all the most consistent ending would be her death.
>
> (*Louisville Courier-Journal*, 8 December 1883)

The most notorious of these adaptations was the English version of *A Doll's House*, performed by Beerbohm-Tree in 1884 under the title of *Breaking a Butterfly*. Although greeted with mixed reviews, the critical consensus was that this play – and, since it was taken to correspond to Ibsen's text which was not yet available in translation, the original too – was unimportant and trifling. However, those English critics familiar with Ibsen's text condemned the adaptation as a travesty. Arguing that "Ibsen's drama is, in short, a plea for woman's rights – not for her right to vote and prescribe medicine, but for her right to exist as a responsible member of society" William Archer pointed out that the adaptation had cut Nora's children, removing the source of her anguish. In addition, a comic sister for Nora's husband is substituted for the sombre figure of the dying Doctor; and Mrs. Linde, the woman who plays on the blackmailer's better nature and persuades him to send back the forged document, is replaced by a book-keeper who steals the "fatal paper". As one critic (Edward Aveling) pointed out, "the authors of this conventional little play have succeeded in the Herculean labour of making Ibsen appear common-place" and the type of alterations "are a sad reminder of the condition of our bourgeois morality generally" in reducing social analysis to standard melodrama:

> ... the whole moral of the Norwegian play is lost in the English version by Helmer taking upon himself the crime supposed to have been committed . . . It is however in the ending that the dramatists have most deeply sinned. Whatever may be thought of Ibsen's ending, it is not conventional . . . the ending is as unhappy as it is truthful, and British audiences require the last words of a play to part of a chorus of general congratulations.
>
> (*Today*, 1884)

4.3.2 Henrik Ibsen, the revised ending to *A Doll's House*

Translated by Richard Badger

NORA.   That our life together would be a real marriage. Goodbye. (*She is about to go.*)

HELMER.   (*Takes her by the arm.*) Go, if you must, but see your children for the last time.

NORA.   Let me go. I don't want to see them. I cannot.

HELMER.   (*Draws her towards the door at the left.*) You must see them. (*Opens the door and says softly:*) Do you see – there they sleep carefree and quietly. Tomorrow when they awaken and call for their mother, they will have none . . .

NORA.   (*Trembling.*) No mother . . .

HELMER.   As you have had none.

NORA.   No mother! (*An internal struggle. She lets her bag fall and says:*) Oh, I am sinning against myself, but I cannot leave them. (*She sinks down at the door.*)

HELMER.   (*Happy, says softly:*) Nora!

(*The curtain falls.*)

4.3.3 Henrik Ibsen, letter to the *Nationaltidende*, 17 February 1880

MUNICH, 17*th February* 1880.

To the EDITOR

SIR, – In No.1360 of your esteemed paper I have read a letter from Flensburg, in which it is stated that *A Doll's House* (in German *Nora*) has been acted there, and that the conclusion of the play has been changed – the alteration having been made, it is asserted, by my orders. This last statement is untrue. Immediately after the publication of *Nora*, I received from my translator, Mr. Wilhelm Lange, of Berlin, who is also my business manager as far as the North German theatres are concerned, the information that he had reason to fear that an "adaptation" of the play, giving it a different ending, was about to be published and that this would probably be chosen in preference to the original by several of the North German theatres.

In order to prevent such a possibility, I sent to him, for use in case of absolute necessity, a draft of an altered last scene, according to which Nora does not leave the house, but is forcibly led by Helmer to the door of the children's bedroom; a short dialogue takes place, Nora sinks down at the door, and the curtain falls.

This change I myself, in the letter to my translator, stigmatise as "barbaric violence" done to the play. Those who make use of the altered scene do so entirely against my wish. But I trust that it will not be used at very many German theatres.

As long as no literary convention exists between Germany and the Scandinavian countries, we Scandinavian authors enjoy no protection from the law here, just as the German authors enjoy none with us. Our dramatic works are, therefore, in Germany exposed to acts of violence at the hands of translators, theatrical directors, stage-managers, and actors at the smaller theatres. When my works are threatened, I prefer, taught by experience, to commit the act of violence myself, instead of leaving them to be treated and "adapted" by less careful and less skilful hands. – Yours respectfully,

HENRIK IBSEN.

4.3.4 Henrik Ibsen, letter to Moritz Prozor, 23 January 1891

Translated by Mary Morrison

MUNICH, 23rd January 1891.

DEAR COUNT PROZOR, – Mr. Luigi Capuana has, I regret to see, given you a great deal of trouble by his proposal to alter the last scene of *A Doll's House* for performance in the Italian theatres.

I do not for a moment doubt that the alteration you suggest would be distinctly preferable to that which Mr. Capuana proposes. But the fact is that I cannot possibly directly authorise any change whatever in the ending of the drama. I may almost say that it was for the sake of the last scene that the whole play was written.

And, besides, I believe that Mr. Capuana is mistaken in fearing that the Italian public would not be able to understand or approve of my work if it were put on the stage in its original form. The experiment ought, at any rate, to be tried. If it turns out a failure, then let Mr. Capuana, on his own responsibility, employ your adaptation of the closing scene; for I cannot formally authorise, or approve of, such a proceeding.

I wrote to Mr. Capuana yesterday, briefly expressing my views on the subject; and I hope that he will disregard his misgivings until he has proved by experience that they are well founded.[1]

At the time when *A Doll's House* was quite new, I was obliged to give my consent to an alteration of the last scene for Frau Hedwig Niemann-Raabe, who was to play the part of Nora in Berlin. At that time I had no choice. I was entirely unprotected by copyright law in Germany, and could, consequently, prevent nothing. Besides, the play in its original, uncorrupted form, was accessible to the German public in a German edition which was already printed and published. With its altered ending it had only a short run. In its unchanged form it is still being played.

The enclosed letter from Mr. Antoine I have answered, thanking him for his intention to produce *The Wild Duck*, and urging him to make use of your translation. Of course I cannot tell what he will decide. But as the Théâtre Libre is really of the nature of a private society, it is probably not possible to procure a legal injunction. There are, besides, reasons which would render the taking of such a step inadvisable, even if possible. However, I leave the decision of this question entirely to you, assured that you will act in the best way possible.

*

In a sense even such extreme adaptations as *Breaking a Butterfly* were simply an attempt to make sense of an action – not only Nora's exit from her marriage, but abandoning her children – which denied accepted attitudes and expectations of the time to such an extent that Nora's motivation appeared incomprehensible. Even in Germany, the country most open to Ibsen's naturalistic drama, critical response was initially unfavorable. For instance, the reviewers of *Die Gegenwart* (18, 1880) and *Deutsche Rundschau* (26, 1881) saw the play as clearly didactic, dealing with a serious subject, but were confused about the actual message, and attacked the character development of Nora, finding the woman of the final act incompatible with the child-mother of the opening. However, attitudes changed in Germany after the publication of a monograph on Ibsen – by L. Passarge in 1883, the very first to appear, predating Shaw's study by almost a decade. Indeed it was only when more extensive analyses of Ibsen's work were published that the integrity of the original ending was recognized, and then became the standard staging.

In England William Archer's production of *A Doll's House* in his own translation preceded Shaw's lectures on *The Quintessence of Ibsenism*. It was a popular success, and although the play itself was heavily attacked by all the critics, even unsympathetic reviews praised the performance:

The interest was so intense last night that a pin might have been heard to drop. Miss Janet Achurch received the enthusiastic congratulations she so

---

[1] Luigi Capuana (born 1839), an Italian novelist and dramatic critic, translated *A Doll's House* into Italian. It was the famous actress, Eleonora Duse, who wished him to alter the last scene of the play; but she finally accepted and acted it in the original form.

well deserved, and when the curtain fell there was such cheering that Mr. Charrington promised to telegraph the happy result to Henrik Ibsen. We cannot doubt that all who desire to become better acquainted with the author's new-fangled theories, and to see them put into practice in the most satisfactory manner, will crowd the Novelty Theatre for the next few evenings. If they cannot agree with the author, they will, at any rate, see some admirable acting.

(*Sunday Times*, 7 June 1889)

The play had already become a "vehicle" for star actresses, such as Helena Modjeska – as reviews of her 1883 performance indicate:

The production last evening was a novelty, curiosity to see Modjeska in a new role, as well as admiration for the great actress arousing more than ordinary interest in the performance . . . Her portrayal of the innocent, gay, true-hearted *Thora* is full of beauty and varying charm, reaching in the second act a nervous intensity and strength and yet maintaining a rare delicacy and grace which seem in the power of none so well as this actress . . . The character, indeed, is a beautiful one, and in that pure womanliness, that exquisite art necessary for its interpretation, where is the actress so gifted as Modjeska? Modjeska, in truth, was the performance.

(*Louisville Courier-Journal*, 8 December 1883)

Indeed it was *A Doll's House* that made Janet Achurch a star, attracting the attention of Bernard Shaw, who wrote *Candida* (his "counterblast" to Ibsen, showing that in the typical doll's house "it is the man who is the doll") for her.

Among others who saw Janet Achurch's performance in 1889 was the actress/producer Elizabeth Robins, who was inspired by this to become the leading interpreter of Ibsen in America; and Achurch's rendering of Nora remained the standard against which English critics measured other actresses who took up the role – notably Eleonora Duse. But if *A Doll's House* became a star vehicle, it was because, like Ibsen's other naturalistic plays, this was one of the few challenging leading roles for women in contemporary drama.

Ibsen was not only an advocate of woman's rights (despite his own disclaimers). His plays also reversed gender stereotypes by making the actress the central figure in performance; and, as Archer argued, *A Doll's House* was the play that had the most impact of all Ibsen's work, especially in spreading the new drama to England and North America.

4.3.5 William Archer, Producing *A Doll's House* (Letter to Charles Archer)

13 *June*, '89

We have fought a good fight for the Old Min [pet name for Ibsen], and have won a really glorious victory. It would take me a day's hard writing to give you full details, but I shall send along with this a budget of press notices. Of course most of them are silliness itself; but still the play has been the great event of the week– almost of the season. It has been more talked about and written about than even *The Profligate*. It holds the B.P. like a vice – and what's more, they pay to see it. The receipts are not large – between £35 and £45 a performance – but that, for an out-of-the-way house, is by no means bad, especially as it is scarcely advertised at all. Of course Miss Achurch has the lioness's share in the success. She is really a delightful Nora – not ideal; her voice and tricks of utterance forbid that – but she *feels* the part right through, and is often very fine and even noble. In short she is *a* Nora and a very beautiful one, though not quite *the* Nora. It is by far the biggest thing she has ever done; compliments and offers of engagements have poured in upon her; no actress for years has made such a success. She varies rather from night to night. I always go to see the last scene, which is to me *the* great thing of the piece and one of the Old Min's biggest achieve-ments; and once or twice I have seen her play it *perfectly*. At other times she goes in for motiveless *fortes* and *pianos* which mar the smoothness of it. On the first night Waring (Helmer) got a little wrong in his lines and didn't say the speech: "I would work for you, etc.; but no man sacrifices his honour even for one he loves" – so that of course she couldn't get in her *Millions of women have done that*. I was mad at that, for she speaks it beautifully – it was almost the one misfortune of a glorious evening. Since then we have of course got the passage put right, and the B.P. now rises to the occasion unfailingly . . . . But *what* a scene that is! Every speech in it rings like a clarion. They may call it pure logic if they like, but it is logic saturated with emotion. I cry over it every night. It's very curious, the first time I saw Miss A. rehearse it she was deadly – querulous, whimpering, wretched. I arranged to meet her half an hour before the next rehearsal and go through the scene with her; but that day she was ill and didn't come to rehearsal at all; so I told Charrington what I thought was wrong, and he said he would go through it with her. The next rehearsal I sat in the stalls and listened to it – the thing was totally different. It gripped me line by line and simply thrilled me with intellectual pleasure and intense emotion. At the end she came to the footlights and said: "How was that?" I said: "If that scene moves the audience half as much as it has moved me to-day, the play's all right" – and it was! There was another rather amusing thing about that scene. X. Y., the acting manager, a Philistine of the Philistines, happened to see it one day at rehearsal. At the end he said: "You'll excuse me, Miss Achurch, it's no business of mine, but I can't help saying that that scene's splendid – most interesting – certain to go." She rushed across the stage and almost embraced him, and we were all delighted to have conquered the doughty Y. But next day he came to me and said: "It was rather good, my going into raptures over that scene. *I* had no idea it was the last act. *I* thought it was the first act, and it was all going to be cleared up . . . ."

Fru Gundersen of the Xiania Theatre, who is over here just now, told me Miss A. was the best Nora she had ever seen, and she had no reason to put it as strongly as that if she didn't think so. In short we have had a splendid week, and whatever else comes of it, Ibsen has triumphed.

4.3.6 Elizabeth Robins, *Ibsen and the Actress*

In dealing with Ibsen's significance to the acting profession, I naturally think of one actress in particular whose view would have been immensely interesting. I mean, of course, the woman to whom belongs the lasting honour of being the first person to play a great Ibsen part in England – Janet Achurch. As she is not here, I was going to say – but in a sense she is here, vivid in the consciousness of all who ever saw her act. As she cannot, however, speak to you, I think the makeshift-best I can do in this direction is to tell you about my own recollection of the first production of *A Doll's House*, for that occasion, in addition to so much else, stood for Ibsen and at least three actresses: Janet Achurch, Marion Lea, and myself, plus I don't know how many more, who were to be affected by that day's happening. I do not know whether I had ever heard Ibsen's name till the afternoon when I went with my friend Marion Lea to see her friend act *A Doll's House*.

I cannot think such an experience was ever ushered in with so little warning. There was not a hint in the pokey, dingy theatre, in the sparse, rather dingy audience, that we were on the threshold of an event that was to change lives and literatures. The Nora of that day must have been one of the earliest exceptions – she was the first I ever saw – to the rule that an actress invariably comes on in new clothes, unless she is playing a beggar. This Nora, with her home-made fur cap on her fair hair, wore the clothes of Ibsen's Nora, almost shabby, with a touch of prettiness.

I never knew before or since anybody strike so surely the note of gaiety and homeliness as Janet Achurch did in that first scene. You saw her biting into one of the forbidden macaroons, white teeth flashing, blue eyes full of roguery, her entire *Wesen* inviting you to share that confidence in life that was so near shipwreck. The unstagey effect of the whole play (and that must have owed much to Charles Charrington) made it, to eyes that first saw it in '89, less like a play than like a personal meeting – with people and issues that seized us and held us, and wouldn't let us go.

I remember Marion Lea wanted desperately to play Nora – in the provinces, in America, anywhere. Strangely, it didn't take me like that. Janet Achurch's acting had carried me clean out of myself. I didn't even feel on that first occasion, as I did later, that the Tarantella dance was, from the point of view of the theatre, somehow a mistake. But the famous lines: "Millions of women have done so" and ". . . it burst upon me that I had been living here these eight years with a strange man, and had borne him three children" – for all time they should be said just as they were first said, and by just that person.

4.3.7 William Archer, *A Doll's House* and the Ibsen Revolution

If we may measure fame by mileage of newspaper comment, Henrik Ibsen has for the past month been the most famous man in the English literary world. Since Robert Elsmere left the Church, no event in 'coëval fictive art' (to quote a modern stylist) has exercised men's, and women's, minds so much as Nora Helmer's departure from her Doll's House. Indeed the latter exit may be said to have awakened even more vibrant echoes than the former; for, while Robert made as little noise as possible Nora slammed the door behind her. Nothing could be more trenchant than her action, unless it be her speech. Whatever its merits or defects, *A Doll's House* has certainly the property of stimulating discussion. We are at present bandying the very arguments which hurtled around it in Scandinavia and in Germany nine years ago. When the play was first produced in Copenhagen, some one wrote a charming little satire upon it in the shape of a debate as to its tendency between a party of little girls around a nursery tea-table. It ended in the hostess, aged ten, gravely declaring that had the case been hers, she would have done exactly as Nora did. I do not know whether the fame of *A Doll's House* has reached the British nursery, but I have certainly read some comments on it which might very well have emanated from that abode of innocence.

Puerilities and irrelevances apart, the adult and intelligent criticism of Ibsen as represented in *A Doll's House*, seems to run on three main lines. It is said, in the first place, that he is not an artist but a preacher; secondly, that his doctrine is neither new nor true; thirdly, that in order to enforce it, he oversteps the limits of artistic propriety.

[. . .]

For my part, looking at his dramatic production all round, and excepting only the two great dramas in verse, *Brand* and *Peer Gynt*, I am willing to admit that his teaching does now and then, in perfectly trifling details, affect his art for the worse. Not his direct teaching – that, as it seems to me, he always inspires with the breath of life – but his proclivity to what I may perhaps call symbolic side-issues. In the aforesaid dramas in verse this symbolism is eminently in place; not so, it seems to me, in the realistic plays. I once asked him how he justified this tendency in his art; he replied that life is one tissue of symbols. 'Certainly,' I might have answered; 'but when we have its symbolic side too persistently obtruded upon us, we lose the sense of reality, which, according to your own theory, the modern dramatist should above all things aim at.' There may be some excellent answer to this criticism; I give it for what it is worth. Apart from these symbolic details, it seems to me that Ibsen is singularly successful in vitalising his work; in reproducing the forms, the phenomena of life, as well as its deeper meanings. Let us take the example nearest at hand – *A Doll's House*. I venture to say – for this is a matter of fact rather than of opinion – that in the minds of thousands in Scandinavia and Germany, Nora Helmer lives with an intense and palpitating life such as belongs to few fictitious characters. Habitually and instinctively men pay Ibsen the compliment (so often paid to Shakespeare) of discussing her as though she were a real woman, living a life of her own, quite apart from the poet's creative intelligence. The very critics who begin by railing at her as a puppet end by denouncing her as a woman. She irritates, troubles, fascinates them as no puppet ever could. Moreover, the triumph of the actress is the dramatist's best defence. Miss Achurch might have the genius of Rachel and Desclée in one, yet she could not transmute into flesh and blood the doctrinary doll, stuffed with sawdust and sophistry, whom some people declare Nora to be. Men do not shudder at the agony or weep over the woes of an intellectual abstraction. As for Helmer, I am not aware that any one has accused him of unreality. He is too real for most people – is commonplace, unpleasant, objectionable. The truth is, he touches us too nearly; he is the typical husband of what may be called chattel matrimony. If there are few Doll's-Houses in England, it is certainly for lack of Noras, not for lack of Helmers. I admit that in my opinion Ibsen has treated Helmer somewhat unfairly. He has not exactly disguised, but has omitted to emphasize, the fact that if Helmer helped to make Nora a doll, Nora helped to make Helmer a prig. By giving Nora all the logic in the last scene (and she is not a scrupulous dialectician) he has left the casual observer to conclude that he lays the whole responsibility on Helmer. This conclusion is not just, but it is specious; and so far, and so far only, I grant that the play has somewhat the air of a piece of special pleading. I shall presently discuss the last scene in greater detail; but even admitting for the moment that the polemist here gets the better of the poet, can we call the poet, who has moved freely through two acts and two-thirds, nothing but a doctrinary polemist?

[. . .]

The second line of criticism is that which attacks the substance of Ibsen's so-called doctrines, on the ground that they are neither new nor true. To the former objection one is inclined to answer curtly but pertinently, 'Who said they were?' It is not the business of the creative artist to make the great generalisations which mark the stages of intellectual and social progress. Certainly Ibsen did not discover the theory of evolution or the doctrine of heredity, any more than he discovered gravitation. He was not the first to denounce the subjection of women; he was not the first to sneer at the 'compact liberal majority' of our pseudo-democracies. His function is to seize and throw into relief certain aspects of modern life. He shows us society as Kean was said to read Shakespeare – by flashes of lightning – luridly, but with intense vividness. He selects subjects which seem to him to illustrate such and such political, ethical, or sociological ideas; but he does not profess to have invented the ideas. They are common property; they are in the air. A grave injustice has been done him of late by those of his English admirers who have set him up as a social prophet, and have sometimes omitted to mention that he is a bit of a poet as well. It is so much easier to import an idea than the flesh and blood, the imagination, the passion, the style in which it is clothed. People have heard so much of the 'gospel according to Ibsen' that they have come to think of him as a mere hot-gospeller, the Boanerges of some strange social propaganda. As a matter of fact Ibsen has no gospel whatever, in the sense of a systematic body of doctrine. He is not a Schopenhauer, and still less a Comte. There never was a less systematic thinker. Truth is not, in his eyes, one and indivisible; it is many-sided, many-visaged, almost Protean. It belongs to the irony of fate that the least dogmatic of thinkers – the man who has said of himself, 'I only ask: my call is not to answer' – should figure in the imagination of so many English critics as a dour dogmatist, a vendor of social nostrums in pilule form. He is far more of a paradoxist than a dogmatist. A thinker he is most certainly, but not an inventor of brand new notions such as no one has ever before conceived. His originality lies in giving intense dramatic life to modern ideas, and often stamping them afresh, as regards mere verbal form, in the mint of his imaginative wit.

The second allegation, that his doctrines are not true, is half answered when we have insisted that they are not put forward (at any rate by Ibsen himself) as a body of inspired dogmas. No man rejects more consistently than he the idea of finality. He does not pretend to have said the last word on any subject. 'You needn't believe me unless you like,' says Dr. Stockmann in *An Enemy of the People*, 'but truths are not the tough old Methuselahs people take them to be. A normally constituted truth lives, let us say, some seventeen or eighteen years; at most twenty.' The telling of absolute truths, to put it in another way, is scarcely Ibsen's aim. He is more concerned with destroying conventional lies, and exorcising the 'ghosts' of dead truths; and most of all concerned to make people think and see for themselves. Here again we recognise the essential injustice of regarding a dramatic poet as a sort of prophet-professor, who means all his characters say and makes them say all he means. I have been asked, for example, whether Ibsen intends us to understand by the last scene of *A Doll's House* that awakened wives ought to leave their husbands and children in order to cultivate their souls in solitude. Ibsen intends nothing of the sort. He draws a picture of a typical household; he creates a man and woman with certain characteristics; he places them in a series of situations which at once develop their characters and suggest large questions of conduct; and he makes the woman, in the end, adopt a course of action which he (rightly or wrongly) believes to be consistent with her individual nature and circumstances. It is true that this course of action is so devised as to throw the principles at stake into the strongest relief; but the object of that is to make people thoroughly realise the problem, not to force upon them the particular solution arrived at in this particular case. No two life-problems were ever precisely alike, and in stating and solving one, Ibsen does not pretend to supply a ready-made solution for all the rest. He illustrates, or, rather, illumines, a general principle by a conceivable case; that is all. To treat Nora's arguments in the last scene of *A Doll's House* as though they were the ordered propositions of an essay by John Stuart Mill is to give a striking example of the strange literalness of the English mind, its inability to distinguish between drama and dogma. To me that last scene is the most moving in the play, precisely because I hold it the most dramatic. It has been called a piece of pure logic – is it not rather logic conditioned by character and saturated with emotion? Some years ago I saw *Et Dukkehjem* acted in Christiania. It was an off season; only the second-rate members of the company were engaged; and throughout two acts and a half I sat vainly striving to recapture the emotions I had so often felt in reading the play. But the moment Nora and Helmer were seated face to face, at the words, 'No, that is just it; you do not understand me; and I have never understood you – till to-night' – at that moment, much to my own surprise, the thing suddenly gripped my heart-strings; to use an expressive Americanism, I 'sat up;' and every phrase of Nora's threnody over her dead dreams, her lost illusions, thrilled me to the very marrow. Night after night I went to see that scene; night after night I have watched it in the English version; it has never lost its power over me. And why? Not because Nora's sayings are particularly wise or particularly true, but because, in her own words, they are so true *for her*, because she feels them so deeply and utters them so exquisitely. Certainly she is unfair, certainly she is one-sided, certainly she is illogical; if she were not, Ibsen would be the pamphleteer he is supposed to be, not the poet he is. 'I have never been happy here – only merry. . . . You have never loved me – you have only found it amusing to be in love with me.' Have we not in these speeches the very mingling of truth and falsehood, of justice and injustice, necessary to humanise the character and the situation? After Nora has declared her intention of leaving her home, Helmer remarks, 'Then there is only one explanation possible – You no longer love me.' 'No,' she replies, 'that is just it.' 'Nora! can you say so?' cries Helmer, looking into her eyes. '*Oh, I'm so sorry, Torvald,*' she answers, '*for you've always been so kind to me.*' Is this pamphleteering? To me it seems like the subtlest human pathos. Again, when she says 'At that moment it became clear to me that I had been living here for eight years with a strange man and had borne him three children – Oh, I can't bear to think of it! I could tear myself to pieces' – who can possibly take this for anything but a purely dramatic utterance? It is true and touching in Nora's mouth, but it is obviously founded on a vague sentiment, that may or may not bear analysis.

94

Nora postulates a certain transcendental community of spirit as the foundation and justification of marriage. The idea is very womanly and may also be very practical; but Ibsen would probably be the first to admit that before it can claim the validity of a social principle we must ascertain whether it be possible for any two human beings to be other than what Nora would call strangers. This further analysis the hearer must carry out for him, or her, self. The poet has stimulated thought; he has not tried to lay down a hard-and-fast rule of conduct. Again, when Helmer says, 'No man sacrifices his honour even for one he loves,' and Nora retorts, '*Millions of women have done that!*' we applaud the consummate claptrap, not on account of its abstract justice, but rather of its characteristic injustice. Logically, it is naught; dramatically, one feels it to be a masterstroke. Here, it is the right speech in the right place; in a sociological monograph it would be absurd. My position, in short, is that in Ibsen's plays, as in those of any other dramatist who keeps within the bounds of his form, we must look, not for the axioms and demonstrations of a scientific system, but simply for 'broken lights' of truth, refracted through character and circumstance.[1] The playwright who sends on a Chorus or a lecturer, unconnected with the dramatic action, to moralise the spectacle and put all the dots on all the i's, may fairly be taken to task for the substance of his 'doctrines.' But that playwright is Dumas, not Ibsen.

Lastly, we come to the assertion that Ibsen is a 'coarse' writer, with a morbid love for using the theatre as a physiological lecture-room. Here again I can only cry out upon the chance which has led to so grotesque a misconception. He has written some twenty plays, of which all except two might be read aloud, with only the most trivial omissions, in any young ladies' boarding-school from Tobolsk to Tangiers. The two exceptions are *A Doll's House* and *Ghosts* – the very plays which happen to have come (more or less) within the ken of English critics. In *A Doll's House* he touches upon, in *Ghosts* he frankly faces, the problem of hereditary disease, which interests him, not in itself, but simply as the physical type and symbol of so many social and ethical phenomena. *Ghosts* I have not space to consider. If art is for ever debarred from entering upon certain domains of human experience, then *Ghosts* is an inartistic work. I can only say, after having read it, seen it on the stage, and translated it, that no other modern play seems to me to fulfil so entirely the Aristotelian ideal of purging the soul by means of terror and pity. In *A Doll's House*, again, there are two passages, one in the second and one in the third act, which Mr. Podsnap could not conveniently explain to the young lady in the dress-circle. Whether the young lady in the dress-circle would be any the worse for having them explained to her is a question I shall not discuss. As a matter of fact, far from being coarsely treated, they are so delicately touched that the young person suspects nothing and is in no

---

It so happens that two or three formal generalisations of Ibsen's have recently been going the round of the press; but they are all taken from letters or speeches, not from his plays.

way incommoded. It is Mr. Podsnap himself that cries out – the virtuous Podsnap who, at the French theatre, writhes in his stall with laughter at speeches and situations *à faire rougir des singes*. I have more than once been reproached, by people who had seen *A Doll's House* at the Novelty, with having cut the speeches which the first-night critics pronounced objectionable. It has cost me some trouble to persuade them that not a word had been cut, and that the text they found so innocent contained every one of the enormities denounced by the critics. Mr. Podsnap, I may add, has in this case shown his usual alacrity in putting the worst possible interpretation upon things. Dr. Rank's declaration to Nora that Helmer is not the only man who would willingly lay down his life for her, has been represented as a hideous attempt on the part of a dying debauchee to seduce his friend's wife. Nothing is further from the mind of poor Rank, who, by the way, is not a debauchee at all. He knows himself to be at death's door; Nora, in her Doll's House, has given light and warmth to his lonely, lingering existence; he has silently adored her while standing with her, as with her husband, on terms of frank comradeship; is he to leave her for ever without saying, as he puts it, 'Thanks for the light'? Surely this is a piece either of inhuman austerity or of prurient prudery; surely Mrs. Podsnap herself could not feel a suspicion of insult in such a declaration. True, it comes inaptly at that particular moment, rendering it impossible for Nora to make the request she contemplates. But essentially, and even from the most conventional point of view, I fail to see anything inadmissible in Rank's conduct to Nora. Nora's conduct to Rank, in the stocking scene, is another question; but that is merely a side-light on the relation between Nora and Helmer, preparatory, in a sense, to the scene before Rank's entrance in the last act.

In conclusion, what are the chances that Ibsen's modern plays will ever take a permanent place on the English stage? They are not great, it seems to me. [. . .] On the other hand I have not the remotest doubt that Ibsen will bulk more and more largely as years go on in the consciousness of all students of literature in general, as opposed to the stage in particular. The creator of *Brand* and *Peer Gynt* is one of the great poets of the world.

4 *HEDDA GABLER*

The play

Ibsen's preliminary notes for *Hedda Gabler* are more detailed than for any of his other plays, and allow analysis of his working methods. They show the development from an initial concept (probably late summer 1889), to a complete outline (spring 1890), along with many scattered jottings, and a detailed scenario for Acts I and II which was probably written after the first draft of Act I. This full-length draft – published in vol. XII of *The Works of Henrik Ibsen* (edited by William Archer, New York 1912) – was begun in mid-July, thoroughly revised in October and published on December 4, 1890. There are real-life analogues to the main characters. Løvborg was based on Julius Hoffory, a Norwegian professor who went insane in 1890; and Ibsen's earliest notes revolve around Camilla Collett, the Norwegian novelist and woman's rights advocate, who had complained that Ibsen used her as a model for the central figure in *The Lady from the Sea*:

> A married woman more and more imagines that she is an important personality, and as a consequence feels compelled to create for herself a sensational past –
>
> If an interesting female character appears in a new story or in a play, she believes it is she who is being portrayed.
>
> The masculine environment helps to confirm her in this belief.
>
> The two lady friends agree to die together. One of them carries out her end of the bargain, but the other one who realizes what lies in store for her loses her courage. This is the reversal.
>
> 'He has such a disgusting way of walking when one sees him from behind.'
>
> She hates him because he has a goal, a mission in life. The lady friend has one too, but does not dare to devote herself to it. Her personal life treated in fictional form.
>
> In the second act the manuscript that is left behind –
>
> The 'lost soul' apologizes for the man of culture. The wild horse and the race horse . . . Revolution against the laws of nature – but nothing stupid, not until the position is secure.

The issue of a woman's lack of real outlets for personal fulfillment in a male dominated society was carried over into subsequent versions, together with the female protagonist's jealousy of a man with a mission in life, and contrasting male figures. In addition certain of the plot details from these first jottings survive into the final play – such as a misplaced manuscript, and a double suicide, botched by one of the participants. However, the protagonist was to change completely; and a slightly later note encapsulates the central elements of the character who emerges as Hedda:

4.4.1 Notes to *Hedda Gabler*

Translated by Evert Sprinchorn; pages 98–100 translated by A.G. Chater

¶ The pale, apparently cold beauty. Expects great things of life and the joy of life.

The man who has now finally won her, plain and simple in appearance, but an honest and talented, broad-minded scholar.

[. . .]

¶ The manuscript that H. L. leaves behind contends that man's mission is: Upward, toward the bearer of light. Life on the present foundations of society is not worth living. Therefore he escapes from it through his imagination. By drinking, etc. – Tesman stands for correct behavior. Hedda for blasé oversophistication. Mrs. R. is the nervous-hysterical modern individual. Brack represents the personal bourgeois point of view.

¶ Then H. departs this world. And the two of them are left sitting there with the manuscript they cannot interpret. And the aunt is with them. What an ironic comment on humanity's striving for progress and development.

¶ But Holger's double nature intervenes. Only by realizing the basely bourgeois can he win a hearing for his great central idea.

¶ Mrs. Rising is afraid that H., although "a model of propriety," is not normal. She can only guess at his way of thinking but cannot understand it. Quotes some of his remarks –

¶ One talks about building railways and highways for the cause of progress. But no, no, that is not what is needed. Space must be cleared so that the spirit of man can make its great turnabout. For it has gone astray. The spirit of man has gone astray.

¶ *Holger:* I have been out. I have behaved obscenely. That doesn't matter. But the police know about it. That's what counts.

¶ H. L.'s despair lies in that he wants to master the world but cannot master himself.

¶ Tesman believes that it is he who has in a way seduced H. L. into indulging in excesses again. But that is not so. It is as Hedda has said: that it was *he* she dreamed of when she talked about "the famous man." But she does not dare tell Tesman this.

¶ To aid in understanding his own character, L. has made notes in "the manuscript." These are the notes the two of them should interpret, want to interpret, but *cannot* possibly.

¶ Brack is inclined to live as a bachelor, and then gain admittance to a good home, become a friend of the family, indispensable –

¶ They say it is a law of nature. Very well then, raise an opposition to it. Demand its repeal. Why give way. Why surrender unconditionally –

¶ In conversations between T. and L. the latter says that he lives for his studies. The former replies that in that case he can compete with him. – (T. lives *on* his studies) that's the point.

¶ L. (Tesman) says: I couldn't step on a worm! "But now I can tell you that I too am seeking the professorship. We are rivals."

⸻

¶ NB! Brack had always thought that Hedda's short engagement to Tesman would come to nothing.

Hedda speaks of how she felt herself set aside, step by step, when her father was no longer in favor, when he retired and died without leaving anything. Then she realized, bitterly, that it was for his sake she had been made much of. And then she was already between twenty-five and twenty-six. In danger of becoming an old maid.

She thinks that in reality Tesman only feels a vain pride in having won her. His solicitude for her is the same as is shown for a thoroughbred horse or a valuable sporting dog. This, however, does not offend her. She merely regards it as a fact.

Hedda says to Brack that she does not think Tesman can be called ridiculous. But in reality she finds him so. Later on she finds him pitiable as well.

Tesman: Could you not call me by my Christian name?

Hedda: No, indeed I couldn't – unless they have given you some other name than the one you have.

Tesman puts Løvborg's manuscript in his pocket so that it may not be lost. Afterward it is Hedda who, by a casual remark, with tentative intention, gives him the idea of keeping it.

Then he reads it. A new line of thought is revealed to him. But the strain of the situation increases. Hedda awakens his jealousy.

¶ In the third act one thing after another comes to light about Løvborg's adventures in the course of the night. At last he comes himself, in quiet despair. "Where is the manuscript?" "Did I not leave it behind me here?" He does not know that he has done so. But after all, of what use is the manuscript to him now! He is writing of the "moral doctrine of the future"! When he has just been released by the police!

¶ Hedda's despair is that there are doubtless so many chances of happiness in the world, but that she cannot discover them. It is the want of an object in life that torments her.

When Hedda beguiles T. into leading E. L. into ruin, it is done to test T.'s character.

¶ It is in Hedda's presence that the irresistible craving for excess always comes over E. L.

Tesman cannot understand that E. L. could wish to base his future on injury to another.

¶ *Hedda:* Do I hate T.? No, not at all. I only find him boring.

¶ *Brack:* But nobody else thinks so.

Hedda: Neither is there any one but myself who is married to him.

Brack: . . . not at all boring.

Hedda: Heavens, you always want me to express myself so correctly. Very well then, T. is not boring, but I am bored by living with him.

Hedda: . . . had no prospects. Well, perhaps you would have liked to see me in a convent (home for unmarried ladies).

Hedda: . . . then isn't it an honorable thing to profit by one's person? Don't actresses and others turn their advantages into profit. I had no other capital. Marriage – I thought it was like buying an annuity.

Hedda: Remember that I am the child of an old man – and a worn-out man too – or past his prime at any rate – perhaps that has left its mark.

Brack: Upon my word, I believe you have begun to brood over problems.

Hedda: Well, what cannot one take to doing when one has gone and got married.

¶ Notes: One evening as Hedda and Tesman, together with some others, were on their way home from a party, Hedda remarked as they walked by a charming house that was where she would like to live. She meant it, but she said it only to keep the conversation with Tesman going. "He simply cannot carry on a conversation."

The house was actually for rent or sale. Tesman had been pointed out as the coming young man. And later when he proposed, and let slip that he too had dreamed of living there, she accepted.

He too had liked the house very much.

They get married. And they rent the house.[1]

But when Hedda returns as a young wife, with a vague sense of responsibility, the whole thing seems distasteful to her. She conceives a kind of hatred for the house just because it has become her home. She confides this to Brack. She evades the question with Tesman.

¶ The play shall deal with "the impossible," that is, to aspire to and strive for something which is against all the conventions, against that which is acceptable to conscious minds – Hedda's included.

[. . .]

¶ Very few true parents are to be found in the world. Most people grow up under the influence of aunts or uncles – either neglected and misunderstood or else spoiled.

¶ Hedda rejects him because he does not dare expose himself to temptation. He replies that the same is true of her. The wager! . . . He loses . . . ! Mrs. Elvsted is present. Hedda says: No danger – He loses.

¶ Hedda feels herself demoniacally attracted by the tendencies of the times. But she lacks courage. Her thoughts remain theories, ineffective dreams.[2]

¶ The feminine imagination is not active and independently creative like the masculine. It needs a bit of reality as a help.

¶ Løvborg has had inclinations toward "the bohemian life." Hedda is attracted in the same direction, but she does not dare to take the leap.

¶ Buried deep within Hedda there is a level of poetry. But the environment frightens her. Suppose she were to make herself ridiculous!

Both of them, each in his and her own way, have seen in their common love for this house a sign of their mutual understanding. As if they sought and were drawn to a common home.

Then he rents the house. They get married and go abroad. He orders the house bought and his aunt furnishes it at his expense. Now it is their home. It is theirs and yet it is not, because it is not paid for. Everything depends on his getting the professorship. (Ibsen's note)

This note is omitted in the Centennial Edition. It is translated from Else Høst, *Hedda Gabler: En monografi* (Oslo: 1958), p. 82.

¶ Hedda realizes that she, much more than Thea, has abandoned her husband.

¶ The newly wedded couple return home in September – as the summer is dying. In the second act they sit in the garden – but with their coats on.

¶ Being frightened by one's own voice. Something strange, foreign.

¶ NEWEST PLAN: The festivities in Tesman's garden – and Løvborg's defeat – already prepared for in the 1st act. Second act: the party –

¶ Hedda energetically refuses to serve as hostess. She will not celebrate their marriage because (in her opinion, it isn't a marriage)

¶ *Holger:* Don't you see? I am the cause of your marriage –

¶ Hedda is the type of woman in her position and with her character. She marries Tesman but she devotes her imagination to Eilert Løvborg. She leans back in her chair, closes her eyes, and dreams of his adventures. . . . This is the enormous difference: Mrs. Elvsted "works for his moral improvement." But for Hedda he is the object of cowardly, tempting daydreams. In reality she does not have the courage to be a part of anything like that. Then she realizes her condition. Caught! Can't comprehend it. Ridiculous! Ridiculous!

¶ The traditional delusion that one man and one woman are made for each other. Hedda has her roots in the conventional. She marries Tesman but she dreams of Eilert Løvborg. . . . She is disgusted by the latter's flight from life. He believes that this has raised him in her estimation. . . . Thea Elvsted is the conventional, sentimental, hysterical Philistine.

¶ Those Philistines, Mrs. E. and Tesman, explain my behavior by saying first I drink myself drunk and that the rest is done in insanity. It's a flight from reality which is an absolute necessity to me.

¶ *E. L.:* Give me something – a flower – at our parting. Hedda hands him the revolver.

¶ Then Tesman arrives: Has he gone? "Yes." Do you think he will still compete against me? No, I don't think so. You can set your mind at rest.

¶ Tesman relates that when they were in Gratz she did not want to visit her relatives –

¶ He misunderstands her real motives.

¶ In the last act as Tesman, Mrs. Elvsted, and Miss Rysing are consulting, Hedda plays in the small room at the back. She stops. The conversation continues. She appears in the doorway – Good night – I'm going now. Do you need me for anything? Tesman: No, nothing at all. Good night, my dear! . . . The shot is fired –

¶ CONCLUSION: All rush into the back room. Brack sinks as if paralyzed into a chair near the stove: But God have mercy – people don't *do* such things!

¶ When Hedda hints at her ideas to Brack, he says: Yes, yes, that's extraordinarily amusing – Ha ha ha! He does not understand that she is quite serious.

¶ Hedda is right in this: there is no love on Tesman's part. Nor on the aunt's part. However full of love she may be.

Eilert Løvborg has a double nature. It is a fiction that one loves only *one* person. He loves two – or many – alternately (to put it frivolously). But how can he explain his position? Mrs. Elvsted, who forces him to behave correctly, runs away from her husband. Hedda, who drives him beyond all limits, draws back at the thought of a scandal.

¶ Neither he nor Mrs. Elvsted understands the point. Tesman reads in the manuscript that was left behind about "the two ideals." Mrs. Elvsted can't explain to him what E. L. meant. Then comes the burlesque note: both T. and Mrs. E. are going to devote their future lives to interpreting the mystery.

¶ Tesman thinks that Hedda hates E. L.

Mrs. Elvsted thinks so too.

Hedda sees their delusion but dares not disabuse them of it. There is something beautiful about having an aim in life. Even if it is a delusion –

She cannot do it. Take part in someone else's.

That is when she shoots herself.

The destroyed manuscript is entitled "The Ethics of Future Society."

¶ Tesman is on the verge of losing his head. All this work meaningless. New thoughts! New visions! A whole new world! Then the two of them sit there, trying to find the meaning in it. Can't make any sense of it. . . .

¶ The greatest misery in this world is that so many have nothing to do but pursue happiness without being able to find it.

¶ "From Jochum Tesman there developed a Jørgen Tesman – but it will be a long, long time before this Jørgen gives rise to a George."

¶ The simile: The journey of life = the journey on a train.

H.: One doesn't usually jump out of the compartment.

No, not when the train is moving.

Nor stand still when it is stationary. There's always someone on the platform, staring in.

[. . .]

¶ NB: The mutual hatred of women. Women have no influence on external matters of government. Therefore they want to have an influence on souls. And then so many of them have no aim in life (the lack thereof is inherited) –

¶ Løvborg and Hedda bent over the photographs at the table.

He: How is it possible? *She:* Why not? *L.:* Tesman! You couldn't find words enough to make fun of him. . . . Then comes the story about the general's "disgrace," dismissal, etc. The worst thing for a lady at a ball is not to be admired for her own sake . . . *L.:* And Tesman? He took you for the sake of your person. That's just as unbearable to think about.

¶ Just by marrying Tesman it seems to me I have gotten so unspeakably far away from him.

¶ *He:* Look at her. Just look at her! . . . *Hedda:* (stroking her hair) Yes, isn't she beautiful!

¶ Men and women don't belong to the same century. . . . What a great prejudice that one should love only *one!*

[. . .]

¶ The demoniacal element in Hedda is this: She wants to exert her influence on someone – But once she has done so, she despises him. . . . The manuscript?

¶ In the third act Hedda questions Mrs. Elvsted. But if he's like that, why is he worth holding on to. . . . Yes, yes, I know –

¶ Hedda's discovery that her relations with the maid cannot possibly be proper.

¶ In his conversation with Hedda, Løvborg says: Miss H – Miss – You know, I don't believe that you are married.

¶ *Hedda:* And now I sit here and talk with these Philistines – And the way we once could talk to each other – No, I won't say any more. . . Talk? How do you mean? Obscenely? Ish. Let us say indecently.

¶ NB!! The reversal in the play occurs during the big scene between Hedda and E. L. *He:* What a wretched business it is to conform to the existing morals. It would be ideal if a man of the present could live the life of the future. What a miserable business it is to fight over a professorship!

Hedda – that lovely girl! *H.:* No! *E. L.:* Yes, I'm going to say it. That lovely, cold girl – cold as marble.

I'm not dissipated fundamentally. But the life of reality isn't livable –

¶ In the fifth act: *Hedda:* How hugely comic it is that those two harmless people, Tesman and Mrs. E., should try to put the pieces together for a monument to E. L. The man who so deeply despised the whole business –

¶ Life becomes for Hedda a ridiculous affair that isn't "worth seeing through to the end."

¶ The happiest mission in life is to place the people of today in the conditions of the future.

L.: Never put a child in this world, H.!

¶ When Brack speaks of a "triangular affair," Hedda thinks about what is going to happen and refers ambiguously to it. Brack doesn't understand.

¶ Brack cannot bear to be in a house where there are small children. "Children shouldn't be allowed to exist until they are fourteen or fifteen. That is, girls. What about boys? Shouldn't be allowed to exist at all – or else they should be raised outside the house."

¶ H. admits that children have always been a horror to her too.

¶ Hedda is strongly but imprecisely opposed to the idea that one should love "the family." The aunts mean nothing to her.

¶ It liberated Hedda's spirit to serve as a confessor to E. L. Her sympathy has secretly been on his side – But it became ugly when the public found out everything then he backed out.

¶ MAIN POINTS:

1. They are not all made to be mothers.
2. They are passionate but they are afraid of scandal.
3. They perceive that the times are full of missions worth devoting one's life to, but they cannot discover them.

¶ And besides Tesman is not exactly a professional, but he is a specialist. The Middle Ages are dead –

¶ *T.:* Now there you see also the great advantages to my studies. I can lose manuscripts and rewrite them – no inspiration needed –

¶ Hedda is completely taken up by the child that is to come, but when it is born she dreads what is to follow –

¶ Hedda must say somewhere in the play that she did not like to get out of her compartment while on the trip. Why not? I don't like to show my legs. . . . Ah, Mrs. H., but they do indeed show themselves. Nevertheless, I don't.

¶ Shot herself! Shot herself!

Brack (collapsing in the easy chair): But great God – people don't *do* such things!

¶ NB!! Eilert Løvborg believes that a comradeship must be formed between man and woman out of which the truly spiritual human being can arise. Whatever else the two of them do is of no concern. This is what the people around him do not understand. To them he is dissolute. Inwardly he is not.

¶ If a man can have several male friends, why can't he have several lady friends?

¶ It is precisely the sensual feelings that are aroused while in the company of his female "friends" or "comrades" that seek release in his excesses.

¶ Now I'm going. Don't you have some little remembrance to give me – ? You have flowers – and so many other things – (the story of the pistol from before) – But you won't use it anyhow –

¶ In the fourth act when Hedda finds out that he has shot himself, she is jubilant. . . . He had courage.

¶ Here is the rest of the manuscript.

¶ CONCLUSION: Life isn't tragic. . . . Life is ridiculous. . . . And that's what I can't bear.

¶ Do you know what happens in novels? All those who kill themselves – through the head – not in the stomach. . . . How ridiculous – how baroque –

¶ In her conversation with Thea in the first act, Hedda remarks that she cannot understand how one can fall in love with an unmarried man – or an unengaged man – or an unloved man – on the other hand –[3]

But, my heavens, Tesm. was unmarried. *H.:* Yes, he was. *Th.:* But you married him. *H.:* Yes, I did. *Th.:* Then how can you say that . . . Well now –.

¶ Brack understands well enough that it is Hedda's repression, her hysteria that motivates everything she does.

¶ On her part, Hedda suspects that Brack sees through her without believing that she understands.

¶ *H.:* It must be wonderful to take something from someone.

¶ When H. talks to B. in the fifth act about those two sitting there trying to piece together the manuscript without the spirit being present, she breaks out in laughter then she plays the piano – then – d –

¶ Men – in the most indescribable situations how ridiculous they are.

¶ NB! She really wants to live a *man's* life wholly. But then she has misgivings. Her inheritance, what is implanted in her.

¶ Loving and being loved by aunts . . . Most people who are born of old maids, male and female.

¶ This deals with the "underground forces and powers." Woman as a minor. Nihilism. Father and mother belonging to different eras. The female underground revolution in thought. The slave's fear of the outside world.

¶ NB!! Why should I conform to social morals that I know won't last more than half a generation. When I run wild, as they call it, it's my escape from the present. Not that I find any joy in my excesses. I'm up to my neck in the established order. . . .

¶ Hedda: Slender figure of average height. Nobly shaped, aristocratic face with fine, wax-colored skin. The eyes have a veiled expression. Hair medium brown. Not especially abundant hair. Dressed in a loose-fitting dressing gown, white with blue trimmings. Composed and relaxed in her manners. The eyes steel-gray, almost lusterless.

¶ Mrs. Elvsted: weak build. The eyes round, rather prominent, almost as blue as water. Weak face with soft features. Nervous gestures, frightened expression –

¶ See above. E. L.'s idea of comradeship between man and woman. . . . The idea is a life-saver!

¶ If society won't let us live morally with them (women), then we'll have to live with them immorally –

¶ *Tesman:* the new idea in E. L.'s book is that of progress resulting from the comradeship between man and woman.

¶ Hedda's basic demand is: I want to know everything, but keep myself clean.

¶ I want to know everything – everything – everything –
H.: – –
H.: If only I could have lived like him!

¶ Is there something about Brabant? *B.:* What on earth is that? . . .

¶ The wager about the use of both pistols.

¶ *Miss T.:* Yes, this is the house of life and health. Now I shall go home to a house of sickness and death. God bless both of you. From now on I'll come out here every day to ask Bertha how things are –

¶ In the third act H. tells E. L. that she is not interested in the great questions – nor the great ideas – but in the great freedom of man. . . . But she hasn't the courage.

¶ The two ideals! *Tesman:* What in the name of God does he mean by that? What? What do we have to do with ideals?

¶ The new book treats of "the two ideals." Thea can give no information.

A complete version of the notes, including detail on their original format, can be found in *The Oxford Ibsen*, vol. VII, ed. James McFarlane (1966).

*

Among "the tendencies of the times" to which Hedda is "demoniacally attracted", is the whole *fin-de-siècle* atmosphere, which forms an oblique background to the play (as it does for Strindberg's *Miss Julie*, written in 1888). The central icon of Decadent art was Salome, and as a summary of the *fin-de-siècle* movement points out:

In literature it led to the characterization of women as passive creatures of emotion and instinct or as dangerously attractive but ruthless dolls, the grown-up children of Schopenhauer's philosophy, whose instinct is to drag men down to their own biological level. When this predatoriness is consciously aggressive, the '*femme fatale*' results, the kind of role so enjoyed by Sarah Bernhardt, which, in turn, is easily associated with the 'gynander' – the unnatural woman who behaves like a man, that for Strindberg was exemplified by the 'bluestocking' heroines of Ibsen.

The attempt of such women to control or usurp male creativity was emblematized by the Decadents in vampires, sphinxes, maenads, willis, and destructive watersprites, but a particularly apt image was discovered in the symbolic castration afforded by decapitation, or decollation. This became one of the most frequent Decadent *topoi*, exemplified not only in the central story of Salome – who is very often conflated with her mother, Herodias – but also by the myths of Judith, Taïs, Delilah, Turandot, Rusalka, and the decapitated Orpheus . . .

The characteristic Decadent stance towards women, then, was the simultaneous urge to self-abasement and to savage domination that is technically known as 'sado-masochism'. This definition was introduced . . . by Richard von Krafft-Ebing in his *Psychopathia Sexualis* (1886), and was taken from the name of Leopold von Sacher-Masoch who in 1870 had published a celebrated novel about bondage, *Venus in Furs*, in which sex is not seen as a pleasure but as a demonic source of pain . . .

(Brian Parker, in *Modern Drama*, 32 [1989])

The image of Hedda given by the notes corresponds closely with such an archetype: "the pale, apparently cold beauty", over-sophisticated and "demonic", masculinarized by the association with her father's pistols, who leads a man to ruin through inspiring an "irresistible craving for excess". Other elements in the play are the "vine leaves" Hedda envisions in Løvborg's hair, as well as his slightly displaced castration – shooting himself in the "stomach" through the agency of her pistol. It is also significant that Sacher-Masoch had been a friend of Ibsen's in Rome.

However, as with the "MAIN POINTS" listed in the notes, which clearly outline a central concern with the position of women, the *fin-de-siècle* Salome theme is present only in the subtext. Although in his correspondence Ibsen insisted on a particular actress – Constance Bruun – for the title figure because of her capacity "to express the demonical basis of the character" (letter to Hans Schrøder, director of the Christiana Theater, 27 December 1890), his commentary on the play stressed that it had no explicit message. For instance, a letter to Moritz Prozor, his German translator, focussed on the psychological basis of the play and its unity as a whole:

> The title of the play is *Hedda Gabler*. My intention in giving it this name was to indicate that Hedda as a personality is to be regarded rather as her father's daughter than as her husband's wife.
>
> It has not been my desire to deal in this play with so-called human problems. What I principally wanted to do was to depict human beings, human emotions, and human desires, upon a groundwork of certain of the social conditions and moral principles of the present day. When you have read the whole, my fundamental idea will be clearer to you than I can make it by entering into further explanations . . .
>
> (4 December 1890)

Other letters, written while the play was in rehearsal at the Christiana Theater, emphasize the dynamics of the action – in particular the monolithic unity of the society that faces Hedda. Writing to Kristina Steen, an actress in the production, Ibsen commented:

> Jørgen Tesman, his old aunts, and the faithful servant Berthe together form a picture of complete unity. They think alike, they share the same memories and have the same outlook on life. To Hedda they appear like a strange and hostile power, aimed at her very being. In a performance of the play the harmony that exists between them must be conveyed.
>
> (14 January 1891)

The same letter stresses that all characters, even an apparently minor figure like the "good-natured, simple, oldish" maid, are equally important and have to be fully realized by the actors to create this unified impression.

Not surprisingly, Ibsen's supporters were quick to see the connection between the Hedda and Nora, and to point to the social criticism embodied in the title figure. One of the best commentaries on *Hedda Gabler*, which analyzes its technique and structure, gives a contemporary reading of Hedda's character as a "*fin de siècle* woman" and identifies its place in the naturalistic movement, is by Edmund Gosse, the English translator of the play.

4.4.2 Ibsen's new drama

The Fortnightly, January–June, 1891

The new drama is the longest which Ibsen has published, with the exception of *The Wild Duck*. In comparison with the seven social plays which have preceded it, its analogies are rather with *A Doll's House* than with the rest. It attempts no general satire of manners, as do *The Pillars of Society* and *An Enemy of the People*. It propounds no such terrible questions in ethics as *Ghosts*; it is almost as perplexing, but not nearly so obscure, as *The Wild Duck*. In style it is a return to Ibsen's old realistic manner, without a trace of the romanticism which cropped up so strangely in *The Lady from the Sea*, and even in *Rosmersholm*; while the dialogue is more rapid and fluent, and less interrupted by long speeches than it has ever been before. In the whole of the new play there is not one speech which would require thirty seconds for its enunciation. I will dare to say that I think in this instance Ibsen has gone perilously far in his desire for rapid and concise expression. The *stichomythia* of the Greek and French tragedians was lengthy in comparison with this unceasing display of hissing conversational fireworks, fragments of sentences without verbs, clauses that come to nothing, adverbial exclamations and cryptic interrogatories. It would add, I cannot but think, to the lucidity of the play if some one character were permitted occasionally to express himself at moderate length, as Nora does in *A Doll's House*, and as Mrs. Alving in *Ghosts*. None the less is the feat of combining a story with a play, and conducting both in meteoric bursts of extremely colloquial chat, one which Ibsen deserves the highest praise for having performed. And, on the stage, no doubt, this rapid broken utterance will give an extraordinary sense of reality.

As is known, Ibsen, like Euripides, does not present his characters to the public until their fortunes are determined. The heightened action of a third act in a "well-made" play is no luxury which he offers himself. But the Norwegian tragic poet cannot present a herald to his audience, or send Hermes down to tell the story in heroic verse. He has to explain the situation out of the mouths of his characters, and this he has an unrivalled adroitness in doing. We are never conscious of being informed, but, as we read on, the situation gradually and inevitably becomes patent to us. In the present case the state of affairs is as follows: A promising young man of letters, George Tesman, has gained a stipend, a sort of travelling scholarship, with the vague understanding that when he returns he will be appointed to the vacant Chair of the History of Civilisation, presumably at the University of Christiania. He is now looked upon as the principal rising authority in that science, a friend or rival of his, of far more original genius, one Ejlert Løvborg, having sunken into obscurity through drink and ill-living. Tesman, a sanguine, shallow youth, proposes to marry the beauty of the circle, Hedda Gabler, the orphan daughter of a late General Gabler. Tesman is himself an orphan, having been brought up by two maiden aunts, one of them a confirmed invalid. Hedda Gabler is understood to express a great desire to live in a certain villa. They marry, and they depart for six months on the Continent. A judge (*assessor*), Mr. Brack, who has been an intimate friend of both of them, contrives to secure and to furnish this villa for them during their absence. It seems a little rash that, having no income, they should launch into these expenditures, but it is excused on the score of Tesman's practical certainty of being made a university profes-sor. And their affection is supposed to be, and on Tesman's side is, of so tender and idyllic a character that it is really cruel to disturb them about money. The reader takes it for granted that they are going to be disap-pointed of the Chair, and accordingly ruined, but that does not happen. Ibsen does not play these obvious old games of comedy.

It must now be explained that during the honeymoon of the Tesmans an event has occurred in the literary world. Ejlert Løvborg, who was supposed to have become submerged for good and all, and who was hidden in a mountain parish, has suddenly published a volume on the progress of civil-isation which surpasses all his previous writings, and which creates a wide sensation. It is whispered that a lady up there in the mountains, Mrs. Elvsted, the wife of a sheriff of that name, has undertaken his social restor-ation. Løvborg is once more a dangerous rival to Tesman, who, however, with generous enthusiasm, hastens to pay his tribute of praise to the new publication. The play opens on the morning after the arrival of the Tes-mans at their villa, and the action occupies forty-eight hours, the scene never changing from the suite of apartments on the ground floor. It may be conceived from these brief preliminaries that action, in the ordinary sense, is not the strong point of the drama, the interest of which, indeed, is strictly psychological. It consists, mainly, of the revelation of the complex and morbid character of Hedda Gabler, attended by the satellites of Mrs. Elvsted, Brack, and Løvborg, the husband, Tesman, being in reality a semi-comic character, not much more subtle than Helmer in *A Doll's House*, but no whit the less closely studied.

Hedda is one of the most singular beings whom Ibsen has created. She has a certain superficial likeness to Nora, of whom she is, indeed, a kind of moral parody or perverted imitation. Hedda Gabler is a spoilt child, whose indulgent father has allowed her to grow up without training of any kind. Superficially gracious and pleasing, with a very pretty face and tempting manners, she is in reality wholly devoid of moral sense. She reveals herself, as the play proceeds, as without respect for age or grief, without natural instincts, without interest in life, untruthful, treacherous, implacable in revenge. She is a very ill-conditional little social panther or ocelot, totally without conscience of ill or preference for good, a product of the latest combination of pessimism, indifferentism and morbid selfishness, all claws and thirst for blood under the delicate velvet of her beauty.

[. . .]

Hedda Gabler is a more pronounced type of the *fin de siècle* woman than Ibsen has hitherto created. She is not thwarted by instinctive agencies beyond her authority, like Ellida Wangel; nor drawn aside by overmastering passion, like Rebekka West; personal refinement distinguishes her from Gina Ekdal, and deprives her of an excuse; she is infinitely divided from the maternal devotion of Helene Alving. As I have hinted before, the only figure in Ibsen's rich gallery of full-length portraits which has even a superficial likeness to her is Nora Helmer. But Nora is intended; or else the play is a mere mystification, to be a sympathetic individual. Whatever view we may take of her famous resolve and her sudden action upon it, we have to understand that ignorance of life and a narrow estimate of duty have been the worst of her defects. In her child-like or doll-like sacrifice of principle for her husband she has acted with a native generosity which it would be monstrous to expect husbands, at any rate, wholly to disapprove of. But Hedda Gabler has no such infantile unselfishness; no such sacrifice of self even upon a squalid altar. Curiously enough, when confronted with the terrible act, the destruction of Løvborg's manuscript, which she has committed purely to revenge herself on that personage, she deftly adopts Nora's excuse for the forgery – she has done it for her husband's sake. Here, and not for the first time, Ibsen seems to be laughing, if not at himself, at those fanatic disciples who take his experiments in pathology for lectures on hygiene.

[. . .]

In depicting Hedda Gabler, Ibsen seems to have expended his skill on the portrait of a typical member of that growing class of which M. Jules Simon spoke so eloquently the other day in his eulogy on Caro. To people of this temperament – and it is one which, always existing, is peculiarly frequent nowadays – the simple and masculine doctrines of obedience to duty, of perseverance, of love to mankind, are in danger of being replaced by "a complicated and sophisticated code which has the effect of making some of us mere cowards in the face of difficulty and sacrifice, and of disgusting all of us with the battle of life." In Hedda Gabler we see the religious idea violently suppressed under the pretext of a longing for liberty. She will not be a slave, yet is prepared for freedom by no education in self-command. Instead of religion, morality, and philosophy her head is feverishly stuffed with an amalgam of Buddhism and Schopenhauer. Even the beautiful conventions of manners are broken down, and the suppression of all rules of conduct seems the sole road to happiness. In her breast, with its sickly indifferentism, love awakens no sympathy, age no respect, suffering no pity, and patience in adversity no admiration.

[. . .]

In *Hedda Gabler*, I believe it will be admitted that Ibsen has gone further than ever before in his disdain for the recognised principles of scenic art. In this connection, it is amusing to note that the situation on which his new play is based has a very curious resemblance to that of M. Henri Becque's much-discussed comedy of *La Parisienne*. As in that play, so in *Hedda Gabler*, the three central figures are a wife of seductive manners and acute perceptions, devoid of all moral sense; a husband, who is a man of letters in search of a place; and a lover, who is the sympathetic friend of the husband, and even his defender against the caprices of the wife. The difference between French and Scandinavian convention is shown, indeed, in the fact that while Clotilde is pre-eminently unfaithful, Hedda has no virtue left but this, the typical one. Through the tempest which has raged in her moral garden, *elle a sauvé sa rose*. But in each play the tame lover, Lafont or Brack, eadeavours to restrain the *tendresse* of the wife, Clotilde or Hedda, for an unseen or suspected second lover, Sampson or Løvborg, and to prevent a scandal in the interest of the husband. I do not push the parallel further than this, nor would I affront convinced Ibsenites by comparing so serious a work as *Hedda Gabler* with *La Parisienne*, which is doubtless a trifle, though a very brilliant trifle. But this accidental resemblance to the work of Henri Becque turns up again in the last act of *Hedda Gabler*, where all the personages appear in deep mourning, and irresistibly remind "the inner eye " of the lugubrious *mise-en-scène* of *Les Corbeaux*. Probably the reason why the name of Becque occurs to us once and again as we turn the pages of Ibsen's last drama is, not so much these superficial resemblances of situation as the essential identity of the theatrical ideal in these two dramatists. Each is fighting, in defiance of the Clement Scotts and the Francisque Sarceys, against the tradition of the "well-made" play; each is trying to transfer to the boards a real presentment of life, or of a fraction of life. It is therefore curious, to say the least, to find them hitting upon forms of expression so similar. Unless my memory fails me, a piece of Becque's was acted at the Théàtre Libre in Paris on the same night, or nights, on which *Ghosts* was performed there. It must have been very interesting to compare work so like and yet so *essentially dissimilar*. [. . .]

What the moral of *Hedda Gabler* is, what "gospel" it preaches, and what light it holds out to poor souls tossing in our sea of "hysterical mock-disease," I will not pretend to conjecture. Doubtless there will be scarcely less discussion over the ethics of Hedda's final resolve than there was over those of Nora, when she slammed the front-door so vigorously eleven years ago. These are matters which, I conceive, interest the great magian at Munich less than they do his disciples. He takes a knotty situation, he conducts it to its extreme logical conclusion, he invites the world to fight over it, and then he retires for another two years of solitary meditation.

Hedda Gabler: chronology of major early performances

January 1891 Munich	Residenztheater	Hedda: Clara Heese
February 1891 Berlin	Lessing Theatre	Hedda: Anna Haverland
February 1891 Copenhagen	Royal Theatre	Hedda: Betty Hennings
April 1891 London	Vaudeville Theatre	Hedda: Elizabeth Robins
December 1891 Paris	Théâtre du Vaudeville	Hedda: Mme. Brandes
May 1893 London	Opera Comique	Hedda: Janet Achurch
March 1898 New York	5th Avenue Theatre	Hedda: Elizabeth Robins
February 1899 Moscow	Moscow Art Theatre	Hedda: Maria F. Andreeva
October 1903 London	Adelphi Theatre	Hedda: Eleonora Duse
October 1903 New York	Manhattan Theatre	Hedda: Minnie Maddern Fiske
November 1906 St. Petersburg	Komissarzhevshaya Theatre	Hedda: Vera Komissarzhevskaya
November 1906 New York	Princess Theatre	Hedda: Alla Nazimova
March 1907 London	Court Theatre	Hedda: Mrs Patrick Campbell

Performance and reception

Given the subtext of *Hedda Gabler* outlined in Ibsen's notes – that "the play shall deal with 'the impossible'" and with "'underground forces and powers'", plus the association of women with "Nihilism" – it is hardly surprising to find both actors and audiences uncomprehending. Both the world premiere in Germany at the Residenztheater (13 January 1891) and the first Paris performance (17 December 1891) at the Théâtre du Vaudeville were judged disastrous. The popular Munich actress Marie Conrad-Ramlo played Hedda in a conventionally histrionic and declamatory style, while the French comedienne Marthe Brandès presenting her as a stereotypical seductress was forced to close the production after a single matinee performance. Even the Norwegian public was confused, despite Ibsen's involvement in the Christiana production.

When the play was presented in England by Elizabeth Robins (Vaudeville Theatre, 20 April 1891), the response was moral outrage, as William Archer's

Figure 4.2 Studio portrait of Elizabeth Robins as Hedda Gabler, London, 1891

summary of the reviews shows. The tone of these criticisms echoed the reactions to earlier productions of *A Doll's House*, and particularly *Ghosts*, indicating the way that any play by Ibsen became a battleground between conservative and reformist forces in the period. Indeed, this selection of criticism by Archer also documents the campaign for Ibsen, and is highly selective in omitting the praise of Robins' performance by even the most antagonistic reviewers – such as Clement Scott, who acknowledged a "morbid attraction" in Robins' "sublime study of deceit and heartlessness ... What changes of expression! What watchfulness! ... She has fascinated us with the savage" (*Illustrated London News*, 25 April 1891).

4.4.3 Susan Mason, *Hedda Gabler* at the Christiana Theater, 26 February 1891

The production was received without enthusiasm by the public and by the critics who, for the most part, found the play confusing. The main criticism of Miss Bruun's Hedda was that she was too cold. The critic for *Aftenposten* wrote that she has created an individual out of "the problematic female character" and that she brought out the "aristocratic, blasé, boredom with life and the cold passion" but did not bring out the other aspects. The *Dagbladet* critic wrote that Hedda should be like "champagne on ice" and that Miss Bruun served the ice but forgot the champagne. He also commented on the confusion in the audience and one member asking, "Don't these people ever eat breakfast?"

The *Dagbladet* critic continues that Miss Bruun lacked "the finer shadings" which a few more rehearsals would have achieved. Given the still relatively short rehearsal period, there is probably some truth in this observation. In addition, he felt Miss Bruun's Hedda had already decided to kill herself by the first act and "she is too blasé and too finished with life from the first to the last." He thought that unhappy love was Hedda's tragedy and her failure to win back Eilert should have been played as the cause of her suicide. Furthermore, he was confused by the relationship between Hedda and Brack. She played the earlier scene about the train both "secretive and promising" which made it confusing at the ending when she was so opposed to being in his power.

Although the *Dagbladet* reviewer found the overall performance lacking fullness and intensity, he noted the difficulty of the role, and suggested Miss Bruun's admirable performance would improve. Several months later when Ibsen attended, this same reviewer wrote that now "there is an intensity and clear development . . . a fully formed figure."

The critic for *Morgenbladet* wrote that Miss Bruun had understood the role's various sides, and the reviewer for *Skillings Magazin* mentions her intellectual grasp of the role. However the latter was critical of the actress' spontaneity – "letting the demonic out everywhere, lightly and playfully" and "supplementing his [Ibsen's] strict style with the kind of spontaneity not really appropriate. . . ." He also mentions the ensemble acting, especially noting the scenes between Hedda and Brack and "how far our stage has reached in the last few years in the direction of natural speech." Olaf Hansson, who played Brack, was known for his naturalistic line delivery and movement. One historian even asserts that Hansson was the first Norwegian actor who seriously turned his back to the public.

Because Bjørn Bjørnson directed this production and because he was such an exacting director, his comments on Hedda may indicate how he instructed Miss Bruun to play the role. He wrote that Hedda was "too weak to let herself go until she threw herself into death – the single, heedless,

integrated courageous thing in her whole messed up life." He also wrote
that Miss Bruun's tendency was toward coolness but that in the scene in
front of the fire she was "hysterically wild." By Bjørnson's account, Ibsen
later told him, "That is how pregnant women can become." Also, the words
about "dying in beauty with vine-leaves in the hair – are from the same
workshop." As in an earlier reference, Ibsen attributed much of Hedda's
behavior to her pregnancy.

4.4.4 William Archer, The English Reception of *Hedda Gabler*

"The Mausoleum of Ibsen", *Fortnightly Review*, 1 July 1893

Ghosts was produced at the first performance of the Independent Theatre.
The frenzy of execration with which it was greeted must be within the
memory of all my readers. [. . .]

  Nothing daunted by the tempest, Miss Elizabeth Robins and Miss Marion Lea produced *Hedda Gabler* only five weeks later (April 20th, 1891). This
time the "suburban Ibsen," the "egotist and bungler," was found by the
Daily Telegraph to have produced a "ghastly picture beautifully painted."
"It was like a visit to the Morgue. . . . There they all lay on their copper
couches, fronting us, and waiting to be owned. . . . There they all were, false
men, wicked women, deceitful friends, sensualists, egotists, piled up in a
heap behind the screen of glass, which we were thankful for. . . . There were
the dead bodies, and no one could resist looking at them. Art was used for
the most baleful purpose. It is true that the very spectacle of moral corruption was positively fascinating. . . . Would indeed that, after this Morgue
inspection, after this ghastly spectacle of dead bodies and suicides, after this
revolting picture of human frailty and depravity, there could be a break in
the cloud. . . . But alas! there is no gleam to be seen in the dark raincloud of
Ibsenite pessimism! . . . What a horrible story! What a hideous play!" Most
of my readers are probably aware that there is only one dead body in *Hedda
Gabler*, seen for something like a quarter of a minute just as the curtain falls.
But what must the readers of the *Daily Telegraph* have gathered from the
outburst I have just quoted? "I should like so much to see the piece you're
in," a lady said to Mr. Scott Buist, the excellent Tesman of the cast, "but I
don't think I could stand anything so horrible." "Horrible! How do you
mean?" he inquired. "Why, you have the Morgue on the stage, haven't
you?" was the reply. And I have no doubt many thousands of people were
under the same impression, on that 21st (not 1st) of April. The other critics,
if less imaginative, were no less denunciatory.

> "Ibsen's plays regarded as masterpieces of genius by a small but
> noisy set of people, but . . . the tastes of English playgoers are sound
> and healthy, and the hollowness and shams of the Ibsen cult need
> only be known to be rejected."– *Standard.*

"Dr. Ibsen's social dramas have yet to prove their power to interest cultivated audiences; for the limited number of worshippers who proclaim these productions as masterpieces of art and stagecraft . . . cannot be accepted as a fair sample even of the educated public." – *Daily News.*

"Robust common-sense of ordinary English audiences will confirm the adverse judgment pronounced upon the morbid Norwegian dramatist by all save a clique of faddists anxious to advertise themselves by the aid of any eccentricity that comes first to hand. . . . Already, we fancy, the craze has had its day." – *Sporting and Dramatic News.*

"One left the theatre filled with depression at the sorry spectacle that had been set before them (*sic*)." – *Reynolds' Newspaper.*

"A few steps out of the hospital-ward and we arrive at the dissecting-room. Down a little lower and we come to the deadhouse. There, for the present, Ibsen has left us. . . . Miss Elizabeth Robins has done what no doubt she fully intended to do (!). She has made vice attractive by her art. She has almost ennobled crime. She has glorified an unwomanly woman," &c., &c. Mr. C. SCOTT in the *Illustrated London News.*

"Hideous nightmare of pessimism . . . The play is simply a bad escape of moral sewage-gas. . . . Hedda's soul is a-crawl with the foulest passions of humanity." – *Pictorial World.*

"The piece is stuff and nonsense; poor stuff and 'pernicious nonsense.' It is as if the author had studied the weakest of the Robertsonian comedies, and had thought he could do something like it in a tragic vein." – *Punch.*

"It is not, possibly, so utterly repulsive as others that have been seen, but, nevertheless, it is offensive." – *Lloyd's News.*

"The more I see of Ibsen, the more disgusted I am with his alleged dramas." *London.*

"Utterly pessimistic in its tedious turmoil of knaves and fools. . . . Other plays from the same tainted source." – *The People.*

"Full of loathsomeness." – *The Table.*

"Things rank and gross in nature alone have place in the mean and sordid philosophy of Ibsen. . . . Can any human being feel happier or better from a contemplation of the two harlots at heart who do duty in *Hedda Gabler?* . . . Insidious nastiness of photographic studies of vice and morbidity. . . . It is free from the mess and nastiness of *Ghosts,* the crack-brained maunderings of *Rosmersholm,* the fantastic, short-sighted folly of *A Doll's House.* . . The blusterous little band of Ibsen idolaters. . . ." – *Saturday Review.*

"Strange provincial prigs and suburban chameleons. . . . The funereal clown who is amusing us . . is given to jokes in very questionable taste. We are reminded again and again of Goethe's famous stage direction, '*Mephistopheles macht eine unaständige Geberde*,' and it is a coarseness of this sort which, I fear, constitutes Ibsen's charm for some of his disciples. . . . For sheer unadulterated stupidity, for inherent meanness and vulgarity, for pretentious triviality . . . no Bostonian novel or London penny novelette has surpassed *Hedda Gabler*."

Mr. ROBERT BUCHANAN in the *Illustrated London News*.

*

The reception of *Hedda Gabler* in England, which was widely recognized as a vindication of Ibsen's theatre despite the attacks on what was seen as the immorality and pessimism of the play's vision, was largely due to the psychological character study on which Robins based her performance. This was outlined in her commentary forty years later in *Ibsen and the Actress*. The feminist implications of her interpretation were indeed overlooked (as she indicates); even Lady Bell, whom she mentions as one of her strongest women supporters, focuses solely on the "corrosiveness" and "tragic" nature of the characterization:

> Who that saw it will ever forget what Elizabeth Robins did with the second act? The crouching figure by the fire, Lovborg's book in her terrible maleficent grasp, the firelight flickering on the sinister triumph of hatred in her eyes, as handful by handful she cast the manuscript into the flames, the intensity of her sibilant whisper shuddering through the air – 'Your child, Thea! Your child and Eilert Lovborg's. . . now I am burning the child!'
>
> (*Landmarks*, 1929)

Significantly this highpoint in the performance departed from Ibsen's text – as Archer notes Robins also did at other key moments. In her marked acting script for the production Robins crossed out Ibsen's detailed and specific stage directions, substituting her own actions and lines to intensify the pathological destructiveness and emotion:

> Hedda holds out her hands, wavering a little as he [Løvborg] goes out. She utters a broken cry, grasps curtains, looks back at desk where manuscript is and whispers hoarsely, '*Thea! Thea!*' – again and again as she crosses the room, takes out ms with eager hands, catches sight of stove, glides to it and drops before it opening door and muttering, '*Who? child, the child*' – crushes some leaves and burns them during '*How I love burning your child*'.

Henry James was first exposed to Ibsen by seeing Elizabeth Robins in *Hedda Gabler*. His description of the production used her rendering of the role as a basis to interpret Ibsen's work, pointing out:

> It is the portrait of a nature, the story of what Paul Bourget would call an *état à âme*, and of a state of nerves as well as soul, a state of temper, of

disappointment, of desperation. *Hedda Gabler* is in short the study of an exasperated woman ... We receive Hedda ripe for her catastrophe, and if we ask for antecedents and explanations we must simply find them in her character. Her motives are simply her passions.

(*The New Review*, June 1891)

James defined Ibsen's "great quality" as "dealing essentially with the individual caught in the fact" – and the wide influence of his essay effectively imposed this performance as the standard view of Hedda's character.

Whatever its subsequent critical importance, however, at the time the effect of this production was perhaps more limited than Robins' supporters – who included Shaw as well as Archer and James – claimed. As one reviewer noted on revisiting *Hedda Gabler* towards the end of its run, the English audience for Ibsen was limited to an educated and politically radical elite:

Remarkable, indeed, has been the fate of *Hedda Gabler* at the Vaudeville. Only last week this pretty theatre was unto the worshippers at the shrine of Ibsen as a sort of temple, and the denizens of the stalls and dress circle were even more interesting than the odd drama itself. Their enthusiasm for their idol used to inspire his interpreters; and certainly the matinee performances of *Hedda Gabler* were vastly superior to those which take place now nightly at Mr. Thorne's theatre, although the cast remains unaltered. Before the lic [common public], which pays its shillings and its pence to enjoy an amusing or be thrilled by an exciting play, the aspect of things changed as if by magic. The pit and the gallery watched in blank amazement the vagaries of the lunatic Hedda, and listened to the crudely coarse dialogue with stupefaction. But little applause followed the fall of the curtain, and Miss Elizabeth Robins and Miss Marion Lea [Thea] both felt the chilly influence, and their old magic spell seemed broken.

(*Saturday Review*, 16 May 1891)

4.4.5 Elizabeth Robins, on playing Hedda

Ibsen and the Actress, Hogarth Press, 1928

I have somewhere several sets of page proofs of *Hedda Gabler* as they left the hands of the translators; one set scored over in Marion Lea's handwriting, one with mine, and our final agreed recommendations. These Mr Archer fully criticised, sometimes denounced and utterly declined; but the final result was, I think, a very speakable, very playable version, no less faithful – I have always held more faithful – to Ibsen [. . .]

The press notices were a palpitating excitement, especially those we jeered at – with anxiety in our hearts. But we put on a bold front. Mr Clement Scott understand Hedda? – any man except that wizard Ibsen

118

really understand her? Of course not. That was the tremendous part of it. How should men understand Hedda on the stage when they didn't understand her in the persons of their wives, their daughters, their women friends? One lady of our acquaintance, married and not noticeably unhappy, said laughing, "Hedda is all of us."

Hedda was not all of us, but she was a good many of us – so Mr Grant Allen told the public. Anyway, she was a bundle of the unused possibilities, educated to fear life; too much opportunity to develop her weakness; no opportunity at all to use her best powers [. . .]

Hedda is first represented to us as an enviable person. We hear of what General Gabler's daughter had "been accustomed to"; how fond she was of dancing, and shooting at a mark and riding with her handsome father – she "in her long black habit and with feathers in her hat." "So beset with admirers," Aunt Julia says – who would have dreamt she would marry a mere professor? Well, she wasn't on the scene sixty seconds before it was clear she knew there was joy in life that she hadn't been able to grasp, and that marriage only emphasised what she was missing.

It was never any wish of mine to whitewash General Gabler's somewhat lurid daughter. Even in the heat and glamour of that first personal contact with a great Ibsen part, I was under no temptation to try to make her what is conventionally known as "sympathetic." One surviving recollection bears witness to that. Among those who never much cared about Ibsen, but always came to see him acted, was Lady Bell. At the first performance of *Hedda* she was thought by her companion to be in danger of lending herself too much to the glamour of the play; so this friend of Lady Bell's youth warned her: "It's all very exciting, but I wouldn't trust her round the corner – that woman playing Hedda."

I had the best of reasons for not trying to mitigate Hedda's corrosive qualities. It was precisely the corrosive action of those qualities on a woman in Hedda's circumstances that made her the great acting opportunity she was – in her revolt against those commonplace surroundings that the bookworm she had married thought so "elegant"; her unashamed selfishness; her scorn of so-called womanly qualities; above all, her strong need to put some meaning into her life, even at the cost of borrowing it, or stealing the meaning out of someone else's.

Hedda's first and dearest dream had been to find contacts with life through the attractive young man of letters, Eilert Løvborg. That hope ended in driving him from her at the point of a pistol – not, as one eminent critic has said, "in the ostentation of outraged purity which is the instinctive defence of women to whom chastity is not natural." Hedda drove Løvborg from her in disgust; disgust at the new aspects of vulgar sensuality which her curiosity about life had led him to reveal. She never denied it was her doing that he revealed these things; it was not her doing that he had them to reveal. They made her gorge rise. The man who had wallowed in that filth must not touch Hedda Gabler – certainly not fresh from the latest orgy. The effect of that experience, plus the conditions of her own life and upbringing, was to throw her into marriage with the least ineligible man she can find who is decent, and no one can deny that poor Tesman was entirely decent.

The result was not peculiar to Ibsen characters. In one form or another, as we all know, it is a commonplace in the history of people whose nervous system generates more force than the engine of their opportunity can use up. Hedda speculates, like many another woman, on the opportunity politics would give to her husband, and, through him, give to her; but she is too intelligent to have much hope of Tesman in that direction. She is no sooner home from her boring honeymoon than she finds that a girl she had looked down on and terrorised at school – shrinking, gentle Mrs Elvsted – has reclaimed the dissipated Løvborg. More than that, largely by her faith in him, she has helped him to write what they are calling a work of genius. The timid Thea Elvsted has actually left her husband and her home to watch over Løvborg, so that he may not fall into evil courses again. How on earth had it all come about? Hedda, by turns, worms and coerces the facts out of Thea; "He gave up his old habits not because I *asked* him to, for I never dared do that; but he saw how repulsive they were to me – so he dropped them."

As simple as that! None of those shady stories told to Thea – but the pretty little fool has his dreams in her keeping; she has helped to turn them into reality. And Hedda has lost him. For Hedda there would be "others." The insinuating Judge Brack, with his aristocratic profile and his eyeglass, is already at the door – but never the man whose faith in his own genius, faith in life, had given Hedda the one respite she had known from mean standards, mean fears.

Those had been times for Løvborg, too, of respite from his meaner self. Hedda's passion for external material beauty was not the only kind of beauty that swayed her. Løvborg in his moods of poetic exaltation had given her, too, a glorious sense of freedom, of daring. She had her phrase for those high moods of his. It was the phrase that, with a truly Ibsenite irony, became famous in England in a totally different sense. When Hedda asks eagerly, "Did he have vine leaves in his hair?" she was not inquiring whether Løvborg was drunk with the fiery Scandinavian punch, but whether he had been tasting a diviner draught. She was using her symbol for his hour of inspired vision, which had had for her, too, its intoxication. Now she has lost all that – unless – unless she can break the hold of this irritating little goose. Thea had said she'd been so frightened of Hedda at school. Well, she should be frightened again!

It is a commentary on actress psychology that though in those days I accepted, and even myself used, the description of Hedda as a "bloodless egoist," I was under no temptation to play her like that. Here I was in debt to Ibsen's supreme faculty for giving his actors the clue – the master-key – if they are not too lofty or too helplessly sophisticated to take it. Ibsen's unwritten clue brought me close enough to the "cold-blooded egoist" to feel her warm to my touch; to see Hedda Gabler as pitiable in her hungry loneliness – to see her as tragic. Insolent and evil she was, but some great celebrators of Ibsen have thought more meanly of Hedda than the text warrants [. . .]

It is perhaps curious Ibsen should have known that a good many women have found it possible to get through life by help of the knowledge that they have power to end it rather than accept certain slaveries. Naturally enough, no critic, so far as I know, has ever noticed this governing factor in Hedda's outlook, her consciousness of one sort of power, anyway – the power of escape. The reason men have not noticed the bearing this had on Hedda's character and fate seems plain enough. Certainly the particular humiliations and enslavements that threaten women do not threaten men. Such enslavements may seem so unreal to decent men as to appear as melodrama.

Ibsen not only knew better; he saw further than the special instance. He saw what we at the time did not; I mean the general bearing of Hedda's story.

4.4.6 William Archer, Letter to Charles Archer, 8 July 1891

I have just been correcting the proofs of the last act of *Hedda* . . . The last act of *Hedda* quite thrilled me as it acted itself before me in the proofs. Miss Robins was really fine in it – she had moments of inspiration. I must tell you what poor old Joe Knight said to me one day. We were talking about Barrie's *Ibsens's Ghost*, which was produced on the afternoon before the last performance of *Hedda*. I said it was rather funny. He said: "Well, yes – but I assure you, Archer, at the point where Miss Vanbrugh changed from Thea into Hedda, and I saw the black figure and the long white arms glimmering through the darkness of the stage, the feeling of the real thing gripped me and thrilled me, and I could hardly resist going back that night and seeing it once more." Certainly it was a big thing, that last act, and how it held even the densest of audiences! They always used to hiss Hedda at the lines "I did it for your sake, George", and "I couldn't bear that anyone should throw *you* in the shade" – and certainly Miss Robins was diabolically feline in those lines. What always fetched me most in her performance was a point in which she departed from Ibsen's strict intention. It is where Hedda is sitting by the stove, absorbed in the contemplation of Løvborg's having "had the will and the courage to turn away from the banquet of life – so early." Instead of starting, where Brack says he must dispel her pleasant illusion, Miss R. used to speak three speeches: "Illusion?" "What do you mean?" and "Not voluntarily!" – quite absently, looking straight in front of her, and evidently not taking in what Brack was saying. She used to draw deep

121

breaths of relief ("befrielse"), quite intent on her vision of Eilert lying "I skonhed" [beautifully], and only woken up at her fourth speech: "Have you concealed something?" Now the old min [Archer's pet name for Ibsen] evidently didn't intend this but it is one of those things I'm sure he would be grateful for, it was so beautiful.

5

ANTON CHEKHOV: 1860–1904

1 CONTEXT

The conditions in Russia during Chekhov's lifetime were quite different from those facing naturalistic dramatists elsewhere. The legislative and judicial as well as executive powers of government were embodied in an absolute monarch. Under the autocracy of the Czar individual liberties were far more restricted than in Western countries at the close of the nineteenth century, social divisions were more extreme and the vast mass of the people impoverished and illiterate. Indeed, up until the year after Chekhov's birth the mass of the Russian population lived under a form of indentured slavery, serfdom only being finally abolished in 1861; and its effects were still working their way through society at the beginning of the twentieth century.

Even more than in England, there was censorship of the stage – both centrally and through official committees attached to major theatres – while any political writing was likely to be suppressed. Although official censorship had only been established in 1804, in 1848 the Czar took over personal control of the system, which forbade any representation of the Czar – causing the banning of Pushkin's *Boris Godunov* – as well as any satire on the social establishment or state officials. Despite a certain arbitrariness (staging of Gogol's *The Inspector General* was permitted because it apparently amused the Czar), any form of overt social criticism was almost automatically censored; and among the more notable plays to be suppressed were Turgenev's *A Month in the Country* and Tolstoi's *The Power of Darkness*.

From today's perspective there seems to be a sharp divide between that era, and the Soviet state established by the October Revolution in 1917. Partly perhaps because of the picture painted in Chekhov's plays, the image of Russian life in the latter part of the nineteenth century seems one of comparative stability. In actuality Chekhov lived through a period of reform and reaction, assassination and repression. The social unrest, which was particularly violent in his student years, led up to the first revolution of 1905 shortly following his death.

All this provides the background to his plays, although it is mainly expressed in mood and tone, and only very obliquely through the speeches of his characters. Similarly, the one brief autobiographical outline of his career completely omits any mention of political or social events, even if political awareness is clearly implied in his fact-finding tour of a penal colony. It is notable that the analysis of the Russian prison system, which came out of this, is the only one of his literary works specifically mentioned by Chekhov. However, this autobiographical statement – written for an album commemorating the alumni of the 1884 graduates from the Medical School of Moscow University, which had been agreed on at an 1899 class reunion that Chekhov attended – does define some of the principles on which his naturalistic plays were based.

5.1.1 Anton Chekhov, Letter to Grigory Rossolimo, 11 October 1899

Translated by Michael Heim

I'm sending a photograph of myself (a pretty poor one, taken when my *enteritis* was at its worst) to your address, registered mail. My autobiography? I have a malady called autobiographophobia. It is real torture for me to read any details whatsoever about myself, to say nothing of writing them up for the press. I am enclosing several dates entirely unadorned on a separate sheet of paper. That's the best I can do. If you like, you may add that on my application to the rector for admission to the university I wrote: The School of Med*a*cine.

[. . .]

Yours,
A. Chekhov

I, A. P. Chekhov, was born on January 17, 1860, in Taganrog. I was educated first at the Greek school of the Church of the Emperor Constantine and then at the Taganrog gymnasium. In 1879 I entered the Medical School of Moscow University. I had a very dim idea of the university at the time, and I do not remember exactly what prompted me to choose medical school, but I have had no reason to regret the choice. During my first year of studies, I began publishing in weekly magazines and newspapers, and by the early eighties these literary activities had taken on a permanent, professional character. In 1888 I was awarded the Pushkin Prize. In 1890 I traveled to the Island of Sakhalin and wrote a book about our penal colony and hard labor. Not counting trial reporting, reviews, miscellaneous articles, short news items and the columns I wrote from day to day for the press and which would be difficult to locate and collect, during the twenty years I have been active in literature I have written and published more than forty-eight hundred pages of novellas and stories. I have written plays as well.

There is no doubt in my mind that my study of medicine has had a serious impact on my literary activities. It significantly broadened the scope of my observations and enriched me with knowledge whose value for me as a writer only a doctor can appreciate. It also served as a guiding influence; my intimacy with medicine probably helped me to avoid many mistakes. My familiarity with the natural sciences and the scientific method has always kept me on my guard; I have tried wherever possible to take scientific data into account, and where it has not been possible I have preferred not writing at all. Let me note in this connection that the principles of creative art do not always admit of full accord with scientific data; death by poison cannot be represented on stage as it actually happens. But some accord with scientific data should be felt even within the boundaries of artistic convention, that is, the reader or spectator should be made to realize that convention is involved but that the author is also well versed in the reality of the situation. I am not one of those writers who negate the value of science and would not wish to be one of those who believe they can figure out everything for themselves.

As for my medical practice, I worked as a student in the Voskresensk Zemstvo Hospital (near the New Jerusalem Monastery) with the well-known *zemstvo* doctor Pavel Arkhangelsky and spent a brief period as a doctor in the Zvenigorod Hospital. During the years of the cholera epidemic (1892 and 1893) I headed the Melikhovo Region of the Serpukhov District.

*

If the absolute rule of an Autocrat – the Czar's official title – was one dominant factor which distinguished Russia from the West in the late nineteenth century, the other unique element was the history of Serfdom. As indentured peasants, the serfs had been tied to the land and literally the property of the landlord or the state. They had been unable to own land (though this had been modified in 1848), subject to 25 years' military service (reduced to 15 years in 1834) and liable to physical punishment by their owners (restricted by a law of 1856). Before its abolition Serfdom had been a significant source of social unrest. There had been major peasant uprisings in the seventeenth and eighteenth centuries, while during the half-century before 1861 there had been over 700 peasant disturbances, and 173 landlords or bailiffs had been killed. Even if this violence was not the sole cause of reforms, which modern historians see as primarily a tool used by the Czar to diminish the independence of the gentry, by 1881 at least 84 percent of former serfs had become owners of the allotments they had been cultivating before 1861. However, the fees they had to pay for "redemption" – advanced by the government at 6 percent interest over 49 years – were calculated on an inflated basis of rents and services owed under Serfdom, rather than the value of the land. The psychological impact of the abolition of Serfdom was immense, both on the gentry and the peasants. But the ex-serfs' general conditions hardly improved. Although gradually entrepreneurs (such as Lopakhin in *The Cherry Orchard*) began to emerge from the peasant class and by the 1880s the process of industrialization had begun in Russia, as an early account of *Daily Life in Russia* indicates, nostalgia for the old system (typified by the servant Firs in Chekhov's play) was common among the older generation.

The widespread absence of any democratic rights, and lack of political equality meant that the position of women had far less prominence in Russia during the latter part of the nineteenth century than in Scandinavia or Western Europe. At the same time, under the feudal system female property owners had the same (restricted) rights as men. Perhaps as a result, while women characters are no less central in Chekhov's plays, unlike other naturalistic dramatists there is nothing polemic in the way they are presented. Even so – as a survey on the status of women (conducted shortly after Chekhov's death) shows – women's access to education was at the mercy of arbitrary acts by the Czarist authorities, and although by 1900 they comprised 44 percent of the laboring population, their wages were so minimal that prostitution was an appealing alternative.

> Everywhere the oriental viewpoint has had its effect on the status of women. In general the standards of life are low; therefore the wages of the women are especially wretched . . . The Russian woman's rights movement is forced by circumstances to concern itself chiefly with educational and industrial problems. All efforts beyond these limits are, as a matter of course, regarded as "revolutionary" . . . therefore they are dangerous and practically hopeless . . . In Bialystock, which has the best socialistic organization of women, the women textile workers earn about 18 cents a day; under favorable circumstances $1.25 to $1.50 a week. A skillful woman tobacco worker will earn 32 ½ cents a day. The average daily wages for Russian women labourers are 18 to 20 cents.
>
> (Dr. Kathe Shirmacher, *The Modern Woman's Rights Movement: A Historical Survey*, 1912)

These statistics illuminate the circumstances facing such characters as Varya in *The Cherry Orchard*. Being an adopted child, she is either the orphan of a peasant on the Ranevsky estate, or the illegitimate daughter of Gayev (Madame Ranevsky's brother), and the only marriage open to her would be to one of the very few wealthy members of the peasant class. Refusing Lopakhin, her future is bleak.

5.1.2 Henri Troyat, *Daily Life in Russia*: the Peasants

Translated by Malcolm Barnes

Once there had been two kinds of serfs: those who were tied to the soil (*krepostnye*) and those who were tied to the master (*dvorovye*). The *dvorovye* were not involved in agriculture, but served in the master's house as porters, cooks, valets and coachmen. They could be sold at any moment and into no matter what conditions. The *krepostnye*, however, could not be removed from the soil they cultivated, and if the proprietor sold them properly, they passed under the authority of the purchaser without the boundaries of their fields being affected by it. Thus in the course of centuries the idea had taken deep root in the minds of the moujiks that the land was theirs, although their persons belonged to the master. The master could deprive them of every-thing except the land.[1] When, on February 19, 1861, Alexander II promul-gated the law emancipating the serfs, the latter received the news with a joy that was mixed with anxiety. According to this law, the *dvorovye* must, for two more years, either pay a fee to the master (30 roubles per man and 10 roubles per woman), or guarantee him personal service. After this brief interval they were free but, of course, received no share of the land. Thus a class of permanent servants was created. The treatment of the *krepostnye*, on the other hand, was inspired by the anxiety both to give land to former serfs and to safeguard, as far as possible, the right of the owners. The latter therefore found that they were forced to give the moujiks a part of their domains, but subject to compensation in accordance with a scale annexed to the act. The application of these extremely complex terms was entrusted to an arbitrator, chosen from amongst the nobility. The latter's decisions could be submitted to a special court composed of the nobles of the Government. And it was the Senate, the noble assembly *par excellence*, which judged the differences in the last resort. This aspect of the reform aroused the suspicions of the moujiks; dimly convinced that they were the owners of the plots they cultivated, they were astonished that they now had to pay for them. Doubtless the owners had distorted the Emperor's generous ideas! One day the truth would out! The Tsar would issue a new 'ukase', written 'in letters of gold', to make clear that he gave the moujiks both their liberty and their land.

But the years passed; the 'ukase in letters of gold' was slow in appearing, and the moujiks reckoned that, although they were freed from bodily servi-tude, other restraints weighed upon them. In fact, to make it possible for them to acquire their enclosures and portions (*nadel*) rapidly, the State had granted them long-term loans. It was the State which, in their stead, had paid the purchase price (*obrok*) to the landowners in letters of credit. Afterwards, the State turned to the moujiks to claim an annual payment of six kopecks for every rouble advanced, the capital being fully redeemed in forty-nine years. Thereafter every connection was broken between the former masters and the peasants. But the latter remained debtors to the State which, to secure its debt, imposed responsibility for payment upon the commune, represented by the popular assembly known as the *mir*. Formerly, it had been the master who had accepted the responsibility for tax collection: if he was harsh he flogged the negligent payer, but ended by sending the taxes where they were intended; if he was a good man, he might pay the debt himself out of laziness or pity. But the *mir* was intractable. This assembly of peasants accepted no

---

The Russian peasants were enslaved and tied to the master's land only at the end of the sixteenth century by a decision of the Tsar Boris Gudonov.

excuses from their fellows who, by misfortune or mistake jeopardized the interests of the community. According to Paul Egorovitch Sychkin, many moujiks, overwhelmed by care, felt a nostalgia for the days of serfdom. Once they had been like children, without rights, vaguely oblivious and without initiative; but now they had become adults overnight, with instructions to steer their own way through life. 'Things were better in the masters' days,' the old folk said. 'At least, we didn't have to worry about the future. We were sure of eating our fill. The master did the thinking for us. . . .'

*

Chekhov trained as a doctor (attending the Moscow University Medical School, where he began writing the short stories that established his reputation as an author, from 1879–1884); and in the 1870s medical students had become a centre of radical activity, particularly at St. Petersburg where Kropotkin had become their spokesman. In 1874 between 1,000 and 2,000 socialist students from Moscow and St. Petersburg had spread out across Russia, following Bakunin's theories in forsaking self-education for political action, to become rural agitators. The signal failure of this populist movement led radical socialists to advocate terrorism as an instrument of political change. After a wave of assassinations in 1878, including the attempted shooting of the Governor-General of St. Petersburg and the killing of General Mezentsev, the head of the gendarmes, the extremist People's Will (*Narodnaia Volia*) organization was founded in 1879 – the year Chekhov entered medical school. In 1881 they assassinated Czar Alexander II, by throwing a bomb at the Royal coach as he returned from inspecting the guards, and sent an open letter to the new Czar justifying his father's killing.

Chekhov hardly ever refers to political issues in his correspondence – an exception being his support for Dreyfus in 1897, while living in France – and (following a similar line to Ibsen) rejects all brands of politics in favor of individual liberty:

I am neither liberal, nor conservative, nor gradualist, nor monk, nor indifferentist . . . I hate lies and violence in all their forms . . . Pharisaism, dullwittedness and tyranny reign not only in merchant's homes and police stations. I see them in science, in literature, among the younger generation . . . I look upon tags and labels as prejudices. My holy of holies is the human body, health, intelligence, talent, inspiration, love and the most absolute freedom imaginable, freedom from violence and lies, no matter what form the latter two take. Such is the program I would adhere to if I were a major artist.

(Letter to Alexei Plehcheyev, 4 October 1888)

Indeed, politics form only the most muted subtext in his plays, the most obvious example being the polemic speech of the student radical in Act II of *The Cherry Orchard*.

However, Chekhov was certainly aware of the ideological ferment that increasingly preoccupied the Russian intelligentsia from the mid-1880s, leading up to the

1905 revolution. He saw the political activist Vladimir Korolenko, whose writing was largely protest literature devoted to the liberation of the common people, as a close colleague. He corresponded with Maxim Gorki, and resigned from the Russian Academy together with Korolenko when Gorki's election was cancelled in 1902. His rejection of overtly political commentary in art expresses a position familiar to more contemporary political writers:

> I sometimes preach heresies, but I haven't gone so far as to deny that prob-
> lematic questions have a place in art . . . You are right to demand that an
> author takes conscious stock of what he is doing, but you are confusing two
> concepts: answering the questions and formulating them correctly. Only the
> latter is required of an author.
>
> (Letter to Alexei Suvorin, 27 October 1888)

In 1872 the first volume of Marx's *Das Kapital* had been translated into Russian; and in 1883 Plekhanov founded the first Russian Marxist group, the "Emancipa-tion of Labour". By the 1890s large numbers of (legally published) books and journals were propagating Marxist ideas – among them G.V. Plekhanov's *The Monist View of History* (1895), and *The Development of Capitalism in Russia* (1899) by V.I. Ulianov (Lenin). Clandestine Marxist groups of intelligentsia and industrial laborers were formed in several major cities, leading to the founding of the Russian Social Democratic Workers' Party in 1898, with its official paper, *Iskra* (*The Spark*), being published abroad and secretly distributed in Russia. At the same time, a populist movement (the Agrarian Socialist League) emerged in the prov-inces, establishing "peasant brotherhoods" in various villages from which the Party of Socialist Revolutionaries emerged in 1901, calling for "the nationali-zation of land and communal, planned socialist organization of production" (Chernov, *The Immediate Question of the Revolutionary Cause*, 1900). In addition, the growing student population became increasingly radicalized. When a student demonstration in St. Petersburg was violently broken up by police in 1899, protest strikes and riots erupted across university campuses, in 1901 one of the students expelled for taking part assassinated the minister of public education, and continuing agitation among the students led into the revolution of 1905.

The socialist ideas that preoccupied so many of Chekhov's contemporaries form a background to his early naturalistic drama (*Ivanov*, 1887; *The Wood Demon*, 1889). It becomes still more evident in his last plays, *The Three Sisters* (1901) and *The Cherry Orchard* (1904), each of which deal on a very broad level with the destruction of the old establishment.

The influence of revolutionary theories, coupled with reactionary policies in the wake of Alexander II's assassination, the effects of famine in 1891–2, and the economic miseries of rapid industrialization, compounded by the unpopular and militarily disastrous war with Japan – the result of Russian Imperial expansion in the Far East – produced the revolution of 1905. Although over a year after the writing of *The Cherry Orchard*, it was the culmination of the political situation indirectly symbolized by "the sound of a breaking harp-string, mournfully dying away" and the appearance of a drunken beggar in Act II. The spark was a peaceful march of striking workers through the streets of St. Petersburg on 22 January 1905, led by a priest carrying a petition to Nicholas II. Barred from the Winter Palace by police, they were fired on before they could present their grievances and demands to the Czar. Scores were killed, hundreds wounded; "Bloody Sunday" triggered nationwide protest demonstrations, anti-government strikes and mutinies. Together with continuing military and naval defeats in the war with Japan, the widespread insurrection forced the Czar to grant "civic freedom based on the principles of genuine personal inviolability, freedom of conscience, speech, assemblies and associations." The same proclamation promised "that no law shall become effective without confirmation by the State Duma", which would now include representatives of "all those classes of the population which presently are completely deprived of voting rights" (*The October Manifesto*). A month later the Czar canceled all the redemption payments imposed on the peasants by the Emancipation bill of 1861.

5.1.3 A Letter from the Revolutionary Executive Committee of the Narodnaia Volia to Alexander III: 22 March 1881

Translated by Basil Dmytrshn

Basil Dmytrshn, *Imperial Russia*, Holt, Rinehart, Winston, 1974

Your Majesty:

[. . .]

The tragedy enacted on the Ekaterínski canal [the assassination of the Tsar] was not a mere casualty, nor was it unexpected. After all that had happened in the course of the previous decade it was absolutely inevitable; and in that fact consists its deep significance for a man who has been placed by fate at the head of governmental authority. Such occurrences can be explained as the results of individual malignity, or even of the evil disposition of "gangs," only by one who is wholly incapable of analyzing the life of a nation. For ten whole years – notwithstanding the strictest prosecution; notwithstanding the sacrifice by the late Emperor's Government of liberty, the interests of all classes, the interests of industry and commerce, and even its own dignity; notwithstanding the absolute sacrifice of everything in the attempt to suppress the revolutionary movement – that movement has obstinately extended, attracting to itself the best elements of the country – the most energetic and self-sacrificing people of Russia – and the revolutionists have carried on, for three years, a desperate partizan warfare with the administration.

You are aware, your Majesty, that the Government of the late Emperor could not be accused of a lack of energy. It hanged the innocent and the guilty, and filled prisons and remote provinces with exiles. Tens of so-called "leaders" were captured and hanged, and died with the courage and tranquility of martyrs; but the movement did not cease – on the contrary it grew and strengthened. The revolutionary movement, your Majesty, is not dependent upon any particular individuals; it is a process of the social organism; and the scaffolds raised for its more energetic exponents are as powerless to save the out-grown order of things as the cross that was erected for the Redeemer was powerless to save the ancient world from the triumph of Christianity. The Government, of course, may yet capture and hang an immense number of separate individuals, it may break up a great number of separate revolutionary groups, it may even destroy the most important of existing revolutionary organizations; but all this will not change, in the slightest degree, the condition of affairs. Revolutionists are the creation of circumstances; of the general discontent of the people; of the striving of Russia after a new social framework. It is impossible to exterminate the whole people; it is impossible, by means of repression, to stifle its discontent. Discontent only grows the more when it is repressed. For these reasons the places of slain revolutionists are constantly taken by new individuals, who come forth from among the people in ever-increasing numbers, and who are still more embittered, still more energetic. These persons, in order to carry on the conflict, form an association in the light of the experience of their predecessors, and the revolutionary organization thus grows stronger, numerically and in quality, with the lapse of time. This we actually see from the history of the last ten years. Of what use was it to destroy the Dolgú-shintsi, the Chaikóftsi, and the workers of 1874? Their places were taken by much more resolute democrats. Then the awful repressive measures of the Government called upon the stage the terrorists of 1878–1879. In vain the Government put to death the Kováslkis, the Dubróvins, the Ossînskis, and the Lisobúbs. In vain it destroyed tens of revolutionary circles. From among those incomplete organizations, by virtue of natural selection, arose only stronger forms, until, at last, there has appeared an Executive Committee with which the Government has not yet been able successfully to deal.

A dispassionate glance at the grievous decade through which we have just passed will enable us to forecast accurately the future progress of the revolutionary movement, provided the policy of the Government does not change. The movement will continue to grow and extend; deeds of a terroristic nature will increase in frequency and intensity, and the revolutionary organization will constantly set forth, in the places of destroyed groups, stronger and more perfect forms. [. . .] A terrible explosion, a bloody hurly-burly, a revolutionary earthquake throughout Russia, will complete the destruction of the old order of things. Upon what depends this terrible prospect? [. . .] It arises, your Majesty, from the lack in Russia of a real government in the true sense of that word. A government, in the very nature of things, should only give outward form to the aspirations of the people and effect to the people's will. But with us – excuse the expression – the Government has degenerated into a mere camarilla, and deserves the name of a usurping "gang" much more than does the Executive Committee.

Whatever may be the intentions of the Tsar, the actions of the Government have nothing in common with the popular welfare, or popular aspirations. The Imperial Government subjected the people to serfdom, put the masses into the power of the nobility, and is now openly creating the most injurious class of speculators and jobbers. All of its reforms result merely in a more perfect enslavement and a more complete exploitation of the people. It has brought Russia to such a pass that, at the present time, the masses of the people are in a state of pauperism and ruin; are subjected to the most humiliating surveillance, even at their own domestic hearths; and are powerless even to regulate their own communal and social affairs. The protection of the law and of the Government is enjoyed only by the extortionist and the exploiter, and the most exasperating robbery goes unpunished. But, on the other hand, what a terrible fate awaits the man who sincerely considers the general good! You know very well your Majesty, that it is not only socialists who are exiled and prosecuted. Can it be possible that the *Government* is the guardian of such "order"? Is it not rather probable that this is the work of a "gang" – the evidence of a complete usurpation?

These are the reasons why the Russian Government exerts no moral influence, and has no support among the people. These are the reasons why Russia brings forth so many revolutionists. These are the reasons why even such a deed as Tsaricide excites in the minds of a majority of the people only gladness and sympathy. Yes, your Majesty! Do not be deceived by the reports of flatterers and sycophants – Tsaricide, in Russia, is popular.

From such a state of affairs there can be only two exits: either a revolution, absolutely inevitable and not to be averted by any punishments, or a voluntary turning of the Supreme Power to the people. In the interest of our native land, in the hope of preventing the useless waste of energy, in the hope of averting the terrible miseries that always accompany revolution, the Executive Committee approaches your Majesty with the advice to take the second course. Be assured, so soon as the Supreme Power ceases to rule arbitrarily, so soon as it firmly resolves to accede to the demands of the people's conscience and consciousness, you may, without fear, discharge the spies that disgrace the administration, send your guards back to their barracks, and burn the scaffolds that are demoralizing the people. The Executive Committee will voluntarily terminate its own existence, and the organizations formed about it will disperse, in order that their members may devote themselves to the work of culture among the people of their native land.

[. . .]

The conditions that are prerequisite to a change from revolutionary activity to peaceful labor are created, not by us, but by history. These conditions, in our opinion, are two.

1. A general amnesty to cover all past political crimes; for the reason that they were not crimes but fulfillments of civil duty.
2. The summoning of representatives of the whole Russian people to examine the existing framework of social and governmental life, and to remodel it in accordance with the people's wishes.

We regard it as necessary, however, to remind you that the legalization of the Supreme Power, by the representatives of the people, can be valid only in case the elections are perfectly free. For this reason such elections must be held under the following conditions.

1. Delegates are to be sent from all classes, without distinction, and in number are to be proportionate to the number of inhabitants.
2. There shall be no limitations, either for voters or delegates.
3. The canvass and the elections shall be absolutely unrestricted, and therefore the Government, pending the organization of the National Assembly, shall authorize, in the form of temporary measures; (a) Complete freedom of the press; (b) Complete freedom of speech; (c) Complete freedom of public meeting; (d) Complete freedom of election program. This is the only way in which Russia can return to the path of normal and peaceful development.

We declare solemnly, before the people of our native land and before the whole world, that our party will submit unconditionally to the decisions of a National Assembly elected in the manner above indicated, and that we will not allow ourselves, in future, to offer violent resistance to any Government that the National Assembly may sanction.

And now, your Majesty, decide! Before you are two courses, and you are to make your choice between them. We can only trust that your intelligence and conscience may suggest to you the only decision that is compatible with the welfare of Russia, with your own dignity, and with your duty to your native land.

The Executive Committee

5.1.4 Father George Gapon, Petition to Nicholas II: 22 January 1905

Translated by Basil Dmytrshn

Sovereign!

We, the workers and the inhabitants of various social strata of the city of St. Petersburg, our wives, children, and helpless old parents, have come to you, Sovereign, to seek justice and protection. We are impoverished; our employers oppress us, overburden us with work, insult us, consider us inhuman, and treat us as slaves who must suffer a bitter fate in silence. Though we have suffered, they push us deeper and deeper into a gulf of misery, disfranchisement, and ignorance. Despotism and arbitrariness strangle us and we are gasping for breath. Sovereign, we have no strength left. We have reached the limit of endurance. We have reached that terrible moment when death is preferable to the continuance of unbearable sufferings.

And so we left our work and informed our employers that we shall not resume work until they meet our demands. We do not demand much; we only want what is indispensable to life and without which life is nothing but hard labor and eternal suffering. Our first request was that our employers discuss our needs jointly with us. But they refused to do this; they even denied us the right to speak about our needs, saying that the law does not give us such a right. Also unlawful were our requests to reduce the working day to eight hours; to set wages jointly with us; to examine our disputes with lower echelons of factory administration; to increase the wages of unskilled workers and women to one ruble per day; to abolish overtime work; to provide medical care without insult; to build shops in such a way that one could work there and not die because of awful drafts, rains, and snow.

Our employers and factory administrators considered all this to be unlawful; they regarded every one of our requests as a crime and interpreted our desire to improve our condition as audacity.

Sovereign, there are thousands of us here; outwardly we resemble human beings, but in reality neither we nor the Russian people as a whole enjoy any human right, have any right to speak, to think, to assemble, to discuss our needs, or to take measures to improve our conditions. They have enslaved us and they did it under the protection of your officials, with their aid and with their cooperation. They imprison and [even] send into exile any one of us who has the courage to speak on behalf of the interests of the working class and of the people. They punish us for our good heartedness and sympathy as if for a crime. [. . .]

Sovereign! Is all this compatible with God's laws, by the grace of which you reign? And is it possible to live under such laws? Wouldn't it be better for all of us if we, the toiling people of all Russia, died? Let the capitalist-exploiters of the working class, the bureaucratic embezzlers of public funds, and the pillagers of the Russian people live and enjoy themselves. Sovereign, these are the problems that we face and these are the reasons that we have gathered before the walls of your palace. Here we seek our last salvation. [. . .] It is not arrogance that forces us to speak but the realization of the need to escape from a situation unbearable for all of us. Russia is too great, her needs too diverse and numerous to be administered by bureaucrats only. It is essential to have a popular representation; it is essential that the people help themselves and that they govern themselves. Only they know their real needs. Do not spurn their help; accept it; decree immediately to summon at once representatives of the Russian land from all classes, from all strata, including workers' representatives. Let there be present a capitalist, a worker, a bureaucrat, a priest, a doctor, and a teacher – let everyone regardless of who they are elect their own representatives. Let everyone be equal and free to elect or be elected, and toward that end decree that the elections to the Constituent Assembly be carried out on the basis of universal, secret, and equal suffrage.

*

Perhaps because the political subtext of Chekhov's plays is so ambiguous, his drama is generally seen as associated with pre-revolutionary society. Indeed, all his full-length plays deal with the leisured classes, and are set outside the centres of power and political struggle, on Russian country estates (with the exception of *The Three Sisters*, which takes place in a provincial town). At first sight there is little sign of the growing revolutionary ferment, and Chekhov's characters appear to be insulated from political events by their geographical distance from Moscow – though the three sisters who sigh so heavily for Moscow are in fact living only just outside the capital. This apolitical association of Chekhov with the values of the pre-revolutionary elite stems partly from Stanislavsky's description of a performance of *The Cherry Orchard* on the eve of the October Revolution.

At the same time, writing his memoirs under Stalinism, Stanislavsky promoted a specific political meaning in Chekhov's plays. The political sensitivity of Chekhov's work is also indicated by the Russian editions of his correspondence (1944–51, and 1963–4). In these a letter which quoted a passage from Porfiry Uspensky, a nineteenth-century Bishop – "Standing armies . . . are the lawless defenders of unjust and unfair laws, of privilege and of tyranny" (6 February 1899) – had a note stating that Bishop Porfiry, who wrote in 1848, was commenting solely on the armies of capitalist countries. Another letter referring disparagingly to "Marxists with their self-important faces" [26 December 1900] was either omitted altogether, or had a note claiming that Chekhov was only referring to those Marxists "officially sanctioned" by the Czarist state – not to the Marxist–Leninists who had founded the Soviet state. So Stanislavsky's proto-revolutionary interpretation has to be seen as a way of justifying the close association of the Moscow Art Theatre with Chekhov's work, by showing his characters as prefiguring the "heroes" of the 1917 Communist revolution:

Astrov and Uncle Vanya are not simple and small men, but ideal fighters against the terrible realities of the Russia of Chekhov's time . . . when the plot of the play drags him and his heroes into the sad dark life of the eighties of the last century, then the happy laughter of the men [of the post-revolutionary audience] serves but to make clearer the hardships that were borne in Russia by the great men who became heroes in the days of revolution. I cannot

135

believe that a man like Astrov would remain unrecognized at a moment of national uplift in Russia.

(Konstantin Stanislavsky, *My Life in Art* 1926)

Despite the tone of special political pleading, Stanislavsky does point to a major motif that runs through all Chekhov's plays in the longing for a better life expressed – in a very general and undefined way – by so many of his characters.

5.1.5 Konstantin Stanislavsky, Chekhov and Russian Politics

Translated by J. J. Robbins

"[. . .] our art is not eternal, but it is the most inescapable of all arts so far as our contemporaries are concerned. What strength there is in it! Its action is created not by one man, but simultaneously by a group of actors, artists, stage directors, and musicians; not by one art, but simultaneously by many most diverse arts, music, drama, painting, declamation, dancing. This theatrical action is received not by one man, but simultaneously by a crowd of human beings which develops a mass emotion that sharpens the moments of receptivity. This collectivity, that is, the simultaneous creation of many different artists, this comprehensivity, that is, the action not of one, but of many arts at one time, this herd feeling of receptivity, show their full strength in the impression they make on this new, unspoiled, trusting, and unsophisticated spectator."

This force of the scenic power over the spectator was shown in strongest relief at one performance which I will always remember. This performance was given almost on the eve of the Third Revolution. On that night the soldiery was gathering around the Kremlin, mysterious preparations were being made, gray-clad mobs were walking somewhere, some of the streets were completely empty, the lanterns were out, the police patrols removed, and in the Solodovnikovsky Theatre there gathered a thousand-headed crowd of the common people to see Chekhov's "Cherry Orchard", in which the life of that class against whom the common people were preparing for final revolt was painted in deep and sympathetic tones.

The auditorium, filled almost exclusively by the common people, buzzed with excitement. The mood on both sides of the footlights was one of worry. We actors, in our make-ups, waiting for the performance to begin, stood near the curtain and listened to the buzzing of the audience in the thickened atmosphere of the auditorium.

"We won't be able to finish the performance," we said to each other. "There will be a scandal. Either they will drive us from the stage or they will attack us."

When the curtains parted, our hearts beat in the expectation of a possible excess. But – the lyricism of Chekhov, the eternal beauty of Russian poetry,

136

the life-mood of country gentility in old Russia, caused a reaction even under the existing conditions. It was one of our most successful perform-ances from the viewpoint of the attention of the spectators. It seemed to us that all of them wanted to wrap themselves in the atmosphere of poetry and to rest there and bid peaceful farewell forever to the old and beautiful life that now demanded its purifying sacrifices. The performance was ended by a tremendous ovation, and the spectators left the theatre in silence, and who knows – perhaps many of them went straight to the barricades. Soon shoot-ing began in the city. Hardly able to find cover, we made our way to our homes in the night. In the darkness I ran into a priest, and thought:

"They are shooting there, and we are in duty bound to go, he to the church, I to the theatre. He to pray, I to create for those who seek respite."

2 CHEKHOV'S NATURALISTIC DRAMA

While there is no direct evidence that he knew of Zola's theories, when Chekhov came across *J'Accuse!* – Zola's polemic pamphlet defending Dreyfus – in 1898, he characterized Zola as "a noble soul" and stressed that he was "delighted by his outburst" (Letter to Alexei Suvorin, 4 January 1898). Chekhov certainly knew, and admired Ibsen's naturalistic plays, and his commitment to objectivity follows the basic principle of Naturalism:

> It is not the writer's job to solve such problems as God, pessimism, etc.; his job is merely to record who, under what conditions, said or thought what about God or pessimism. The artist is not meant to be a judge of his characters and what they say; his only job is to be an impartial witness
>
> (Letter to Alexei Suvorin, 30 May 1888)

However, just as Strindberg rejected "photographic realism", he expressed his impatience with realistic writers who "describe life as it is and . . . have neither immediate nor remote goals". In his definition all good writers

> have one highly important trait in common: they're moving towards something definite and beckon you to follow . . . The best of them are realistic and describe life as it is, but because each line is saturated with the conscious-ness of its goal, you feel life as it should be in addition to life as it is . . .
>
> (Letter to Alexei Suvorin, 25 November 1892)

Comments to other writers on their work, scattered through his correspondence, offer insights on his own methods of dramatic composition. These indicate that Chekhov based his writing on images – which he collected in his mind independ-ent of any specific story or play – and began by creating a framework of character relationships, building up minor figures to create a context that delineated the nature of the protagonists.

137

These elements control the meaning in Chekhov's plays, most obviously the images, which he singled out as "best, that I love and jealously hold on to so as not to waste" on more minor work (Letter to Alexei Suvorin, 27 October 1888). These infuse his drama on several levels. There are the explicit, global images of the seagull or the cherry orchard: similar to Ibsen's doll's house or wild duck, but even more pervasive. They give the titles to the plays, are present on the stage, identified with by one of the characters, referred to in the dialogue (and intensified in their effect by being destroyed – shot like the bird, or chopped down like the trees). There is the transposition or expansion of the dramatic situation into musical terms, as with the street musicians in Act IV of *The Three Sisters*, whose nostalgic interplay of harp and violin speak for the silent listening characters, or the retreating sound of the military band – and the openly symbolic breaking harp-string in *The Cherry Orchard*. Chekhov also had clear visual images in mind for the specific moments in the stage action, as in his directive to Stanislavsky during the rehearsals for *The Three Sisters*:

> You write that when Natasha is making the rounds of the house at night in Act Three she puts out the lights and looks under the furniture for burglars. It seems to me, though, that it would be better to have her walk across the stage in a straight line without a glance at anyone or anything à la Lady Macbeth with a candle – that way it would be much briefer and more frightening.
>
> (Letter, 2 January 1901)

As with this analogy to Lady Macbeth, these images contradict what is usually assumed to be a fundamental principle of Naturalism, in substituting interpretive symbolism for the observed behavior of ordinary people in daily life.

In the way he used images, Chekhov can be seen as borrowing techniques from the Symbolist movement; and indeed there are references to the symbolists in his plays. Gayev talks of "the Decadents" (the common term for symbolist writers) in *The Cherry Orchard*, while the play that Nina performs in Act I of *The Seagull* – "the talented work of Treplev" which Stanislavsky refers to as "real art" (*My Life in Art*) – corresponds to the quintessential qualities of Symbolism. These were defined by Arthur Symons, who took *Axël* by Villiers de L'Isle-Adam as his prime example of symbolist drama:

> The religious ideal, the occult ideal, the passionate ideal, all are presented one after the other, in these dazzling and profound pages; Axël is the disdainful choice from among them, the disdainful rejection of life itself, of the whole illusion of life, "since infinity alone is not a deception" . . . And the play is written, throughout in a particular kind of eloquence, which makes no attempt to imitate the level of speech of every day, but which is a sort of ideal language in which beauty is aimed at exclusively as if it were written in verse . . .
>
> The ideal, to Villiers, being the real, spiritual beauty being the essential beauty, and material beauty its reflection or its revelation, it is with a sort of

fury that he attacks the materialising forces of the world: science, progress, the worldly emphasis on "facts," on what is "positive," "serious," "respectable."

(Arthur Symons, *The Symbolist Movement*, 1899)

Just as the extreme theory of Naturalism traced passions to physiology, which substituted for the soul, Symbolism denied the validity of physical existence. Chekhov combines elements of both, to create what has been called "poetic naturalism" – and indeed it was this quality that Stanislavsky singled out as the basis of his naturalistic "System" of acting:

Chekhov discovered to us the life of things and sounds, thanks to which all that was lifeless, dead and unjustified in the details of production, all that in spite of our desires created an outward naturalism, turned of itself into living and artistic realism, and the properties on the stage took on an inner relationship with the soul of the actor. Chekhov, like no one else, was able to create inward and outward artistic truth.

(*My Life in Art*, 1926)

This balance was difficult for even the Moscow Art Theatre to achieve. As Stanislavsky admits in his memoirs, the over-emphasis on external Naturalism in his productions (even in *The Cherry Orchard* after extensive experience with Chekhov's plays) caused Chekhov to propose adding a speech – "How wonderful! We hear no birds, no dogs, no cuckoos, no owls, no clocks, no sleigh-bells, no crickets" – in protest against all the contextual background being introduced in the staging.

There is also another major element in Chekhov's naturalistic plays that transgresses generally accepted boundaries – his combination of comedy, sometimes verging on farce, with intrinsically serious themes, even tragedy. (Death is a consistent theme in his mature plays, ranging from the suicide of a major character, shooting in a duel – albeit off stage – or the final image of an abandoned servant dying of old age, to a failed – and therefore farcical – attempted murder; and none has a "happy" outcome.) This caused repeated misunderstandings, even with Stanislavsky. Despite the themes of unrequited love, the tragic fate of Nina, the young actress, sexually exploited and discarded, and the final suicide of Treplev together with his unsuccessful attempt to kill himself earlier in the play, *The Seagull* was conceived as a "comedy" – as Chekhov wrote to his publisher, "flagrantly disregarding the basic tenets of the stage" (Letter to Alexei Suvorin, 21 October 1895). *The Cherry Orchard* too is explicitly labeled a comedy, and Chekhov complained "Why is the play so persistently called a drama [as distinct from a comedy] in posters and newspaper advertisements? Nemirovich and Stanislavsky definitely see . . . something absolutely different from what I have written" (Letter to Olga Knipper, 10 April 1904).

Indeed Stanislavsky showed a consistent confusion about the degree of humor in Chekhov's plays, asserting for instance that the Moscow Art Theatre cast of *The*

Three Sisters "considered the play a tragedy and even wept over it", angering Chekhov who insisted he "had written a happy comedy" (*My Life in Art*). In fact, as recent scholarship has shown, the only source for a comic interpretation of this play – which is contradicted by Chekhov's letters, where *The Three Sisters* is always referred to as a drama (i.e. a serious play) – is Stanislavky's memoirs, and these contain numerous misconceptions and inaccuracies about both Chekhov's personality and his plays (see Michael Heim, notes to *The Letters of Anton Chekhov*).

Given the potential for misunderstanding in these two central elements of his dramaturgy, Chekhov tried to keep close control over the staging of his plays. For instance, he asserted with reference to *Ivanov*, "(1) the play is the author's property, not the actors'; (2) where the author is present, casting the play is his responsibility; (3) *all* my comments to date have improved the production, and they have all been put into practice . . . (4) the actors themselves ask for my comments" (Letter to Nicholai Leykin, 15 November 1887). Even so, circumstances prevented him from having much influence on the way his plays were performed. Up until the founding of the Moscow Art Theatre his aims were frustrated by theatrical conditions of the time. In the case of *Ivanov*, for instance, Chekhov complained that the producer "promised me ten rehearsals and gave me only four" – making the close attention to detail required for any degree of Naturalism all but impossible – while only two of the cast "knew their parts; the rest of them relied on the prompter and inner conviction" (Letter to Alexander Chekhov, 20 November 1887). With Stanislavsky's productions Chekhov attended rehearsals when his health allowed, and in other cases commented on every aspect of the staging through correspondence with Stanislavsky, Stanislavsky's wife (the actress Maria Lilina), Vladimir Nemirovich-Danchenko (the dramaturge and co-director of the Moscow Art Theatre) and Olga Knipper (the leading actress in Stanislavsky's ensemble, who became Chekhov's wife). Despite this extensive consultation, however, the letters show that his detailed instructions for casting were often ignored, while even his stage-directions for the setting were not always followed – as he reluctantly conceded to Stanislavsky, "please do just as you like about the scenery" for *The Cherry Orchard* (Letter, 10 November 1903).

Largely because of confusion about the nature of his plays, Chekhov's work was delayed in appearing on the stage outside of Russia. Another contributing factor for this neglect was the apparent absence of the challenge to conventional morality or relevance to the movement for social reform, with which the naturalist movement in Europe had identified itself. In England, for example, although *The Seagull* was performed in Glasgow in 1909, the first London production of a Chekhov play was in 1911, when the Stage Society presented *The Cherry Orchard* at Bernard Shaw's insistence. Even then, the play was widely dismissed as actionless and presenting dull or grotesque characters (*Academy & Literature*, 3 June 1911, *Daily Telegraph* and *The Times* 30 May 1911, *Nation*, 22 June 1911), while even critical supporters singled out qualities with little public appeal, such as praise for the way "every piece of irrelevance is relevant to the dramatic impression of irrelevance" (*Saturday Review*, 3 June 1911). In all there were only five British productions of Chekhov's plays – one of which was his short farce, *The Bear* – before the First World War. As a result, Chekhov had little influence on other naturalistic playwrights – with the single exception of one play by Bernard Shaw (*Heartbreak House*).

Following the death toll of the First World War, which devastated the society of Western Europe as well as allowing the Communists to seize power in the Russian Revolution, and hollowed out the establishment even in England, Chekhov's plays were perceived as having a new relevance. There were numerous productions in London during the 1920s, and reviewers showed a deeper understanding of Chekhov's poetic art. At the same time, the themes of the plays were distorted to fit an English context. Thus in response to a 1920 performance of *The Cherry Orchard*, one reviewer saw "an identity between the circumstances of Madame Ranevskaia and any lady of the governing class in Ireland" (*The Observer*, 18 July 1920). Similarly one of the most serious and long lasting misconceptions of Chekhov was initiated by a review of *The Seagull* in 1919: "these Russians of Chekhov's . . . are like grown-up children, entirely without self-control, flaring into sudden 'tempers', and as abruptly cooling down again, all talking at once and no one listening . . . The play is really a picture, somber, ironical, masterly of the solitariness of human lives in a crowd" (*The Times*, 2 June 1919). The assumption that Chekhov portrays the failure of communication, corresponding to the feeling that in the aftermath of the Great War social discourse had broken down, was reflected in English productions at least up until the 1950s and became a critical cliché.

In particular, Chekhov's use of humor has caused difficulties, and is still problematic in productions of his plays outside Russia. However, his combination of comedy and realism had been recognized as early as 1904 in a review of the first English translation of his plays, which is still relevant for its insights:

> Chekhov . . . recorded life with a mocking tenderness, a mixture of satire and sadness, which has no parallel in the literature of his own, or any other country. Those who indulge in definitions call him a pessimist. In point of fact, he never took sides, he never passed judgement. The rest might preach, he wished only to paint. If his palette was grey, if the monotony of the steppe, the disillusion and disenchantment of the Russian soul coloured his canvas, it is because they were factors in contemporary life. Chekhov always remained resolutely true to conditions around him . . .
>
> The sum total of all this misery and stupidity Chekhov lays by subtle inference at the door of the Russian system. The individual he never condemns. It is society in the broadest sense of the term that he indicts . . . So flawless is Chekhov's exposition that though a moralist he never betrays his purpose. He believed that if only the facts of life are placed in proper relation and sequence the conclusion will be inevitable.
>
> (Christian Brinton, *The Critic*, October 1904)

3 *THE SEAGULL*

The play

Little material survives relating to the composition of *The Seagull*. While writing the play, Chekhov gave a brief description: "I'm flagrantly disregarding the basic tenets of the stage. It is a comedy with three female parts, six male, four acts, a landscape (view of a lake), lots of talk on literature, little action and tons of love" (Letter to Alexei Suvorin, 21 October 1895). Nemirovich-Danchenko, who claims to have advised Chekhov on "the architectonics of the piece, its stage form", also offers one detail about its development:

> In the version which I criticized the first act ended in a great surprise: in the scene between Masha and Dr Dorn it was suddenly revealed that she was his daughter. Not a word was again said in the play concerning this circumstance. I said that one of two things must be done: either this idea must be developed, or it must be wholly rejected, all the more so if the first act was to end with this scene. According to the very nature of the theatre, the end of the first act should turn sharply in the direction in which the drama is to develop.
>
> Chekhov said: 'But the public likes seeing a loaded gun placed before it at the end of an act!'
>
> 'Quite true,' I said, 'but it is necessary for it to go off afterwards, and not be merely removed in the intermission!' It seems to me that Chekhov more than once repeated this rejoinder. He agreed with me. The end was changed.
>
> (*My Life in the Russian Theatre*, 1934)

The Seagull marks the breakthrough to Chekhov's mature naturalistic style, and was initially greeted with incomprehension even by Stanislavsky, who records: "Only a few people at that time understood Chekhov's play, although now it seems so simple to most of us. It seemed that it was not scenic, that it was monotonous and boresome . . . I, like the others, had found *The Seagull* strange and monotonous after its first reading" (*My Life in Art*, 1926). The standard view of the conventionally trained theatrical establishment is well represented by the report of the Theatrical Literary Committee of the Alexandrinsky Theatre where the play was first performed. (All plays performed at imperial theatres had to be vetted, and this government-appointed committee comprised a playwright – A.A. Potemkin – a drama critic, and a literary historian.)

5.3.1 First Responses to *The Seagull*

Theatrical Literary Committee Report minutes, 14 September 1896

This comedy, written, needless to say, in a good literary style, as is to be expected from such a writer as Chekhov, and including a few characters delineated with fine humour (for example, the teacher Medvyédenko, the landowner Sorin, and the estate manager Shamráyev), and a few scenes of real dramatic quality, suffers none the less from a number of serious defects. To begin with, the "symbolism", or rather "Ibsenism" (in this case Ibsen's influence seems to be particularly in evidence, if we keep in mind the Norwegian dramatist's *Wild Duck*), which runs like a red thread through the whole of the play, creates a painful impression, all the more so since there is no real need for it (except, perhaps, to show that Konstantin, being a literary decadent, was partial to symbolism); and, indeed, if the "seagull" theme were altogether eliminated, the comedy would not have suffered in the least, nor would its plot have been affected in any way, while keeping the "seagull" theme, the play certainly loses a great deal of its appeal. Furthermore, it is impossible not to animadvert upon the lack of clarity in the characterisation of certain of the *dramatis personae* (for instance, Konstantín Treplyov, who is sometimes represented as a comic character and sometimes as a character who partly arouses, or at any rate is meant by the author to arouse, a serious and sympathetic attitude), the insufficient characterisation of some (for instance, Arkádina and Trigórin), and the staleness of others (for instance, Dr. Dorn), and so on; the same applies to the detailed characterisations of certain persons in the play which are entirely unnecessary, and, indeed, are likely to produce quite a different effect from what the author had intended, as, for instance, Masha's taking snuff and her drinking habits. A serious defect of the play is its faulty dramatic technique as a whole, and the crudities of certain details, unimportant though they be. In this connexion, a certain negligence and haste in workmanship is to be observed: some of the scenes seem to have been thrown off by accident, without being really germane to the plot or having any dramatic significance for its subsequent development.

At the same time – corresponding to the Theatrical Literary Committee's appreciation of "a few scenes of real dramatic quality" – *The Seagull* retains some standard dramatic elements. It is clearly a transitional work. Like his first full-length play *Ivanov*, it concludes with a conventionally climactic suicide – in contrast to Chekhov's later plays where dramatic events are successively minimized. Uncle Vanya fires a pistol, but misses; Tusenbach's death occurs off stage in *The Three Sisters* – and these events neither change the characters' situation, nor are given dramatic emphasis by concluding the action. A further conventional element in *The Seagull* is the inclusion of a *raissoneur* from the French tradition: Dr Dorn, who (like Dr Remonin in *L'Étranger*) is in some ways a surrogate for the author, acts as an objective commentator. But *The Seagull* marks a distinct advance on his earlier full-length plays in the obliqueness of the dialogue – where underlying meanings are communicated through the relationship between various speeches, or the gap between what is said and the speaker's situation or the reaction of other characters – as well as in the absence of the political or ecological polemics, that form the spine of *Ivanov* and *The Wood Demon*.

The Seagull also signals its status as a new stylistic beginning, in being a statement about the nature of art, and the artistic personality, as well as the role of theatre in society. It contrasts two generations of artists, one creative (the playwright Treplev versus the older novelist Trigorin) the other interpretive (two actresses – the young ingenue Nina versus the star Arkadina), with the older pair representing success through fulfilling conventional expectations, and the younger holding to originality and innovation but failing to gain recognition. The play also explicitly presents two antithetical contemporary artistic positions, both of which are rejected in favor of a third (unstated) alternative that it embodies. The book Arkadina reads from and dismisses as "uninteresting and wrong" at the beginning of Act II is *Sur l'eau*, in which Guy de Maupassant comments on the writer's art in passages almost paraphrased by Trigorin in his following speeches about artistic vision. The play that Treplev stages in Act I, which is attacked by Arkadina as "decadent" and ridiculed by all the on-stage observers, is an exaggeratedly symbolist drama, corresponding all too closely with what W.B. Yeats was to define as the symbolist ideal: an "art of the flood" where

one distinguishes devices to exclude or lessen character, to diminish the power of that daily mood . . . If the real world is not altogether rejected, it is but touched here and there, and into the places we have left empty we summon rhythm, balance, pattern, images that remind us of vast passions, the vagueness of past times, all the chimeras that haunt the edge of trance . . . And when we love, if it be in the excitement of youth, do we not also, that the flood may find no stone to convulse, no wall to narrow it, exclude character or the signs of it by choosing that beauty which seems unearthly because the individual woman is lost amid the labyrinth of its lines as though life were trembling into stillness and silence, or at last folding itself away?

(*The Cutting of an Agate*, 1910)

The Seagull: chronology of major early performances

October 1896 St. Petersburg	Aleksandrinsky Theater (benefit performance for Y.I. Levkeyeva)	Konstantin Treployov: Roman Apollonsky Nina Zaretchny: Vera Komissarzhevskaya
December 1898 Moscow	Moscow Art Theatre (the company's first season) Director: Konstantin Stanislavsky	Konstantin Treployov: Vsevolod Meyerhold Irina Arkadina: Olga Knipper Boris Trigorin: Konstantin Stanislavsky Nina Zaretchny: M.L. Roksanova

March 1912 London	Adelphi Society Little Theatre	Nina Zaretchny: Gertrude Kingston Boris Trigorin: Maurice Elvey Irina Arkadina: Lydia Yavorska (Princess Bariatinsky)
May 1916 New York	Washington Square Players Bandbox Theater Translator: Marian Fell	Masha: Florence Enright Konstantin Treployov: Roland Young Nina Zaretchny: Mary Morris Irina Arkadina: Helen Westley Boris Trigorin: Ralph Roeder
April 1929 New York	A Co-operative Company Comedy Theater Director: Leo Bulgakov	Masha: Dorothy Yockel Konstantin Treployov: Lewis Leverett Nina Zaretchny: Barbara Bulgakova Irina Arkadina: Dorothy Sands Boris Trigorin: Walter Abel
September 1929 New York	Civic Repertory Theater Translator: Constance Garnett Settings and Costumes: Aline Berstein	Masha: Eva Le Gallienne Konstantin Treployov: Robert Ross Nina Zaretchny: Josephine Hutchinson Boris Trigorin: Jacob Ben- Ami Irina Arkadina: Merle Maddern
March 1938 New York	The Theater Guild Shubert Theatre Director: Robert Milton Translator: Stark Young Settings and Costumes: Robert Edmond Jones	Masha: Margaret Webster Konstantin Treployov: Richard Whorf Nina Zaretchny: Uta Hagen Boris Trigorin: Alfred Lunt

Performance and reception

It was this play that came to define the essence of Stanislavsky's Moscow Art Theatre (initially named the Popular Art Theatre) which placed the emblem of a seagull on its stage-curtain. Although in fact Stanislavsky's newly founded theatre had already mounted several earlier productions in 1898, the production of *The Seagull* was taken to mark its real beginning as the standard bearer for a new style of drama. Consequently a proprietorial myth became established, which has distorted the stage-history of the play.

The generally accepted history of the first performance of *The Seagull* in St. Petersburg in 1896 is only partly correct. The standard version – promoted by Nemirovich-Danchenko in *My Life in the Russian Theatre*, and by Stanislavsky in *My*

Life in Art – classes the opening night of *The Seagull* with the other famous fiascos that greeted masterpieces such as Bizet's *Carmen* or Stravinsky's *The Rite of Spring*. Chekhov, distraught, became ill and determined to quit the theatre, declaring "The actors played abominably, stupidly. The moral: one should not write plays" (Letter to Michael Chekhov, 18 October 1896) – and two years later the Moscow Art Theatre rescued the play from obscurity over Chekhov's unwilling protests. The first production had been a blow to his already precarious health, and a second failure would have killed him.

The audience at the first Alexandrinsky Theater performance – packed with admirers of the popular comic actress Yelizaveta Leveyeva, since the opening night had been billed as a benefit performance for her – would have been expecting something along the lines of Chekhov's popular one-act farces, and certainly expressed their disapproval. The reviews were indeed savage, deeply dismaying Chekhov, and the management took the play off after only five performances. However, the second night (21 October, four days later and after some minor changes in the *mise en scène*) was a triumph as Vera Komissarzhevskaya, who played Nina, wrote immediately after leaving the theatre: "The play is a complete, unanimous success, just as it ought to be, just as it had to be" (Letter to Chekhov, 21 October 1896). This was confirmed by the third performance, described by the writer Bibilin as "a huge success: the house was sold out and there were long curtain calls for the actors" (Letter to Chekhov, 25 October 1896); and another highly successful production followed at Kiev in November 1896. In addition, the play was staged by a number of provincial companies in 1897, and as Nemirovich-Danchenko himself noted, "The enthusiastic reviews in Kharhov and Odessa newspapers are quite unprecedented" (Letter to Chekhov, 12 May 1898). It had also been translated into Czech, and had its first foreign performance in Prague in 1898: all before the Moscow Art Theatre production.

5.3.2 Anatoly Koni/Anton Chekhov, Letters

Translated by Michael Heim

7 November 1896

My letter may surprise you, but even though I'm drowning in work, I cannot resist writing you about your *Seagull*, which I finally found time to see. I heard (from Savina) that the public's attitude to the play upset you greatly. Let one member of the audience – uninitiated as I may be in the secrets of literature and dramatic art but acquainted with life as a result of my legal practice – tell you that he thanks you for the deep pleasure your play afforded him. *The Seagull* is a work whose conception, freshness of ideas and thoughtful observations of life situations raise it out of the ordinary. It is life itself on stage with all its tragic alliances, eloquent thoughtlessness and silent sufferings – the sort of everyday life that is accessible to everyone and understood in its cruel internal irony by almost no one, the sort of life that is so accessible and close to us that at times you forget you're in a theater and you feel capable of participating in the conversation taking place in front of you. And how good the ending is! How true to life it is that not she, the seagull, commits suicide (which a run-of-the-mill playwright, out for his audience's tears, would be sure to have done), but the young man who lives in an abstract future and "has no idea" of the why and wherefore of what goes on around him. I also very much like the device of cutting off the play abruptly, leaving the spectator to sketch in the dreary, listless, indefinite future for himself. That's the way epic works end or rather turn out. I won't speak of the production, in which Komissarzhevskaya is marvelous. But Sazonov and Pisarev, or so it seems to me, didn't understand their roles and don't play the characters you meant to portray.

Perhaps you are shrugging your shoulders in amazement. Of what concern is my opinion to you, and why am I writing all this? Here is why. I love you for the moments of stirring emotion your works have given and continue to give me, and I want to send you a random word of sympathy from a distance, a word which as far as I know may be quite unnecessary.

11 November 1896

You can't imagine how happy your letter made me. I saw only the first two acts of my play from out front. After that I went backstage, feeling all the while that *The Seagull* was failing. After the performance, that night and the following day, people kept assuring me that my characters were all idiots and that my play was dramatically unsound, ill-considered, incomprehensible, even nonsensical, and so on and so forth. You can see the situation I was in. It was a failure I couldn't have imagined in my worst dreams. I was embarrassed and chagrined, and left Petersburg filled with all sorts of doubts. I thought that if I had written and staged a play so obviously abounding in monstrous shortcomings, then I had lost all sensitivity and that consequently my mechanism had run down once and for all. When I got home, I had word from Petersburg that the second and third performances had been successful. I received several letters, both signed and anonymous, that praised the play and berated the critics. Reading the letters gave me pleasure, but I was still embarrassed and chagrined, and it unwittingly came to me that if kind people found it necessary to console me, then I was certainly in a bad way. But your letter had a very decisive effect on me. I've known you for a long time, I respect you highly, and I believe you more than all the critics put together. You felt as much while you wrote your letter, which is why it is so beautiful and convincing. I am reassured now and can think about the play and the production without revulsion.

Komissarzhevskaya is a marvelous actress. At one of the rehearsals many people wept as they watched her, and they said she is the best actress in all Russia today. Yet on opening night even she succumbed to the general mood of hostility to my *Seagull* and seemed to grow frightened and was barely audible. Our journalists are undeservedly cold to her and I feel sorry for her.

Let me thank you for the letter from the bottom of my heart. Believe me, the feelings that prompted you to write it are more valuable to me than I can express in words, and I will never, never forget, no matter what may happen, the concern you call "unnecessary" at the end of the letter.

*

Although the majority of rehearsals in 1898 were conducted by Nemirovich-Danchenko, the co-producer of the new Moscow Art Theatre, every detail of the staging had been prepared by Stanislavsky in advance. Moves and blocking, gestures and tone of voice, together with sound effects were meticulously noted and illustrated by sketched stage plans on blank pages interleaved with the script. In particular Chekhov's brief stage directions were expanded into complete pictures or extended sequences of action. Thus, the opening stage direction of the play reads:

> A section of the park on Sorin's estate. A wide path leading upstage into the depths of the park, to the lake, is intersected by a stage, hurriedly thrown together for a domestic production, which totally obscures the lake. Bushes to the right and the left of the stage. Some chairs, a little table. The sun has just set. On the stage, behind the curtain, Yakov and the other workmen; a cough, a hammer blow; Masha and Medvedenko enter from the left, returning from a walk.

Alongside this strictly practical description of the setting, Stanislavky evokes a drawn out mood through typical sounds and lighting effects:

> The play opens in darkness, an August evening. The dull glow of a lantern, distant, drunken singing, the distant barking of a dog, croaking frogs, a landrail calls, the infrequent peal of a distant church bell – this helps the audience feel the melancholy monotony of the characters' lives. Harvest lightning, barely audible thunder far away. A ten second pause after curtain-up. After the pause, Yakov hammers in a nail (into the stage); having done so, he moves about there, touching the curtain and humming.
>
> (Translated by Elena Polyakova in *Stanislavsky*, 1982)

The precision of Stanislavsky's visualization of the action in performance is well indicated by the close of the scene between Nina and Konstantin in Act IV. Where Chekhov's stage directions state simply that Nina "*Embraces* KONSTANTIN *impulsively and runs out through the french window . . . During the next two minutes* KONSTANTIN *tears up all his manuscripts and throws them under the desk; then he unlocks the door on the right and goes out*", Stanislavsky creates an extremely detailed narrative sequence that focuses on highly emotional effects.

Figure 5.1 The Seagull, Moscow Art Theatre: 1898 (directed by Stanislavsky). Nina's performance in Act I

Figure 5.2 The dining room of Act III

Figure 5.3 The reversed view of Act IV: study with dining room beyond

The whole of Nina's speech is made to the accompaniment of the howling wind.

Once again she leans against the jamb of the door and bursts out crying. A pause of ten seconds, during which can be heard the distant tolling of a church bell (as in Act I during the performance of Konstantin's play – a rather stale stage effect!). She gives him a quick hug and runs off. One half of the door slams (a pane breaks, so powerfully did the wind slam it), then the other half of the french window shuts; the footsteps on the terrace die away. Noise of the wind, tolling of church-bell, knocking of night-watchman, a louder burst of laughter in the dining-room. For fifteen seconds Konstantin stands without moving, then he lets fall the glass from his hand (this, too, is a rather cheap stage effect!). Konstantin crosses slowly over to the writing desk. Stops. Goes to where his manuscript lies, picks it up, holds it for a moment in his hand, then tears it up. Sits down, picks something up and tries to read it, but tears it up after reading the first line. Falls into a reverie again, rubs his forehead disconsolately, looks around as though searching for something, gazes for a moment at the heap of manuscripts on his desk, then starts tearing them up with slow deliberation. Gathers up all the scraps of paper and crosses over to the stove with them (noise of opening the stage door). Throws the scraps of paper into the stove, leans against it with his hand, looking for some time at the flames devouring his works. Then he turns round, something occurs to him, he rubs his forehead, then crosses over to his desk quickly and opens a drawer. He takes out a bundle of letters and throws it into the fire. Walks away from the stove, ponders for a second, looks around the room once more – and walks out thoughtfully, unhurriedly.

Sound of chairs being pushed back and of loud, merry conversation in the dining-room. The dining-room door begins to give. They knock at the door, shouting, 'Konstantin!' A pause. There is no reply.

(Translated by Elena Polyakova in *Stanislavsky*, 1982)

Stanislavsky later disowned this method of pre-set directing as ignoring "the inner emotions of the actor", but it has the advantage of preserving a fairly accurate picture of how the play appeared on the Moscow Art Theatre stage. Sending his *mise en scène* for the fourth act to Moscow, Stanislavsky commented "I approached it at random, so do anything you like with the planning" – however the reply from Nemirovich-Danchenko indicates that Stanislavsky's directions were precisely followed, although some of the more obtrusive naturalistic detail might have been omitted: "Your *mise en scène* turned out perfectly. Chekhov is in raptures about it . . . [but] there are places that could easily create an awkward impression . . . for example the 'frogs croaking' all the way through Treplev's play . . . At times one should not distract the audience's attention, divert them by prosaic details" (Letters, 11 and 12 September 1898). Excerpts of Stanislavsky's production notes have been selected from Act III to illustrate the way ordinary activities established character relationships and exposed the subtext in the dialogue.

V.A. Simov, the Moscow Art Theatre set-designer, created scenery based on the mood of the play. His memoirs show that he focussed on "the contrast between the happy comfort of the first half of the play and the depressing emptiness, hollowness and discord in the lives of the people in the play in the last two acts" – so that in Act IV "[t]he room had to bear the stamp of impermanency. Outside it is cold, damp, windy; but there is no warmth in the room either. I began with the furniture, arranging it in every possible way so as to obtain the effect of mental disequilibrium" (Translated by David Magarshak in S.D. Balukhaty, *The Seagull Produced by Stanislavsky*, 1952). He also – as Stanislavsky points out – used the placing of a bench as a statement of naturalistic principles.

However, according to Meyerhold (who acted Treplev), when Chekhov attended rehearsals he disapproved of all of the realistic sound effects:

'Realistic!' – repeated Chekhov with a laugh . . . 'The stage is art. There's a genre painting by Kramskoy in which the faces are portrayed superbly. What would happen if you cut the nose out of one of the paintings and substituted a real one? The nose would be "realistic" but the picture would be ruined.'
. . . the stage demands a degree of artifice. . . You have no fourth wall. Besides the stage is art, the stage reflects the quintessence of life, and there is no need to introduce anything superfluous on to it.
(Diary entry, 11 September 1898, translated by Ted Braun, *Meyerhold on Theatre*, 1960)

However, Chekhov was unable to influence Stanislavsky's interpretation at this late stage, and had no opportunity to see *The Seagull* in performance. The production had closed before Chekhov, who was ill and had seen only two early rehearsals, was able to get to Moscow. So a special performance was mounted for him on a different stage, the Nikitsky Theatre, in May 1899.

The interpretation of the play recorded in Stanislavsky's memoirs ignores Chekhov's ironies – and a letter from Maria Chekhova commented: "The Seagull herself acted repulsively, sobbing fit to burst all the time and Trigorin (the literary man) walked about the stage and talked like a paralytic; he has 'no will of his own' and the actor interpreted that in a way that is sickening to behold" (cited in Elena Polyakova, *Stanislavsky*, 1982). As a result, the Moscow Art Theatre performance overstated the creative abilities of the young artists, intensifying the tragic aspect, while Stanislavsky himself was misled into portraying Trigorin as a dashingly successful literary figure.

5.3.3 Konstantin Stanislavsky, production notes for *The Seagull* – Excerpts from Act III

Translated by David Magarshak

SORIN *laughs.*

MISS ARKADINA:[40]   I have no money![41]

SORIN (*whistling*):[42]   I see.[43] Forgive me, my dear. Don't be angry with me. I – I believe you . . .[44] You're such a warmhearted generous woman.

MISS ARKADINA (*crying*):[45]   I have no money![46]

SORIN: Of course if I had any money, I'd give him some myself, but I haven't got anything – not a penny! (*Laughs.*) My agent grabs all my pension[47] and spends it on the estate. He rears cattle, keeps bees, and all my money just goes down the drain. The damned bees die, the damned cows die, and when I ask for a carriage, the horses are wanted for something else . . .

MISS ARKADINA:[48]   Of course I have some money, but you must realise that I'm an actress. Why, my dresses alone are enough to ruin me.

SORIN:[49]   You're very kind, my dear. I – I respect you . . . Indeed, I do.[50] Oh dear, I – I'm afraid – I – I'm not feeling well again – (*Swaying*) my head's going round and round – (*holding on to the table*) afraid I – I'm going to – faint – and – so on.

MISS ARKADINA (*frightened*):[51]   Peter! My dear! (*Trying to support him.*) Peter, darling! (*Shouts.*) Help! Help!

Enter KONSTANTIN *with a dark bandage on his head, followed by* MEDVYEDENKO.

40. Miss Arkádina starts eating vigorously. Sorin gives a loud laugh and gets up.

41. Miss Arkádina says *crossly*[1] and determinedly: 'I haven't any money!'

42. Sorin shakes his head and whistles comically.

43. Sorin waves a hand and starts pacing the room.

44. Sorin speaks a little ironically, as he walks round the table.

45. Miss Arkádina cannot stand it any longer, she throws down her knife (a clatter of dishes on the table) and, like the thoroughly spoilt woman she is, bursts into tears.

46. Miss Arkádina buries her face in a napkin and remains sitting motionless.

47. Walking round the table, Sorin stops at the place where he had been sitting, finishes his glass of wine, then starts walking again.

48. Miss Arkádina has calmed down, but she is still sniffling; to stop it, she pours herself out a glass of water and drinks.

49. As he walks past her, Sorin stops and kisses her on the head.

50. Sorin walks round the table a second time, but on reaching the chair in the foreground of the stage, he clutches at his head, puts a hand over his eyes (he feels dizzy), drops his walking stick and, groping for a chair, gets hold of it – the mimicry of his face changes – his head bends lower and lower, and if Miss Arkádina had not come to his aid, he would have fallen off the chair head foremost and collapsed in a heap on the floor.

51. Miss Arkádina jumps up from her chair and kneels in front of him. She lifts his head with difficulty and puts it on the table; she then runs to pour some water in a glass. At the same time a noise is heard in the front hall. That is Konstantín and Medvyédenko; they have entered, taken off their hats in the hall and are wiping their feet. Miss Arkádina shouts and waves to them. Konstantín runs in, followed by Medvyédenko. Konstantín takes the glass of water from Miss Arkádina and, filling his mouth with water, squirts it over Sorin. Sorin starts. Medvyédenko supports him (lifts Sorin's head) and then feels his pulse. Miss Arkádina picks up Sorin's walking stick.[2]

---

[1] Underlined in ink. (S.B.).

[2] Crossed out: (Medvyédenko and Konstantín come in and wipe their feet on the floor. Miss Arkádina shouts to them. She has already run up to Sorin, who again collapses on top of her. She can hardly manage to hold him up.)

MISS ARKADINA: He's going to faint![52]

SORIN: Oh, it's nothing – nothing. (*Smiles and has a drink of water.*) It's passed off – and – so on.

KONSTANTIN (*to his mother*):[53]   Don't be alarmed, mother. It's nothing serious. Uncle often has these attacks now. (*To his uncle.*) You ought to go and lie down for a bit, uncle.

SORIN: Yes, for a bit . . .[54] But I'm going to town all the same . . . I'll lie down for a bit, and then I'll go . . . I mean, it's pretty obvious, isn't it . . . (*Walks to the door, leaning on his cane.*)[55]

MEDVYEDENKO (*taking his arm*):[56]   Do you know the riddle, sir? In the morning on all fours, in the afternoon on two, in the evening on three . . .

SORIN (*laughs*):[57]   That's right. And at night on his back. Thank you, I can manage myself now . . .

MEDVYEDENKO: Good Lord, sir, this is no time to stand on ceremony, is it?

SORIN *and* MEDVYEDENKO *go out.*

MISS ARKADINA:[58]   Oh, he gave me such a fright!

KONSTANTIN:[59]   It isn't good for him to live in the country. He frets too much.[60] I wish you'd feel munificent for once, mother, and lend him fifteen hundred or two thousand roubles. Then he could manage a whole year in town.

MISS ARKADINA:[61]   I have no money. I'm an actress, not a banker.[62]

A pause.

KONSTANTIN: Please change the bandage for me, mother. You do it so beautifully.

52. *Note to Sorin's fainting fit:* Sorin's face looks as though he were dead. (This scene should be played as realistically as possible, so as to deceive the audience. It should be played in a way to convince the audience that Sorin was dying. That would greatly heighten the suspense of the audience and its interest in what is taking place on the stage.)

53. Kneeling in front of Sorin, Konstantín fans him with a handkerchief, then helps him to wipe his wet face.

54. A pause – Konstantín and Medvyédenko help Sorin to his feet. When Sorin stands up and is given his walking stick, he declares that he will go up to town.

55. Sorin starts walking to the door, Medvyédenko supporting him. Konstantín remains in the same place, while Miss Arkádina accompanies Sorin to the door.

56. Medvyédenko as he walks beside Sorin.

57. Sorin bursts out laughing and, stopping, turns round to Konstantín, let us say, so as to say the amusing phrase facing the audience, for otherwise it might be lost.

58. Miss Arkádina accompanies Sorin to the door and then returns to the table: drinks water after her fright.

59. Sitting down on the chair occupied by Sorin, Konstantín sprawls on it, stretching his legs over the other chair near him. He lies on two chairs, leaning against the table with his right elbow, and with his other against the back of the chair.

60. A pause.

61. Miss Arkádina stops drinking, puts the glass of water on the table, and throws an angry glance at Konstantín.

62. Walks up and down between the cupboard and the table. A pause.

MISS ARKADINA (*takes some iodoform and a box with bandages from the medicine chest*):[63]   The doctor is late today, isn't he?

KONSTANTIN: Yes. Promised to be here at ten, and now it's twelve already.

MISS ARKADINA:[64]   Sit down, dear.[3] (*Takes the bandage off his head.*) You look as if you were wearing a turban. Yesterday a stranger in the kitchen asked what nationality you were.[65] Your wound has almost healed up. Just a little scar left. (*Kisses his head.*) You won't do anything so stupid again while I'm away, will you?

KONSTANTIN: No, mother. I did it in a moment of black despair, when I lost control of myself. It won't happen again. (*Kisses her hand.*)[66] You've got clever fingers, mother. I remember long ago when you were still acting on the Imperial stage – I was a little boy then – there was a fight in our yard, and a washerwoman who lived in our house was badly hurt. Remember? She was unconscious when they picked her up. You looked after her, gave her her medicine and bathed her children. Don't you remember?

MISS ARKADINA: I don't. (*Puts on a fresh bandage.*)

KONSTANTIN: Two ballet dancers lived in our house at the time. They used to come and have coffee with you . . .

MISS ARKADINA: Oh yes, I remember that.[67]

Crossed out by Stanislavsky. (S.B.)

156

63. Walks silently to the low sofa and gets the iodoform and some rags out of the medicine box over the sofa and a clean soup-plate from the sideboard. She then crosses over to Konstantín, moves away the plates, etc., and puts the soup-plate down on the table. Speaks of the doctor while walking from the sideboard to the table.

64. Starts undoing the bandage carefully.

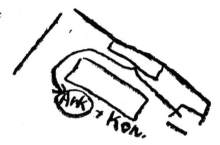

65. Takes off the bandage and examines the wound.

66. He kisses his mother's hand while she is washing his wound.

67. The whole of this scene must be acted with Miss Arkádina and Konstantín kept busy all the time, namely: Miss Arkádina fills a glass with water, pours it into the soup-plate, repeats the process, then shakes up the bottle of disinfectant, pours it into a large spoon and from the spoon into the soup-plate, mixing up the water and the disinfectant in the plate. She then takes a rag, tears it, folds it up, and soaks it in the prepared liquid. She smooths out another folded rag, puts the first rag on his head, the second on top of it, and starts bandaging the head with a fresh roll of bandage. During all this operation, Konstantín is rolling up the old bandage.

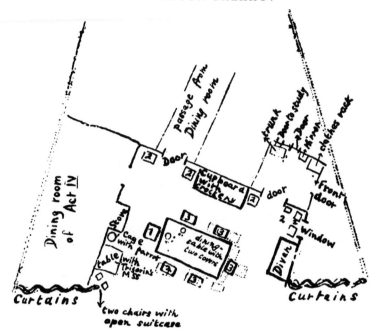

Figure 5.4 Stanislavsky's floor plan for Act III

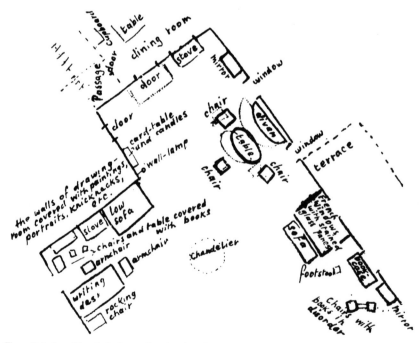

Figure 5.5 Stanislavsky's floor plan for Act IV

5.3.4 Konstantin Stanislavsky, performing *The Seagull*

Translated by J. J. Robbins

Simov understood my plans and purpose of stage direction and began to help me marvellously towards the creation of the mood. On the very fore-stage, right near the footlights, in direct opposition to all the accepted laws and customs of the theatre of that time, almost all the persons in the play sat on a long swinging bench characteristic of Russian country estates, with their backs to the public. This bench, placed in a line with some tree stumps that remained from a destroyed forest, bordered an alley set with century-old trees that stood at a measured distance from each other. In the spaces between their trunks, which seemed mysterious in the darkness of night, there showed something in the form of a proscenium that was closed from sight by a large white sheet. This was the open-air theatre of the unsuccess-ful and unacknowledged Treplev. The scenery and properties of this theatre are poor and modest. But listen to the essence of his art and you find that it is a complete grammar for the actor of today. Treplev speaks of real art in the midst of night, amidst the trees of a damp and ancient park, waiting for the rising of the moon. Meanwhile from the distance there comes the trivial racket of a fashionable and tasteless waltz that changes at times to an even more tasteless but melodious Gipsy song played by Treplev's mother, a provincial actress. The tragedy is self-evident. Can the provincial mother understand the complex longings of her talented son? It is not at all amazing that he runs away from the house to the park so often.

To the accompaniment of tasteless conversation and jokes, the domestic spectators take their places on the long bench and the tree stumps, their backs to the public, very much like sparrows on a telegraph line. The moon rises, the sheets fall, one sees the lake, its surface broken with the silver gleams of the moon. On a high eminence that resembles the base of a monument sits a grief-stricken female figure wrapped in manifold white, but with eyes that are young and shining and cannot be grief-stricken. This is Nina Zarechnaya in the costume of World Grief, the long train of which, like the tail of a snake, is stretched over grass and undergrowth. The wide cloth was a courageous gesture on the part of the artist, a gesture of deep meaning and beautiful generalized form. How talented is this Treplev with the soul of Chekhov and a true comprehension of art.

Nina Zarechnaya is the cause of the failure of Treplev's talented play. She is not an actress, although she dreams of being one so as to earn the love of the worthless Trigorin. She does not understand what she is playing. She is too young to understand the deep gloom of the soul of Treplev. She has not yet suffered enough to perceive the eternal tragedy of the world. She must first fall in love with the scoundrelly Lovelace Trigorin and give him all that is beautiful in woman, give it to him in vain, at an accidental meeting in some low inn. The young and beautiful life is deformed and killed just as meaninglessly as the beautiful white seagull was killed by Treplev because he had nothing to do. Poor Nina, before understanding the depth of what she is playing, must bear a child in secret, must suffer hunger and privation many years, dragging herself through the lower depths of all the provincial theatres, must come to know the scoundrelly attentions of merchants to a young actress, must come to know her own giftlessness, in order to be able in her last farewell meeting with Treplev in the fourth act of the play to feel at last all the eternal and tragic depth of Treplev's monologue, and perhaps for the last and only time say it like a true actress and force Treplev and the spectators in the theatre to shed holy tears called forth by the power of art.

[. . .]

Some of the actors were praised by Chekhov, others received their full meed of blame.

[. . .]

At the special performance he seemed to be trying to avoid me. I waited for him in my dressing-room, but he did not come. That was a bad sign. I went to him myself.

'Scold me, Anton Pavlovich,' I begged him.

'Wonderful! Listen, it was wonderful! Only you need torn shoes and checked trousers.'

He would tell me no more. What did it mean? Did he wish not to express his opinion? Was it a jest to get rid of me? Was he laughing at me? Trigorin in *The Seagull* was a young writer, a favourite of the women – and suddenly he was to wear torn shoes and checked trousers! I played the part in the most elegant of costumes – white trousers, white vest, white hat, slippers, and a handsome make-up.

A year or more passed. Again I played the part of Trigorin in *The Seagull* – and during one of the performances I suddenly understood what Chekhov had meant.

Of course, the shoes must be torn and the trousers checked, and Trigorin must not be handsome. In this lies the salt of the part: for young, inexperienced girls it is important that a man should be a writer and print touching and sentimental romances, and the Nina Zarechnayas, one after the other, will throw themselves on his neck, without noticing that he is not talented, that he is not handsome, that he wears checked trousers and torn shoes. Only afterwards, when the love affair with such 'seagulls' is over, do they begin to understand that it was girlish imagination which created the great genius in their heads, instead of a simple mediocrity. Again, the depth and the richness of Chekhov's laconic remarks struck me. It was very typical and characteristic of him.

The critic, N.E. Efros, who was present at that first performance and helped to create the legend of *The Seagull* and the Moscow Art Theatre, describes the "great uneasiness" of the audience in the opening act at what Gorky had called the "heretical" quality of the play: "the life that was speaking from the stage was a different life, as though life had refined its outer vestures and through them had shown its soul". And by the close of the play "All were shaken. There were no longer sceptics and jokers . . . The Rubicon was crossed. The Art Theatre had irrevocably become Tchekhov's Theatre" (*Theatrical Reminiscences of Tchekhov*, 1927). Nemirovich-Danchenko's letter to Chekhov provides the director's view of the occasion.

The reviews of the Moscow Art Theatre production clearly indicate the amount of attention attracted by the play, with *Novosti* praising the performance as "powerful and irresistible, something that moved the spectator deeply and startled him, upsetting all his preconceived . . . views on art" (No. 9, 1899), and *Novoye Vrema* hailing it as "an important stimulus for the future. The theatre is entering on a new phase" (18 January 1899). There was general criticism of the most extreme naturalistic elements in the staging, both the lighting of Acts I and IV – "dim and ominous, it made it difficult to see and hear" – and particularly the "long bench . . . placed rather awkwardly across the stage, so that the actors sat with their backs to the audience" (*The Courier*, 19 December 1898 and *Stage News*, 13 January 1899). However the analysis of the play itself was surprisingly sensitive and open to the new dramatic qualities introduced in *The Seagull*, with several reviewers commenting on the "delicate mood" of "that particular atmosphere which alone could serve as a true background for the melody of despair" (*Russian News*, 20 December 1898; *Russian Thought*, January 1899; *Theatre and Art*, 10 January 1899).

By contrast, when it finally reached England in 1912, most of the reviewers and the public were clearly confused by the play. In particular Chekhov's type of objectivity conflicted with the moral expectations established for naturalistic drama by Ibsen and particularly Shaw. As a generally sympathetic review of the published text of *The Seagull* (translated by George Calderon) remarked:

> Futility is the characteristic which all his people share . . . They have no force to help life or to hinder it. Implicitly they deny the greatest force in the many of which what we call Life is composed – the spirit and the will of man . . .
>
> Russian melancholy we know; this futility may be another side to it . . . But it is not a feeling which we share in Western Europe, and the difference of temperament may well keep Tchekhov from our affection. Crude, barbaric, and false as our English drama often is, it is all reared on the assumption that men and women either have the chief say in what shall happen to them, or at least are great enough to fight their fate to the end. It exalts passion, ambition, and the will. And it is quite possible that impatience with the flabby people whom Tchekhov shows us yearning vaguely, talking glibly, suffering helplessly, may blind the public in general to the beauty of his work.
>
> (*The Times Literary Supplement*, 1 February 1912)

As the reviews also show, the style of English actors at the time was also unsuitable for the type of ensemble work required by Chekhov. The failure of the play in England, even with a former member of the Moscow Art Theatre troupe in the cast, helps to underline Stanislavsky's achievement.

5.3.5 Vladimir Nemirovitch-Danchenko's report to Chekhov on the first performance

Translated by John Cournos

Dear Anton Pavlovitch!

From my telegrams you already know of the general success of 'The Sea Gull'. In order to paint for you a picture of the first performance, I must tell you that after the third act there reigned behind the wings a kind of drunken atmosphere. As some one has aptly said, it was just as on Easter Day. They all kissed one another, flung themselves on one another's neck; all were excited with the mood of the supreme triumph of truth and honest labour. Just consider the reasons for such joy: the actors are in love with the play, with every rehearsal they discovered in it more and more new pearls of art. At the same time they trembled because the public was so unliterary, so poorly developed, spoiled by cheap stage effects, and unready for a higher artistic simplicity, and would therefore be unable to appreciate the beauty of 'The Sea Gull'. We gave up our whole soul to the play, and we risked everything on this one card. We *régisseurs*, i.e. Alekseiev and I, bent all our efforts and capabilities so that the astonishing moods of the play might be intensified. We had three dress rehearsals, we examined every corner of the stage, we tested every electric-light bulb. For two weeks I lived in the theatre with the decorations, the properties; I made trips to the antique shops, seeking out objects which would give the necessary touches of colour. But why dwell on this? I am speaking of a theatre in which not a single nail has been overlooked.

[. . .]

We played . . . in this order: Knipper is an astonishing, an ideal Arkadina. To such a degree has she merged with the rôle that you cannot tear away from her either her elegance as an actress, or her bewitching triviality, *stinginess*, jealousy, etc. Both scenes in the third act – with Treplev and Trigorin, the first in particular – had a tremendous success. And the departure which concluded the act was an unusual piece of staging, without superfluous people. After Knipper comes Alexeyeva – Masha. A marvellous image! Very characteristic and remarkably touching. She was a great success. Then Luzhsky – Sorin. He played like a major artist. Then Meyerhold. He was tender, touching and definitely a decadent. Then Alekseiev. He used a successfully mild, will-less tone. He spoke the monologues of the second act

162

excellently, marvellously. He was a bit sugary in the third act. Roxanova was not so good; Alekseiev disconcerted her, forcing her to play the rôle of a little fool. I was angry and demanded a return to the previous lyrical tone. The poor woman got all mixed up. Vishnevsky has not yet quite merged with his rôle of the tender-hearted, shrewd, observing and all-experiencing Dorn, who was however very well made up in the style of Alexey Tolstoi and superbly ended the play. The remainder of the cast maintained a harmonious ensemble. The general tone was restrained and highly literary.

The public listened to the play with such absorbed attention as I have rarely witnessed. Moscow is in an uproar over it. In the Small Theatre they are ready to tear us to pieces.

The play is sure of a run. You'd have enjoyed the first act – and, in my opinion, the fourth, in particular.

I am infinitely happy.

I embrace you.

Yours,

VLADIMIR NEMIROVITCH-DANTCHENKO.

What about letting us have 'Uncle Vanya'?

5.3.6 Reception in England

John Palmer, *Saturday Review*, 13 April 1912

Mr. William Archer has dragooned the intellectually accessible public and the junior critics of his time into thinking and writing in a sane and reasonable manner about Ibsen, while Mr. Shaw, who by precept and example has founded a school of dramatic criticism for the intelligent appreciation of his work, has drilled the London playgoer into turning up at his plays for hundreds of nights in succession, and has hypnotised the whole Press into believing that he is an inexhaustible fountain of good copy. [But] . . . If we escape the stigma (of having stoned our own particular prophet of the day), it will be more by good luck than good management. [. . .] That we should look as foolish as every other generation has looked in similar circumstances there is no doubt whatever; for within the last twelve months the most exclusive, superior and advanced audience in London has succeeded, as thousands of audiences similarly qualified have succeeded before it, in looking foolish on a scale which can only be described as small for the reason that its mistake will never be set right so publicly and universally as the mistake that their predecessors made about Ibsen. The mistake of the Stage Society about Chekhov will never be fully discovered in this country; for it is in the interest of no particular group or clique to drill the public into realising it; and Chekhov, not being a social missionary, will never become a watchword with reformers and social prophets.

Chekhov's career in London is disgraceful for all concerned. As one of the most celebrated European dramatists he could not be altogether ignored by the various societies whose mission it is to discover for their members the acknowledged masterpieces of dramatic literature. Nevertheless, Chekhov's first appearance was not in London, but in Glasgow, where Mr. George Calderon was invited to produce 'The Seagull' at Mr. Waring's repertory theatre. I shall always regret that I did not see Mr. Calderon's production; for I believe it was really adequate.

A fortnight ago Mr. Maurice Elvey produced Chekhov's 'The Seagull' at the Little Theatre for the Adelphi Play Society. Players, audience and critics had in the meantime been instructed how to pretend a wisdom if they had it not (which is the true secret of criticism) by Mr. George Calderon's preface to an admirable translation. One might reasonably have expected at the Little Theatre an excellent performance (Chekhov's original heroine was in the cast), an appreciative audience, and critics who were not obviously preparing to denounce a third-rate farcical melodrama. As it turned out, things were a little better in the auditorium; but the performance was worse. [. . .]

The bad character of the Adelphi Society's production was directly measured by the authority and merit of the principal players. I understand that Mr. Maurice Elvey, the Society's producer, is a young man. He would therefore be entirely unable to compel Miss Gertrude Kingston or the Princess Bariatinsky to behave as she should. Anyhow, the play did not seem to have been produced at all. The result will be measured by anyone who has read – with understanding – a line of Chekhov's comedy. . . . Not only does Chekhov's play depend absolutely on the cumulative effect of a method which concerns itself rather with groups than with the individuals composing them; but he has in several passages of the play successfully portrayed group emotions. It is a commonplace of psychology that a group or crowd of people will behave collectively in a manner different from that in which any one of its members would behave. This commonplace, refined at times in the most subtle fashion, Chekhov has successfully illustrated in his comedies. As soon as we realise that the players, all and several, are hero of the piece the play falls naturally into perfect form. I dealt at length, in noticing the Stage Society's production of 'The Cherry Orchard', with Chekhov's technical skill in building up an impression of complete unity of form and idea by means of a style apparently discursive and in defiance of all the commonplaces of structure. Order comes into a superficial chaos as soon as we shift our view from the fortunes of this or that particular person of the play to the fortunes of the group. In the Adelphi Society's production neither Miss Kingston nor the Princess Bariatinsky seemed to realise that her individual part was important only in correlation with the rest. It was not possible to be angry with Miss Kingston, for the whole tradition of British acting, which she so admirably adorns, was against her in this particular venture. But there was no sort of excuse for the Princess Bariatinsky.

I hope I have made it clear how exactly these players offended. They had read their parts with care; they played with energy and skill; individually they were not seriously wrong for more than half the time; and they heavily impressed the audience. In spite of all this – or, rather, because of it – they succeeded in completely upsetting the balance and rhythm of the play. So far as Chekhov's play was concerned my sensations were exactly what they would have been if I saw the two legs of a man I respected suddenly start walking in different directions. . . .

4 *THE CHERRY ORCHARD*

The play

The Cherry Orchard brings together many of the themes from Chekhov's earlier work, but presents them in a new key. The loss of a family estate, which Chekhov himself had experienced in childhood as a result of his own father's mismanagement, had appeared in his earliest play, *Platonov*, and in various short stories during the 1880s, such as "Late Blooming Flowers" or "Other Peoples' Misfortunes". The parody of the semi-educated who have adopted misplaced Western attitudes at the expense of their own culture, embodied here in the servant Yasha, recurs in several stories, as well as (in a more serious form) in *The Three Sisters*. The confusion of values engendered by social displacement in peasants who have attained wealth, like the merchant Lopakhin, had already been explored in such stories as "Three Years". The orchard itself, and its destruction, is a variation on the theme of forests, and the importance of planting trees, that recurs in *The Wood Demon* and *Uncle Vanya*. Chekhov's mistrust of the intelligentsia, given its most memorable expression in *Uncle Vanya*, informs the portrayal of the superannuated student; and the ambiguity of Trofimov's characterization can be traced to comments in Chekhov's correspondence:

> As long as our boys and girls are still students, they're honest and good, they're Russia's future; but as soon as those students have to stand up on their own and grow up, our hope and Russia's future go up in smoke . . . I have no faith in our intelligentsia; it is hypocritical, dishonest, hysterical, ill-bred and lazy. I have no faith in it even when it suffers and complains, for its oppressors emerge from its own midst . . . I see salvation in individuals, scattered here and there, all over Russia, be they peasants or intellectuals.
>
> (Letter to Ivan Orlov, 22 February 1899)

In the same letter Chekhov had expressed hope for the future – "science is inexorably moving forward, social consciousness is on the increase, moral issues are beginning to take on a more disturbing character" – and Anya's optimistic vision has an analogue in one of Chekhov's last stories, "The Bride". There, in sharp contrast to *The Seagull*, *The Three Sisters*, and various stories where young girls are trapped in a stultifying world, the heroine manages to escape from the boredom of provincial life, the restrictions of a fixed social position, and the limitations of a traditional family structure.

As various commentators have noted, in addition several of the characters in *The Cherry Orchard* are based on stock figures in turn of the century Russian drama: the trivial and spendthrift female aristocrat, the greedy social-climbing capitalist, and the naively idealistic revolutionary student. In Ranevskaya, Lopakhin and Trofimov, Chekhov reverses these stereotypes, refusing the standard response to such characters, which confused some of the Moscow reviewers at the time of the first performance. One, for instance, expressed moral indignation at the play's "lack of a clear-cut artistic design", particularly citing Mme Ranevskaya and Trofimov as examples of a missing ethical purpose: "Ranevskaya is an aristocratic slut, of no use to anyone, who departs with impunity to join her Paris gigolo. And yet Chekhov has whitewashed her and surrounded her with a sort of sentimental halo. Similarly, that moldy 'better future' is something incomprehensible and unnatural" (Letter by Vladimir Korolenko, 2 September 1904). At the other extreme, those who took Trofimov as the stereotype of the revolutionary idealist, missing the ironic aspects of Chekhov's characterization, turned the play into a political statement. Thus the censor demanded the deletion of two passages from Trofimov's speeches in Act II – specifically the references to the Russian population living like savages, and to the cherry trees as embodiments of the peasants' suffering in the past. Similarly Karpov, in the first published overview of Chekhov's literary career (1904), and Korelenko, in a memorial article, both interpret *The Cherry Orchard* as the expression of striving for a better world and faith in the future.

There is more secondary information about Chekhov's dramatic intentions in writing *The Cherry Orchard* than for his other plays, through his daily correspondence with his wife during the period of its composition. Having retreated to Yalta for his failing health, Chekhov felt out of touch with what was happening in Moscow. And concern about Stanislavsky's response to the novel qualities in the script, plus garbled newspaper accounts of the nature of the play (spread by an overly enthusiastic critical supporter of Chekhov, N. Efros), also led to an extensive exchange of letters with Stanislavsky, Nemirovich-Danchenko and others associated with the Moscow Art Theatre. Even when writing about production details, Chekhov's letters offer insights into the concept of the play. Thus his comments on casting also summarize his views of the various characters, while the exchanges between Chekhov and Nemirovich-Danchenko help to define the emotional mood, or those with Stanislavky serve to fill in the physical context that Chekhov had envisaged while writing the dialogue. To give a sense of the developing concepts, the selection of extracts from this correspondence is given chronologically.

5.4.1 Correspondence on *The Cherry Orchard*

Translated by Constance Garnett, Elizabeth Hapgood, Michael Heim, Ronald Hingley, S. S. Koteliansky, S. Lederer and Elena Polyakova

Anton Chekhov to M. P. Alexeyeva, 15 September 1903

What has turned out isn't a drama, but a comedy, in places even a farce . . .

Anton Chekhov to Olga Knipper, 21 September 1903

The last act will be joyful, just as the entire play is happy and frivolous.

Anton Chekhov to Olga Knipper, 14 October 1903

Keep well, pony, read the play, read it attentively. There is a horse in my play too [. . .]

I.   Lyubov Andreyevna will be played by you since there is no one else. She is dressed with great taste, but not gorgeously. Clever, very good-natured, absent-minded; friendly and gracious to everyone, always a smile on her face.

II.   Anya. Absolutely must be played by a young actress [. . .]

IV.   Gaev is for Vishnevsky. Ask Vishnevsky to listen to people playing billiards and to note down as many of the terms used as he can. I don't play billiards, or rather did play once but have forgotten it all now and it is all put down at random in my play. We'll talk it over with Vishnevsky later, and I'll put in all that is necessary.

V.   Lopakhin. Stanislavsky [. . .]

VIII.   Charlotta – is a question mark. I will put in some more of her sayings in the fourth act [. . .] Charlotta plays a conjuring trick with Trofimov's galoshes in the fourth act. Rayevskaya could not play it. It must be an actress with a sense of humour [. . .]

If the play will do, say that I will make any alterations required by stage conditions. I have the time, though I confess I am awfully sick of the play. If anything is not clear in it, write and tell me.

The house is an old mansion; at one time people have lived in a very wealthy style in it, and this ought to be felt in the staging. Wealthy and comfortable.

Varya is rather crude and rather stupid, but very good-natured.

Anton Chekhov to Olga Knipper, 19 October 1903

I am most worried about the static quality of the second act and a certain unfinished quality about the student Trofimov. You see Trofimov is in exile from time to time, and now and again thrown out of university, but how can these things be represented?

Konstantin Stanislavsky to Anton Chekhov, 20 October 1903

In my opinion your *Cherry Orchard* is your best play. I have fallen in love with it even more deeply than with our dear *Seagull*. It is not a comedy, not a farce, as you wrote – it is a tragedy, no matter if you do indicate a way out to a better world in the last act. It makes a tremendous impression, and this by means of half-tones, tender water-colour tints. There is a poetic and lyric quality to it, very theatrical: all the parts, including that of the vagrant, are brilliant [. . .] I feel this is all too subtle for the public. It will take time for it to understand all the shadings [. . .] It is so completely a whole that one cannot delete a single word from it. It may be that I am prejudiced, yet I cannot find any defect in this play – except one: it requires too great, too subtle actors to bring out all its charms. We shall never be able to do that. When we had our first reading together I was worried by one thing, I was instantly carried away, and my feelings were caught up in the play. This was not the case with *The Seagull* or *The Three Sisters*. I am accustomed to a rather vague impression from a first reading of your plays. So I was afraid that when I read it for the second time it would not capture me again. Nothing of the sort happened. I wept like a woman, I tried to control myself, but could not. I can hear you say: 'But please, this is a farce' [. . .] No, for the ordinary person this is a tragedy.

Anton Chekhov to Olga Knipper, 21 October 1903

Nemirovich [. . .] has sent me a telegram which describes Anya as being like Irina [in *The Three Sisters*] [. . .] but Anya is as much like Irina as I am like Burdzhalov [a noted comic actor]. Anya is first and foremost a child, happy to the end, who has no awareness of life and isn't at all tearful, apart from Act 2, where she only has tears in her eyes.

Anton Chekhov to Vladimir Nemirovich-Danchenko, 23 October 1903

You were as indignant as I was when I let your theatre have *The Three Sisters* and an announcement about it appeared in *News of the Day*. I spoke with Efros, and he gave me his word it would never happen again. Now I suddenly read that Ranevskaya is living abroad with Anya, that she is living with a Frenchman, that Act 3 takes place somewhere in a hotel, that Lopakhin is a kulak, a son of a bitch, and so on. What could I think [. . .]

Anya doesn't cry once and never speaks in a tearful voice. She has tears in her eyes in Act 2 but her tone is happy and lively. Why do you talk in your telegram of all the crybabies in the play? Where are they? There's only one – Varya – and she is tearful by nature but her tears mustn't arouse a depressing feeling in the spectator. You'll often come across the indication 'through tears' in my stage directions, but this is only an indication of the character's mood, not one of actual tears. There's no graveyard in the second act.

Anton Chekhov to Olga Knipper, 25 October 1903

I never wanted to make Ranevskaya into someone who had calmed down. Death alone can calm such a woman.

Anton Chekhov to Olga Knipper, 28 October 1903

No one but Stanislavsky ought to play the merchant. You see, it is not a merchant, in the vulgar sense of the word, that must be understood [. . .]

Stanislavsky will make a very good and original Gaev, but then who will act Lopakhin? You see, Lopakhin is the central character. If it is not successful the whole play is done for. Lopakhin must not be played as a loud, noisy man; there is no need for him to be typically a merchant. He is a soft man.

Anton Chekhov to Konstantin Stanislavsky, 30 October 1903

Lopakhin may be a merchant, but he is a decent person in every sense; his behaviour must be entirely proper, cultivated and free of pettiness or clowning. I had the feeling you could do a brilliant job of this role, the central role in the play. If you take Gaev, give Lopakhin to Vishnevsky. He won't be an artistic Lopakhin, but he won't be a petty one either [. . .] When you're selecting an actor for the role, don't forget that Varya, a serious and religious young lady, is in love with Lopakhin; she could never have loved a cute little kulak.

Anton Chekhov to Vladimir Nemirovich-Danchenko, 2 November 1903

1. Anya can be played by anyone at all, even a complete unknown as long as she is young and looks like a little girl and speaks in a youthful, vibrant voice [. . .]
2. Varya is a much more important role. What about having Maria Petrovna play her? Without Petrovna the role will seem flat and crude, and I'll have to rework it, tone it down. Maria Petrovna doesn't have to worry about being typecast, because in the first place she is a talented person, and in the second, Varya isn't at all like Sonya or Natasha [in *Uncle Vanya* and *The Three Sisters*]; she wears black, she's a nun, she's slightly simple-minded, a crybaby, and so forth.

3. Gayev and Lopakhin are for Konstantin Sergeyevich [Stanislavsky] to try out and choose from. If he were to take Lopakhin and do well in the role, the play would be a success. Because if Lopakhin is pallid, portrayed by a pallid actor, then both the role and the play are ruined.

[. . .]

5. Charlotta is an important role. You can't give it to Pomyalova, of course. Muratova might be good, but she's not funny. This is Miss Knipper's role.

[. . .]

11. The stationmaster who recites "The Peccatrix" in the third act is for an actor with a bass voice.

Charlotta speaks correct, not broken Russian, but every once in a while she hardens a final soft consonant and uses a masculin adjective with a feminine noun or vice versa. Pischick is a true Russian, an old man afflicted by gout, old age and too much to eat; he is stout and wears a long coat (à la Simov) and boots without heels. Lopakhin wears a white vest and yellow shoes; he takes big steps and waves his arms as he walks. He thinks while he walks and walks in a straight line. Since his hair is rather long, he often tosses his head back. When lost in thought, he strokes his beard from back to front, that is, from neck to mouth. Trofimov is clear I think. Varya wears a black dress with a wide belt.

Konstantin Stanislavsky to Anton Chekhov, 26 October 1903

Should the house be quite, or even very seedy? Lopakhin says he will demolish it. That means it's really good for nothing at all [. . .]

A wooden house, or a stone one? Perhaps the middle part is stone and the wings wooden, the lower part is stone and the top wooden? [. . .]

In summer I recorded a shepherd's horn on my phonograph. The same horn you enjoyed so much at Lyubimovka [. . .] it will come in very useful.

Anton Chekhov to Konstantin Stanislavsky, 5 November 1903

The house is big, solid; wooden – or stone, it makes no difference. It's very old and very large; people do not rent places like that for the summer. Places like that are usually torn down and the materials used to build vacation homes. Antique furniture, stylish, solid; bankruptcy and debt have left the furnishings untouched.

People buy a house like that with the consideration that it is cheaper and easier to build anew than to repair the old.

Your shepherd could certainly play. That exactly fits the bill.

Konstantin Stanislavsky to Anton Chekhov, 2 November 1903

I think I have just found the set for the first act. It is a very difficult set. The windows must be close enough to the front of the stage so that the cherry orchard will be seen from the whole auditorium; there are three doors; one would like to show a bit of Anya's room, bright and virginal. The room is a passageway, but one must be made to feel that here (in the nursery) it is cosy, warm and light. Yet the room has fallen into disuse, there is a sense of emptiness about it. Moreover the set must be comfortable, and contain a number of planned acting areas.

Anton Chekhov to Konstantin Stanislavsky, 10 November 1903

Dunya and Yepikhodov stand in Lopakhin's presence and don't sit down. Lopakhin is very much at ease, behaves like a lord of the manor and is on familiar 'thou' terms with the servants. They use the unfamiliar 'you' form when addressing him.

Konstantin Stanislavsky to Anton Chekhov, 19 November 1903

I have been busy working on the second act and finally have it in shape. I think it will come out charmingly. Let's hope the scenery will be successful: the little chapel, the ravine, the neglected cemetery in the middle of an oasis of trees in the open steppes. The left side and the centre will not have any wings. You will see only the far horizon. This will be produced by a single semi-circular backdrop, with attachments to deepen the perspective. In the distance you see the flash of a stream and the manor house on a slight rise, telegraph poles and a railway bridge. Do let us have a train go by with a puff of smoke in one of the pauses [. . .] Before sundown there will be a brief glimpse of the town, and towards the end of the act, a fog: it will be particularly thick above the ditch downstage. The frogs and corncrakes will strike up at the very end of the act. To the left in the foreground a mown field and a small mound of hay, on which the scene is played by the group out walking. This is for the actors, it will help them get into the spirit of their parts. The general tone of the set is like that of a Levitan painting. The landscape is that of the province of Orel, not of lower Kursk.

The work is now being carried on as follows: Nemirovich-Danchenko rehearsed the first act yesterday and I wrote [the plan for] the following acts [. . .] I am still undecided about the sets for acts three and four. The model is made and came out well; it is full of atmosphere and it is also laid out so that all parts of it are visible to all in the auditorium. Down front there is something like a shrubbery. Further upstage are the stairs and billiard-room. The windows are painted on the walls. This set is more convenient for the ball. Still a small voice keeps whispering in my ear that if we have one set, which we change in the fourth act, it would be easier and cosier to play in.

Anton Chekhov to Olga Knipper, 23 November 1903

Konstantin Sergeyevich wants to bring in a train in Act 2, but I think it would be better to restrain him. He also wants frogs and corncrakes [. . .]

*

As at least one Russian commentator (Ivan Bunin) noted, the whole concept of a cherry orchard was clearly symbolic, since there was nowhere in Russia that cherry trees were grown by themselves, and unlike flowering cherries (which produce no fruit), commercial trees have only small blossoms. Writing to Vera Komissarzhevskaya, Chekhov indicates the significance of the major image in the play, as the starting point for his composition:

(1) I've got an idea for a play and a title for it (*The Cherry Orchard*, but that's still a secret), and I'll most likely settle down to writing no later than the end of February, provided of course I'm well; (2) the central role in the play is that of an old woman.

(27 January 1903)

This serves as a corrective to Stanislavsky's claim that even after the script had been finished and was in rehearsal Chekhov "could not yet decide on the name" of his new play. But the conversation with Chekhov in the autumn of 1903, which Stanislavsky records, bears testimony to the importance of the title image:

'Listen, I have found a wonderful name for the play. A wonderful name,' he declared . . . '*Vishneviy Sad* [The Cherry Orchard],' and he rolled with happy laughter.

I confess that I did not thoroughly understand the reason for his gladness, for I found nothing unusual in the name . . .

'Listen, not *Vishneviy* but *Vishnéviy Sad*,' he stated triumphantly and became all laughter.

At first I did not even understand of what he was speaking, but Chekhov lovingly repeated the word, stressing the tender sound of the 'e' in the word as though he were trying to caress with its help the former beautiful life which was no longer necessary, which he himself lovingly and with tears was destroying in his play. This time I understood the great and yet delicate difference. *Vishneviy Sad* is a commercial orchard which brings in profit. Such an orchard is necessary to life even at the present. But *Vishnéviy Sad* brings no profits. It hides in itself and in all of its flowering whiteness the great poetry of the dying life of aristocracy. The *Vishnéviy Sad* grows for the sake of beauty, for the eyes

172

of spoiled aesthetes. It is a pity to destroy it, but it is necessary to do so, for
the economics of life demand it.

(My Life in Art, 1926)

Chekhov's evident joyfulness and laughter conflicts with the interpretation of the
play that Stanislavsky had already arrived at, and that formed the basis of his
production. And indeed the essentially comic nature of the play was a continuing
point of disagreement and misunderstanding.

In addition to the comedy, and the insights into characterization provided by
Chekhov's suggestions for casting, other aspects of the play that are discussed in
the letters and illuminate his thematic concepts or visualization of the action
include the setting and dramatic weighting of different characters. The correspondence also shows the degree to which, as Olga Knipper later commented,
"The directors and the author could not understand each other could not agree"
– one example being Stanislavsky's introduction of a cemetery into Act II. These
letters contain comments on Chekhov's health, daily activities, views on other
writers (such as Maxim Gorky's plan to found a theatre in Novgorod – "both
theatres for the people and literature for the people are ridiculous . . . What needs
to be done is not lower Gogol to the people's level, but raise the people to Gogol's
level") or critics (particularly Efros). Since most of these topics do not add to our
understanding of the play, they have been omitted. Only directly relevant extracts
are included; and except in one case – where Chekhov's reply is placed immediately after the letter it answers – the correspondence is in chronological order.

Despite his enthusiastic response to early readings of the play – "it is so completely a whole that one cannot delete a single word from it" – Stanislavsky
certainly made at least one alteration to the text. As his memoirs admit, this was
done for solely conventional reasons, to make the structure correspond more to
standard theatrical expectations. This scene was also omitted from the published
version of *The Cherry Orchard*. However, evidence from the manuscript of the play
shows that instead of deleting Charlotta's monologue, as Stanislavsky indicates,
Chekhov transferred it to the beginning of Act II; and that this happened before
the first performance, not in reaction to audience response.

5.4.2 Stanislavsky, Changing Act II of *The Cherry Orchard*

My Life in Art, 1926

[. . .] When we dared to suggest to Anton Pavlovich that a whole scene be
shortened, the whole end of the second act of *The Cherry Orchard*, he became
very sad and so pale that we were ourselves frightened at the pain that we
had caused him. But after thinking for several minutes, he managed to
control himself and said: 'Shorten it.'

Never after did he say a single word to us about this incident. And who
knows, perhaps he would have been justified in reproaching us, because it
may very well be that it was the will of the stage director and not his own

173

which shortened a scene that was excellently written. After the young people left Varya with a great deal of noise, Sharlotta came on the stage with a rifle and lay down in the hay, singing some popular German song. Hardly able to move his feet, there entered Firs, lighting matches, looking in the grass for the fan dropped by his mistress. There takes place a meeting of two lonely people. They have nothing to speak about, but they so want to speak, for a human being must speak to someone. Sharlotta begins to tell Firs of how she worked in her youth in a circus and performed the *salto mortale*, in those very words, which, in our version she says in the beginning of the act when on the stage with Epikhodov, Yasha, and the maid. In answer to her story, Firs talks at length and randomly about something that cannot be understood that happened in the days of his youth, when somebody was taken somewhere in a wagon accompanied by sounds of squeaking and crying, and Firs interprets these sounds with the words cling-clang. Sharlotta does not understand anything in his story, but catches up his cue so that the one common moment in the lives of these two lonely people may not be disturbed. They cry 'Cling-Clang' to each other and both laugh very sincerely. This was the way Chekhov ended the act.

After the stormy scene with the young people, such a lyric ending lowered the atmosphere of the act and we could not lift it again. I suppose that it was mainly our own fault but it was the author who paid for our inability.

The Cherry Orchard: chronology of major early performances

February 1903, Chekhov begins *The Cherry Orchard*, in the spring. He completes the play by autumn.		
January 1904 Moscow (January 17, 1904: Chekhov's 44th birthday and celebrations of the 25th anniversary of his literary work.)	Moscow Art Theatre Directors: Konstantin Stanislavsky and Vladimir Nemirovich-Danchenko	Lopakhin: Leonid Leonidov Anya: Maria Lilina Madame Ranevsky: Olga Knipper Leonid Gayev: Konstantin Stanislavsky Charlotta: E.P. Muratova
1904 Kherson	Companions of New Drama Director: Vsevolod Meyerhold	Trofimov: Vsevolod Meyerhold
1911 London	Aldwych Theatre Producers: Stage Society	Varya: Mary Jerrold Trofimov: Harcourt Williams Pishtchik: Nigel Playfair Epikhodov: Ivan Berlyn
1917 Dublin	Irish Theatre Company Director: Edward Martyn Translator: George Calderon	Lopakhin: Paul Farrel Pishtchik: Oliver Clonabraney Firs: Jimmy O'Dea

| March 1928
New York | Bijou Theatre
Director and Producer:
James B. Fagan
Translator: George
Calderon | Lopakhin: Edwin Maxwell
Anya: Gemma Fagan
Madame Ranevsky: Mary
Grev
Leonid Gayev: James B.
Fagan
Charlotta: Ethel Griffies |
| October 1928
New York | Civic Repertory Theater | Varya: Eva Le Gallienne
Madame Ranevsky: Alla
Nazimova |

Performance and reception

Figure 5.6 The Cherry Orchard, Moscow Art Theatre: 1904 (directed by Stanislavsky). The return in Act I

Figure 5.7 Landscape and graveyard in Act II

175

As for his earlier productions of Chekhov's plays, Stanislavsky created an extremely detailed mise-en-scène for *The Cherry Orchard*. As with *The Seagull*, these notes contain a beat by beat breakdown of moves, gestures and blocking for all the actors, precise indications of complex sound effects and sketches of floor plans. However, here – for the first time – these notes also focus on the motivations of the characters, and on their inner feelings. The way this psychology has been recorded is essentially novelistic, and the technical demands on the actors – the wide register of mental states and swift changes of emotion described – can be seen as a measure of Stanislavsky's growing confidence in the Moscow Art Theatre company. A good example of this is in Act III, when Lopakhin announces that it is he who has purchased the orchard.

> RANEVSKAIA. Has the cherry orchard been sold?
> LOPAKHIN. *(202. Guiltily, examining his handkerchief. Looks down. Doesn't answer at once.)* It has.
> RANEVSKAIA. *(203. Pause, barely audible.)* Who bought it?
> LOPAKHIN. *(204. Pause. Even quieter and more embarrassed.)* I bought it. *(205. Agonizing pause. Lopakhin feels badly and this arouses the beast in him. The awkwardness of his position starts to make him angry. He nervously pulls at his handkerchief . . .)*

After recording the family's response to this, Stanislavsky's notes continue with Lopakhin's reaction to Aria throwing down the keys to the house.

> *(His tone is bitter and insolent as he almost shouts.)* I bought it. *(Pause. Having shouted, Lophakin tears his handkerchief in two and flings it away. He is still for a moment. He calms down. Then he gets up, covers his ears with his hands and crosses*

to the table. [. . .] He sits. [. . .] Pishchick goes to Lophakin and sits on the arm of the sofa. Now, at a distance from Ranevskaia, the feeling of pleasure and commercial pride leads them way over a proper sense of embarrassment and Lophakin begins to boast as a businessman does faced with his brother-merchants or his assistants. The account of the sale (not small minded) with artistic enthusiasm over his skill and efficiency. It is essential to justify Lopakhin that there should be precisely this 'artistic enthusiasm'.) [. . .] Now the cherry orchard is mine. Mine! *(Gross guffaw. He clowns, leaning his head on the table, ruffles his hair, butts Pishchick who is sitting next to him in the chest. Stands up, raises his arms and bears his chest. He continues his speech as he does so. All this clowning is explicable by the force of his character, his unbridled nature, his ecstasy.)* God almighty, gentlemen, the cherry orchard is mine! Tell me I'm drunk, or out of mind, or that I'm imagining all this . . . *(Pause. He thumps the table and the sofa like a kulak. Laughs.)* Don't you dare laugh at me! Don't you laugh, don't you dare! *(Suddenly stops and changes tone. Now he is stern, imperious. The drink is coming into its own. He moves forward. Now he knows no mercy. The drink has gone to his head. He cannot feel Ranevskaia's sorrow and misery. Darkening malice and resentment towards the trials and tribulations of his childhood have been aroused in him. All this will be accepted if the actor goes at it boldly, powerfully, like a warrior, not a bruiser.)*

(Translated by Jean Benedetti, in
Stanislavski, A Biography, 1988)

At the end of this section of the scene Lopakhin is described as feeling twinges of remorse, then undergoing a sudden change of mood at the sight of Ranevskaia's tears, which arouse *"the good and sincere man in him and his tender love for the whole family and her especially"*. However, this tenderness is presented as drunken farce with Lopakhin on his knees, weeping and kissing her skirt *"like a little puppy dog"* – and the tinge of contempt in his analysis of Lopakhin's behaviour suggests why Stanislavsky himself played Gayev instead of this part, despite Chehkov's explicit wishes: "Why then, if he is so tenderhearted, didn't he help Ranevskaia? Because he is a slave to merchant's prejudices, because they would have made him a laughing-stock. *Les affaires sont les affaires*". At the end of the act, as a symbolic way of marking the change in ownership, the "trite polka" of aristocratic balls switches to a crude peasant dance.

From descriptions of the production, Stanislavsky's performance as Gayev was an intriguing combination of dandyish elegance and strong sentimental emotion. It also exemplified Stanislavsky's interpretation of *The Cherry Orchard* as a threnody for the passing of the old order, transferring the focus from the upcoming merchant (for Chekhov the central figure in the play) to the humane but useless aristocrat, and was given a heavily symbolic significance.

Chekhov had complained about the rhythm of the action in the way Stanislavsky had staged *The Cherry Orchard* commenting on two reports he had received: "both say that Stanislavsky acts revoltingly in Act IV, that he drags everything

Figure 5.9 The departure in Act IV

out painfully. How terrible! An act which should last a maximum of twelve minutes lasts forty in your production" (Letter to Olga Knipper, 29 March 1904). The
fast pacing Chekhov wanted carries an automatic comic effect, and is associated
with farce. (Chekhov is undoubtedly exaggerating – a performance that rushed
through the 10 pages of dialogue, with nine distinct scenes and 33 speeches, in just
twelve minutes would be literally breathless – but his intention is clear. By contrast, such protracted slowness was undoubtedly intended to maximize the emotional pathos, reinforcing Stanislavsky's view of the play as a tragedy. This view
was also shared by Meyerhold, though he attributed the slow pacing to a representation of "boredom". Meyerhold's vision of the dancing was "the vortex of a
nightmare" – but he too emphasized the importance of rhythm in the play.

> The following harmony is established in the last act: on one hand, the lamen-
> tations of Ranevskaya with her presentiment of approaching disaster (fate in
> the new musical drama of Chekhov); on the other, the puppet show (not for
> nothing does Chekhov make Charlotta dance among the 'philistines' in a
> familiar puppet theatre costume – black tail-coat and check trousers). Trans-
> lated into musical terms, this is one movement of the symphony. It contains
> the basic elegaic melody with alternating moods in pianissimo, outbursts in
> forte (the suffering of Ranevskaya), and the dissonant accompaniment of the
> monotonous cacophony of the distant dance band and the dance of the living
> corpses (the philistines).
>
> (*Literaturnoe nasledstvo*, 1960)

This reading of the play aligns *The Cherry Orchard* with the symbolist movement. It
is certainly true that Chekhov was contemplating a very different type of drama
right at the end of his life. Stanislavsky gives a brief scenario: a love triangle in
which the two jealous rivals go on a polar expedition, and "the last act portrays a

large ship crushed amid icebergs. The play ends with both friends seeing a white vision slipping over the snow. Apparently this is the shade, soul or symbol of the woman they both love, who has died while they were away" (*My Life in Art*, 1926). This may be the play he spoke of writing, both to Vera Komissarzhevskaya in response to her request for rights to *The Cherry Orchard* ("why don't I write a play for *you* . . . It's an old dream of mine" – Letter, 27 January 1903), and to the touring actor-manager P. N. Orlenov, when he visited Chekhov at Yalta in March 1904. Meyerhold's own production of *The Cherry Orchard* was not overtly symbolist, though as his letter to Chekhov indicates rhythm was an important element of his directorial concept; and his criticism of the Moscow Art Theatre staging is valid.

5.4.3 Vselovod Meyerhold, Letter to Anton Chekhov: 8 May 1904

Translated by Nora Beeson

Tulane Drama Review 25, vol. 9, no. 1

May 8, 1904
(Lopatino)

[. . .] Next year my company will play in Tiflis. Come to see us, because we have grown in an artistic sense. We do *The Cherry Orchard* well. After I saw it at the Moscow Art Theatre, I wasn't ashamed of our production. I did not altogether like the performance in Moscow. In general.

I want to say this. When some author with his genius stirs a theatre to life, then he understands the secret of performing his plays, finds the key [. . .] If the author begins to perfect his technique, gets to the top of his profession, the theatre only loses this key, because it is an association of creators and consequently more cumbersome. The Deutsches Theater in Berlin, for example, has lost the key to performing Hauptmann's plays; the great tragi-comedy *Der rote Hahn*, *Schluck und Jau*, and *Der arme Heinrich* were failures. It seems to me that the Art Theatre was confused when it tackled your *Cherry Orchard*.

Your play is abstract, like a Tchaikovsky symphony. The stage director must above all feel it with his ear. In the third act, against the background of the stupid "stomping" – this "stomping" must be heard – Horror enters unnoticed by anyone.

"The cherry orchard is sold." They dance. "Sold." They dance. And so to the end. When one reads the play, the last act makes the same kind of impression as the ringing in the sick man's ears in your story *Typhus*. Some kind of itch. Gaiety in which sounds of death are heard. In this act there is something Maeterlinck-like frightful. I only use this comparison because I'm incapable of saying it more precisely. You are incomparable in your great work. When one reads plays by foreign authors you appear particularly original. In drama the West should learn from you.

In the Moscow Art Theatre one did not get such an impression from the last act. The background was not concentrated enough and at the same time not remote enough. In the forefront: the story with the billiard cue and the tricks. Separately. All this did not form a chain of "stomping." And in the meantime all the "dancing" people are unconcerned and do not sense the harm. The tempo of this act was too slow in the Art Theatre. They wanted to convey boredom. That's a mistake. One must picture unconcern. There's a difference. Unconcern is more active. Then the tragedy of the act becomes more concentrated.

*

Although the Moscow, and later St. Petersburg audiences were enthusiastic, the reception of the Moscow Art Theatre production by the Russian critics was muted. As Stanislavsky informed Chekhov "connoisseurs are rapturous over play. Newspapers not very understanding" (Telegram, 2 April 1904). There were various criticisms of the acting in individual parts, though the staging was generally approved; and on the whole, the commentaries on the play echoed the emphasis Stanislavsky had given the action. It was accepted as a social tragedy in which the sale of the cherry orchard symbolized the displacement of the old aristocratic establishment – as *The Literary Digest* report on Russian reactions summarized it: "The critics agree that Chekhoff has produced a realistic and poignant drama of modern Russia which is undergoing the transformation pictured in the play" (30 April 1904). In England from the first, the play was misunderstood. While declaring *The Cherry Orchard* would never be outdated as long as human desires remained unfulfilled, George Calderon, the English translator of Chekhov, defined the play as "a picture of the nothingness of hope in all countries and all ages" (*Quarterly Review*, July 1912). The overwhelmingly negative response to the first English production in 1911 can be summed up in the review by *The Times*:

> For anything I see, said Johnson's friend "old" Meynell, foreigners are fools. Russians are foreigners, but even so, it is highly improbable that they are such fools as they seem in the English version of Tchehov's comedy. The fact is, when actors are set to present alien types which they have never seen and which they can only imagine from the necessarily imperfect indications of a translation, they are bound to produce grotesques . . . Mrs. Edward Garnett's *Cherry Orchard* cannot but strike an English audience as something queer, outlandish, even silly. You are shown a family drifting to ruin . . . They all seem children who have never grown up. Genuine comedy and scenes of pure pathos are mixed with knockabout farce.
>
> The players did their best: it was not their fault that the entertainment was not entertaining.
>
> (30 May 1911)

However, this review provoked the novelist Arnold Bennett, who was also a dramatist specializing in naturalistic comedies, to declare that "In naturalism the play is assuredly an advance on any other play that . . . has been seen in England" – asserting that Chekhov achieves "another step in the evolution of the drama" because he "never hesitates to make his personages as ridiculous as in life they would be. In this he differs from every other playwright that I know of. Ibsen for instance; and Henri Becque" (*New Age*, 8 June 1911). Another reaction to the same review shows considerable insight into *The Cherry Orchard*, pointing to a significant change in the appreciation of Chekhov's work.

5.4.4 *The Nation*, 3 June 1911
A Russian comedy of manners

The dramatic critic of the "Times" has never seemed quite happy since, in writing on two interesting plays by Mr. Arnold Bennett and Mr. Fagan, he was asked to believe in the existence of a modern newspaper proprietor. [. . .] But having witnessed nothing in life remotely resembling, say, the illustrious patron of Printing House Square, he was naturally shocked at the *invraisemblance* of these stage pictures of the new journalism. Judge Brack was right; people did *not* do such things, for there were no such people to do them. I see that Mr. Walkley is not less dissatisfied with the psychology of Tchekov's comedy, "The Cherry Orchard." His first impulse is to conceive that the extreme childishness, the irrationality, of the characters in this play are due to the fact that they are foreigners. Then, perhaps on the reflection that they are Russian, and that Russians are at least civilised enough to go to Paris, Mr. Walkley concludes that it is the fault of the translator, and also that British actors cannot impart quite the right touch to a study of Russian types and Russian manners. And then, again, he reverts to the notion that there is something inherently un-English in setting upon the stage what he calls "queer, outlandish, even silly" types of human beings. If, therefore, Mr. Walkley's impeachment be not of Nature herself for thoughtless differentiation from her own average, we must assume that Tchekov's theme and his treatment of it are thoroughly abnormal. "You are shown," he tells us, "a family drifting to ruin." Strange to say, the owner is an "improvident, sentimental, feather-pated creature." She sees the old inheritance, beloved cherry-orchard and all, slipping away, and "can only wring her hands," or offer gold to beggars while her servants' wages are unpaid. This unheard-of character is surrounded by other eccentrics, such as borrowers, drunkards, dreamers who talk and never act, bores, triflers, "doddering" or "knavish" servants, and various creatures that "seem children who have never grown up."

It may occur to a mere unilluminated observer of the processes of things that such persons are the very insignia and provocation of "family ruin"; that it is just through such a procession of harpies, parasites, idlers, fainéants, and "dodderers" that all families, all States, all individuals, all institutions – *e.g.*, the House of Lords, in this year and moment of grace – come to grief; in a word, that if Tchekov's theme is suitable for treatment on the stage, you could not have a more fitly designed group of human accessories than that which Mr. Walkley describes. [. . .] "A Cherry Orchard" is not Bloomsbury, but it is life; and it happens to be a corner of life which has been more closely and brilliantly explored by great literary men than any other part of modern Europe.

So, having led Mr. Walkley thus far, it is possible that we may induce him to go a little farther. The ruin of an old family, who are not fit to last, and who betray themselves to their fall, is not a bad dramatic theme; nay, by the bones of the house of Atreus; it is a good one! And Mr. Walkley, by his *catalogue raisonné* of the characters in "The Cherry Orchard," makes it clear that Anton Tchekov knew exactly what he was doing, and, choosing to make a tragi-comedy of his play, selected the right kind of agents and environment; while, being also a Russian, dealing with Russians, he gives it just that added touch of impracticability, of childlike sentimental helplessness, which we know to be a trifle more obviously Russian than it would be English. But at this point one feels a little difficulty, a little delicacy. For how could a critic of Mr. Walkley's experience and fastidiousness fail to see that Tchekov's characterisation is like fine lace-work as to detail, as well as of all but the greatest ironic power as to general conception and workmanship? Why, Madame Ranevsky is a jewel! She is as perfect an architect of ruin as Lord Rosebery, and her style is his to a T. Miss Katharine Pole gave a very brilliant and charming representation of her, but erred in making her an affected, "precious," fine lady, when, in reality, she is a piece of exquisite nothingness, equally sincere in her adoration of her beautiful orchard and her incapacity to keep it, in her love of Paris and her country home, of her lover and her child, her piety and her intrigue, her sweetness and her tantrums, her selfishness and her considerateness – withal an adorable piece of useless femininity, such as I have thought an amateur of the sex would have loved at first sight. Such a picture of inconstant helplessness would in itself make the fortune of any play with an audience of average wits. But Tchekov has built round his portrait of the lovely Madame Ranevsky the prettiest *predella* of absurdities, such as some Italian artists use to relieve the gravity of their main theme. Such are the ridiculous land-owner, Semyonov-Pishtchik; borrowing (not vainly) of the bankrupt; the German governess, diverting them with silly card tricks; the "doddering" old butler, who thinks he alone keeps the whole rocking concern upright; and, best of all, the shabby, preaching, young-old student, who lolls on his stomach as he discourses of duty, the sanctity of work, and the chastened glories of the society of the future. Such is the cunning ex-peasant, tongue-tied, as Mr. Walkley says, but with the gift of action, which this amiable, moon-struck, talking society lacks; no gentleman, neither a villain nor a hero, but fit to turn the key of the front-door on his old masters and mint the clay of the cherry-orchard into gold.

It seems a little late in the day, not to say a trifle pedantic and irrelevant, to quarrel that the technique of such a play on the ground that it is a

mixture of "pure pathos"and "genuine", comedy and "knock-about farce."
[. . .] It does vary between harsh and delicate effects; indeed, its subject is so
balanced in actual life, for a cause or a social class that falls by its own folly is
by turns pathetic, merely unwise, and wildly ridiculous. Tchekov's irony is at
its root a sad and profound sentiment, as we discern in the closing scene of
"The Cherry Orchard," when as, in the deserted house, doors bang and keys
turn gratingly in the lock, and the shutters are closed, shutting out the
cheerful sounds of life, and only admitting a glint of its day, the poor old
"doddering" white-haired butler, forgotten in the family's hurried half-joyful
departure, creeps into the darkened room, mutters that his master has left his
fur-coat behind, and will assuredly catch cold, and stretches *himself* out in a
sleep that looks like death. And this of course, is the key of the play, which is
thus a comedy and a farce and a tragedy in the sense in which life is all these
things, being made up of change and loss, and a certain sparkling recovery,
and a grimly ludicrous, ironic, riotous play of unknown forces over it all.

H. W. M

*

By the time of the second London production in 1920 – following the trauma of
the First World War, and echoing a general sense of the destruction of European
civilization in its aftermath – Chekhov had become anglicized by adoption.
J. Middleton Murry put it most succinctly in declaring "Today we feel how
intimately Tchekov belongs to us" (*Aspects of Literature*, 1920). Virginia Woolf, for
instance, read her own stream of consciousness writing into *The Cherry Orchard*,
though significantly she picked up on a similar musical analogy to Meyerhold:

It is, as a rule, when a critic does not wish to commit himself or to trouble
himself, that he refers to atmosphere. And, given time, something might be
said in greater detail of the causes which produced this atmosphere – the
strange dislocated sentences, each so erratic and yet cutting out the shape
so firmly, of the realism, of the humour, of the artistic unity. But let the word
atmosphere be taken literally to mean that Chekhov has contrived to shed
over us a luminous vapour in which life appears as it is, without veils, transparent and visible to the depths. Long before the play was over, we seemed to
have sunk below the surface of things and to be feeling our way among submerged but recognizable emotions. 'I have no proper passport. I don't know
how old I am; I always feel I am still young' – how the words go sounding on in
one's mind – how the whole play resounds with such sentences, which
reverberate, melt into each other and pass far away out behind everything! In
short, if it is permissible to use such vague language, I do not know how
better to describe the sensation at the end of *The Cherry Orchard*, than by
saying that it sends one into the street feeling like a piano played upon at last,
not in the middle only but all over the keyboard and with the lid left open so the
sound goes on.

New Statesman, 24 July 1920

The Cherry Orchard remained in the Moscow Art Theatre repertoire as their signature performance, becoming in some ways a museum piece. With Olga Knipper now playing Ranevskaya, it was toured through Europe in 1922, when the young director Michel Saint-Denis saw their production in Paris. His reaction clearly indicates the way Naturalism, already by then becoming the standard for mainstream theatre that young experimental artists fought against, continued to be a vital force in twentieth-century staging, particularly through Chekhov. It is also an early demonstration of the degree to which Chekhov's plays became identified with Stanislavsky's productions, making his acting System so influential. Indeed, though coming out of Jacques Copeau's anti-naturalistic theatre company, Saint-Denis kept his interest in Chekhov, directing a much-praised *Three Sisters* in 1939, and *The Cherry Orchard* in 1961.

A later Moscow Art Theatre tour, which presented *The Cherry Orchard* (as well as *The Three Sisters*) in London in 1938, is a good example of how Stanislavsky's original tragic and political interpretation of the play in the first production had become emphasized to the point of distortion. It also demonstrated, in contrast to the type of naturalistic acting pioneered by André Antoine and apparently promoted in Stanislavsky's theoretical writings, the extent to which the actual style of acting his own productions was declarative and overtly theatrical, corresponding in fact to the style required by Bernard Shaw.

5.4.5 Michel Saint-Denis, Chekhov's impact in Europe

"Style and Reality", *Theatre: The Rediscovery of Style*, Heinemann, 1960

In 1922 Stanislavsky came to Paris with the Moscow Art Theatre. They played at the Théâtre des Champs Elysées. There we all went, all the students together, very smart, a little ready to laugh in advance: we were going to see those realists, those naturalistic people, the contemporaries of old Antoine! We saw *The Cherry Orchard* that night and we stopped laughing very quickly. There is a moment in the first act of *The Cherry Orchard* when all the characters return from a trip to Paris, worn out by days and nights in the train. They enter the nursery; Madame Ranevsky pauses to admire and feel the old room, full of memories, and Anya, her young daughter of seventeen, who has been brought up in that nursery, jumps on to a sofa and, crouching on it, is caught up by a fit of that high-pitched laughter which is induced by a combination of tiredness and emotion. And on that piece of wordless acting the audience of two thousand five hundred people burst into applause. Later on in the third act, Olga Knipper Chekhova, the wife of Chekhov, playing Madame Ranevsky, takes a cup of tea from the old servant while she is engaged in talking to someone else. Her hand shakes, she's burnt by the tea, drops the cup which falls on the ground and breaks. Fresh burst of applause. Why? Because the reality of this action was so complete, so untheatrically managed as to be striking even from a distance.

It was enough to create enthusiasm. I had the opportunity of asking Stanislavski how he had achieved such balanced and convincing reality. He replied, 'Oh it's very stupid. She couldn't get it. We rehearsed for seven months but she still couldn't get it; so one day I told the stage manager to put boiling water in the cup. And he did.' I couldn't help saying – I was twenty-five at the time, (but that man was wonderful) – 'Yes, that was stupid.' He laughed, 'It was absolutely stupid. But you have to do everything, anything, even stupid things, to get what you need in the theatre.'

Earlier that evening we had taken Stanislavski to see *Sganarelle ou Le Cocu Imaginaire* at the Comédie Française. It was a traditional production but there was an extraordinary actor in it, Jean Dehelly, already old, who revealed to me what lightness, what virtuosity can be reached by a juvenile in a classical farce. His performance was exquisitely true in its youthful artificiality – like a butterfly. But Stanislavski did not seem to appreciate this kind of acting. When we went out he said, 'You see my friends, we had a very good example tonight in that old theatre of what not to do.' That was all.

This visit of Stanislavski and his company was of incalculable importance to me. For the first time our classical attitude towards the theatre, our efforts to bring a new reality to acting, a reality transposed from life, were confronted by a superior form of modern realism, the realism of Chekhov. Stanislavski was then at his best; all the great names were in the company; the Russian Revolution was only five years old.

5.4.6 Laurence Kitchin, The Moscow Art Theatre in London, 1938

If the M.A.T. compels readjustment of ideas about Chekhov even when considered at the Saint-Denis level of direction, it makes other productions seem to have borne the relationship to these plays of Pater's dreamy Mona Lisa to Leonardo's portrait; the enigmatic sadness of the original caught and the virile statement, along with the earthiness of the subject, left out. Compared with English productions the lighting alone is as brilliant in impact as the primary colours hitting one for the first time from a masterpiece recently cleaned. [. . .] In *The Cherry Orchard* the tree tops, loaded with blossom and translucent behind crystalline windows, join with a room very sparingly furnished and a dawn as bracing as the opening act of *Oklahoma!* to weigh the scales heavily on the side of youth. Anya, a coltish schoolgirl with pigtails, is at home in this room, more than anyone else. After all, it is still called the nursery.

This play has been out of the repertoire for eleven years, allegedly awaiting a replacement of Kachalov, the last Gaiev. We know Chekhov wanted the brighter side of it emphasized, but certain aspects of this version are questionable. In flat contradiction to the 'oppressive sense of emptiness' asked for in his stage directions to the last act, the set looks even gayer when its meagre furnishings are covered up; it looks suitable, in fact, for conversion to a recreation room in the most hygienic of youth hostels, and in the only movement undeniably external to Chekhov, Anya and Trofimov strike an attitude reminiscent of propaganda posters as they make their final exit. Still, explicitly in the text, she does say good-bye to the old life and he greets the new. The lines ask for attitudes, though perhaps not that one. Then bronzed workmen are glimpsed outside, closing the shutters and leaving Firs to die in a room gently dappled with sunbeams through the apertures. It is as benign a stage death as you ever saw, mellow Shakespearian Chekhov.

If there are some brash lighting and scenic effects hardly to be expected from the 'austere' M.A.T., the sound effects are astounding. Instead of a few apologetic chirps in *The Cherry Orchard*, there is an all-out dawn chorus and later a solo from a cuckoo. [. . .] As for the mysterious sound of a string snapping 'as if out of the sky' in *The Cherry Orchard*, it is deep, plangent, and in context disturbing beyond imagination. Considered side by side with the décor and lighting, this use of sound leads one on to the impression of virile energy – conveyed at times with an almost childish directness as when the clumsy Yepikhodov collides with a door-post – which impregnates the M.A.T.'s acting. Supreme ensemble work was expected of it, but not the rampant individualism attainable within the pattern, not the savage power of Gribov in Chebutikin's drunkenness, not this panache and violence, with more than a hint of Tolstoi and Dostoevsky, in Chekhov; and certainly not the revelation of supposedly minor-key naturalistic plays, even when seen from the back row of Sadler's Wells' circle, is broadly theatrical, at times operatic.

The M.A.T. has developed a way of presenting the intimacies of Chekhov in a pattern of external effects which accommodates all the familiar reticences, hesitations, and interruptions of the dialogue without relying on fleeting, inspirational expressions of the eyes and other minutiae that invite camera close-ups. Whatever Stanislavsky may have taught about ignoring the audience, actors are aligned on it, one often standing behind another when talking to him in a position absolutely meaningless anywhere except on the stage. The relevance of this to drama in general is obvious when you recall the constant attacks on naturalism as something remote, finicky, antitheatrical, and so forth. As practised by the M.A.T. it is none of these things; they behave as if the so-called fourth wall were a crowded auditorium, as it really is. Hence the slight swagger, the hint of conscious artifice admired in public, which prevents the disciplined actions from appearing mechanical; hence the happy, relaxed faces enjoying applause at the finish.

It was this traditionally theatrical projection of voice and gesture, carried over for very different purposes from the kind of drama Stanislavsky despised, which (along with some unashamedly obvious effects) gave the Sadler's Wells performances their inexpected freshness and punch.

[. . .]

For violent impact Lopakhin's assumption of ownership in *The Cherry Orch-ard* is a case in point. Following Chekhov's expectation that Stanislavsky would choose the part for himself, and his reminder that Varya would not love a boor, Lukyanov plays him for the first two acts in a respectable loose-limbed, restless way, exasperated, kind, and impatient. Getting things done in this environment, he lets us know, is like swimming in treacle, the more frustrating the better your normal rhythm. After the sale he comes in unobtrusively and sits quietly on a settee. What sets him off is Varya's action in throwing the keys on the floor, and to mark this she does not just toss them down, but crashes them down directly in front of her, centre stage, with an overarm movement. Alone with Ranevskaya, he begins his tri-umphant tirade sitting down, rises after a few lines as if lifted by his own mounting emotion and picks the keys up. He throws them a yard or so in the air and catches them, right-handed in a movement like a punch which carries his whole body up stage towards the ballroom; he storms into it through the first of two arched openings in the wall.

Inside the ballroom he halts, well in view of the audience through the aperture, and orders the band to play. The pause before it obeys is agon-izing. When the music starts, Ranevskaya, who until now has held a monu-mental 'freeze' while seated on the chair she reached out for on hearing the news, and is alone on the main stage, begins to weep. Lopakhin breaks something in the ballroom with a violence in tune with the sacking of the Czar's palace and comes into full view again, a tall man holding high on to both sides of the second aperture. We see him there, a few yards behind Ranevskaya, wild-eyed and panting, bestially dominant though limp from the emotional effort, until the woman's misery seems to restore his human-ity as a sense of guilt. He staggers miserably into the room and to the opposite side of the table against which she is sitting, like a child seeking reassurance after doing something outrageous. She does not even look at him.

This episode illustrates, among other things, Chekhov's organic use of the stage, including spatial build-up of dynamic movement and use of props every bit as important as the dialogue, and confirms that if Stanislavsky had not existed it would have been necessary to invent him. [. . .] Moreover the preliminary ballroom incidents modify one's response to the climax and deepen its effect, not only by the obvious allusion to fiddling while Rome burns, but by lulling the audience into identification with the family, into their vulnerability. In order to do this, such things as Charlotta's party tricks must be dazzlingly professional and make their own separate effect. We now know why Chekhov made Charlotta a fairground performer in childhood, why he insisted on strong casting for the part. He wanted to draw us into the family circle by direct traditional means.

This seems unwarrantably remote from Lopakhin's big scene, but art on *The Cherry Orchard* level casts wide for its coherence. Lukyanov's acting of the scene has affinities with Stanislavsky's poor relation, the Method, a shaggy quality also present in Trofimov and the Beggar.

*

Perhaps because of its ambiguous nature, and its integration of tragedy, sentiment, comedy and farce, *The Cherry Orchard* has become the most updated of Chekhov's plays on the stage. (In film, of course, there is *Vanya on 42nd Street.*) In some cases these productions have simply been intended to correct Stanislavsky's overemphasis, and focussed on the comic aspect of the play. A case in point is the Tyrone Guthrie production of 1933, with Charles Laughton giving a typically farcical rendition of Lopakhin as "a loutish fellow, with head held on one side and flapping hands" – as one reviewer remarked:

> On its first production in London *The Cherry Orchard* seemed a lugubrious affair. The comic element was submerged. Mr. Tyrone Guthrie has not repeated the mistakes of Mr. Fagan, but in his determination to bring out the farcical extravagance of the dialogue and to dispel the notorious Russian gloom he has swung perilously near the other extreme . . .
>
> (*The Times*, 10 October 1933)

However, Michel Saint-Denis' dry, deliberately unpoetical and farcical production in 1961 was specifically intended to mirror the post-Holocaust, "absurdist" world, aligning *The Cherry Orchard* with Samuel Beckett. It was a challenge to the conventional views of Chekhov:

> The 'connoisseurs' have fallen in love with the scenery, with the dear creatures, representing the threatened past; they mock Trofimov and have little sympathy for Lopakhin; they were bound to resent the degradation of romantic values purposely displayed in my recent production . . . It is my hope that our interpretation has brought many people, particularly among the young, to a new understanding of this many-sided masterpiece.
>
> (Introduction, *Anton Chekhov: The Cherry Orchard*, a version by John Gielgud)

6

BERNARD SHAW
1856–1950

1 CONTEXT

As the prefaces to his plays vigorously assert, Shaw's drama is concerned with current social issues. This is indeed a major distinguishing factor for all naturalistic drama; and Ibsen or Chekhov are as much critics of the status quo as Shaw. But Shaw's focus is far more specific. Ibsen's plays deal with the corruption of individuals under a hypocritical morality and repressive social system. Syphilis may surface in *A Doll's House* and even be central to the action of *Ghosts*, but it is a physiological metaphor for this general moral state. By contrast, syphilis is the explicit subject of one of Eugène Brieux's plays – and Shaw, who compared Brieux to Ibsen, used drama to campaign for specific reforms. Thus his first play, *Widowers' Houses*, has a clearly identifiable subject: the exploitive practices of slum landlords and manipulation of the London County Council for their own profit. Although the door slams decisively at the end of *A Doll's House*, the independence achieved by Ibsen's heroine is a very uncertain quality, whereas Shaw claims that *Widowers' Houses* is "deliberately intended to induce people to vote on the Progressive side at the next Council election in London" (Preface to *Widowers' Houses*, 1893). Similarly, Chekhov documents the decay of the Russian establishment; and the hope for social change expressed by his characters is left undefined. By contrast, in Shaw's version of *The Cherry Orchard*, bombs kill off the representatives of Capitalism, while the remaining characters actively cooperate in the coming destruction of their society (lighting up their house as a beacon for the bombers).

The difference is in the degree of political commitment. Where Ibsen explicitly rejected all political programmes, and Chekhov reflected the ideological ferment of his time without comment, Shaw held strong socialist convictions. The history of Socialism in Britain is complicated. Engels owned factories in England; and Marx – who wrote his political treatises in the British Museum – based much of his analysis of Capitalism on British examples, and anticipated that the proletarian revolution would begin there. Yet Britain, which had been largely unaffected by the revolutions that swept the continent in 1848, remained far more stable than other European nations. This may partly be due to a strong utopian tendency in English radicalism, which found expression from William Blake's *Songs of Innocence and Experience* (1794) through Samuel Butler's *Erewhon* (1872) to William Morris' *News from Nowhere* (1892). But it was also a result of the Fabian movement, founded by Shaw, Sidney Webb, Annie Besant and others in 1884. Initially there were links between the Fabians and the revolutionary Social Democratic Federation, as well as the Socialist League (formed by William Morris, after disagreements with the leadership of the SDF). However, by 1886 the Fabians had broken with the anti-constitutional anarchists and Marxists of the Social Democratic League, and with the Socialist League, to pursue their line of evolutionary socialism.

The Fabians took their name from the Roman general, Fabius Cunctator (the Delayer), who defeated Hannibal by evading battle until the invading Carthagians were worn down. After reading the first volume of *Das Kapital* in 1882, as Shaw later said, he underwent a "complete conversion" to Marxism – but came to fear the "catastrophic policy for simultaneously destroying existing institutions and replacing them with a ready-made Utopia" on which class revolution was based. Instead the Fabian principle of "permeation" (in which key institutions would be infiltrated by socialists) offered a model of revolution that would be "gradual in its operations" (*The Road to Equality*, 1884). This gradualist position was confirmed by "Bloody Sunday" in November 1887, when a revolutionary march, organized by the SDF and addressed among others by Shaw – who called the outcome an "abjectly disgraceful defeat" – was violently crushed by police and troops around Trafalgar Square.

The Fabian political position also has a direct relationship to his drama, since *The Quintessence of Ibsenism*, which in many ways forms a manifesto for his own plays, originated in a lecture Shaw presented to the Fabian Society (1890). This lecture used Ibsen's naturalistic plays as a tool for attacking the "idealist Socialism" of the Marxists, particularly the Social Democratic Federation and the Socialist League; and in a passage omitted from the published version Shaw argued:

> With Ibsen's thesis in one's mind, it is impossible to think without concern of the appalling adaptability of Socialism to idealistic purposes . . . members whose entire devotion to the ideal of Socialism enables them to enlist under the red flag as revolutionary socialists without meaning anything whatever by the word. I know that many of my colleagues believe that we shall never enlist enthusiasm for our cause unless we, like the gentlemen in *Pillars of Society*, hold up the banner of the ideal. Socialism means practically the nationaliza-tion of land and capital, and nothing else. Yet we are told by our own members that we lay too much stress on the economic side of socialism . . . The idealist Socialist always rebels against a reduction of Socialism to practice.

This "practical" approach, combined with the conviction that socialist reform is inevitable and as an evolutionary process requires gradual and orderly develop-ment, is well illustrated by *Fabian Essays in Socialism*, edited by Shaw.

6.1.1 Sidney Webb, Annie Besant: Fabian Socialism

Fabian Essays in Socialism, 1889

The Historic Basis of Socialism: Sidney Webb

[W]e must take even more care to improve the social organism of which we form part, than to perfect our own individual developments. Or rather, the perfect and fitting development of each individual is not necessarily the utmost and highest cultivation of his own personality, but the filling, in the best possible way, of his humble function in the great social machine. We must abandon the self-conceit of imagining that we are independent units, and bend our jealous minds, absorbed in their own cultivation, to this subjection to the higher end, the Common Weal. Accordingly, conscious "direct adaptation" steadily supplants the unconscious and wasteful "indirect adaptation" of the earlier form of the struggle for existence and with every advance in sociological knowledge, Man is seen to assume more and more, not only the mastery of "things", but also a conscious control over social destiny itself.

This new scientific conception of the Social Organism has put completely out of countenance the cherished principles of the Political Economist and the Philosophic Radical. We left them sailing gaily into Anarchy on the stream of *Laisser Faire*. Since then the tide has turned. The publication of John Stuart Mill's "Political Economy" in 1848 marks conveniently the boundary of the old individualist Economics. Every edition of Mill's book became more and more Socialistic. After his death the world learnt the personal history, penned by his own hand,[1] of his development from a mere political democrat to a convinced Socialist.

The change in tone since then has been such that one competent economist, professedly anti-Socialist,[2] publishes regretfully to the world that all the younger men are now Socialists, as well as many of the older Professors. It is, indeed, mainly from these that the world has learnt how faulty were the earlier economic generalizations, and above all, how incomplete as guides for social or political action. These generalizations are accordingly now to be met with only in leading articles, sermons, or the speeches of Ministers or Bishops.[3] The Economist himself knows them no more.

The result of this development of Sociology is to compel a revision of the relative importance of liberty and equality as principles to be kept in view in social administration. In Bentham's celebrated "ends" to be aimed at in a

"Autobiography", pp. 231–2.
Rev. F. W. Aveling, Principal of Taunton Independent College, in leaflet "Down with the Socialists", August. 1888. See also Professor H. Sidgwick on "Economic Socialism" *Contemporary Review*, November, 1886.
That is to say, unfortunately, in nearly all the utterances which profess to guide our social and political action.

civil code, liberty stands predominant over equality, on the ground that full equality can be maintained only by the loss of security for the fruits of labor. That exposition remains as true as ever; but the question for decision remains, how much liberty? Economic analysis has destroyed the value of the old criterion of respect for the equal liberty of others. Bentham, whose economics were weak, paid no attention to the perpetual tribute on the fruits of others' labor which full private property in land inevitably creates. In his view liberty and security to property meant that every worker should be free to obtain the full result of his own labor; and there appeared no inconsistency between them. The political economist now knows that with free competition and private property in land and capital, no individual can possibly obtain the full result of his own labor. The student of industrial development, moreover, finds it steadily more and more impossible to trace what is precisely the result of each separate man's toil. [. . .] For he cannot escape the lesson of the century, taught alike by the economists, the statesmen, and the "practical men", that complete individual liberty, with unrestrained private ownership of the instruments of wealth production, is irreconcileable with the common weal. The free struggle for existence among ourselves menaces our survival as a healthy and permanent social organism. Evolution, Professor Huxley declares, is the substitution of consciously regulated co-ordination among the units of each organism, for blind anarchic competition. Thirty years ago Herbert Spencer demonstrated the incompatibility of full private property in land with the modern democratic State; and almost every economist now preaches the same doctrine. The Radical is rapidly arriving, from practical experience, at similar conclusions; and the steady increase of the government regulation of private enterprise, the growth of municipal administration, and the rapid shifting of the burden of taxation directly to rent and interest, mark in treble lines the statesman's unconscious abandonment of the old Individualism, and our irresistible glide into collectivist Socialism.

The Transition to Social Democracy: Annie Besant

The benefits of such a change as this are so obvious to all except the existing private proprietors and their parasites, that it is very necessary to insist on the impossibility of effecting it suddenly. The young Socialist is apt to be catastrophic in his views – to plan the revolutionary programme as an affair of twenty-four lively hours, with Individualism in full swing on Monday morning, a tidal wave of the insurgent proletariat on Monday afternoon, and Socialism in complete working order on Tuesday. A man who believes that such a happy despatch is possible, will naturally think it absurd and even inhuman to stick at bloodshed in bringing it about. He can prove that the continuance of the present system for a year costs more suffering than could be crammed into any Monday afternoon, however sanguinary. This is the phase of conviction in which are delivered those Socialist speeches which make what the newspapers call "good copy", and which are the only ones they as yet report. Such speeches are encouraged by the hasty opposition they evoke from thoughtless persons, who begin by tacitly admitting that a sudden change is feasible, and go on to protest that it would be wicked. The experienced Social Democrat converts his too ardent follower by first admitting that if the change could be made catastrophically it would be well worth making, and then proceeding to point out that as it would involve a readjustment of productive industry to meet the demand created by an entirely new distribution of purchasing power, it would also involve, in the application of labor and industrial machinery, alterations which no afternoon's work could effect. You cannot convince any man that it is impossible to tear down a government in a day; but everybody is convinced already that you cannot convert first and third class carriages into second class; rookeries and palaces into comfortable dwellings; and jewellers and dressmakers into bakers and builders, by merely singing the "Marseillaise". [. . .] Demolishing a Bastille with seven prisoners in it is one thing: demolishing one with fourteen million prisoners is quite another. I need not enlarge on the point: the necessity for cautious and gradual change must be obvious to everyone here, and could be made obvious to everyone elsewhere if only the catastrophists were courageously and sensibly dealt with in discussion.

What then does a gradual transition to Social Democracy mean specifically. It means the gradual extension of the franchise; and the transfer of rent and interest to the State, not in one lump sum, but by instalments. Looked at in this way, it will at once be seen that we are already far on the road, and are being urged further by many politicians who do not dream that they are touched with Socialism – nay, who would earnestly repudiate the touch as a taint. Let us see how far we have gone. In 1832 the political power passed into the hands of the middle class; and in 1838 Lord John Russell announced finality. Meanwhile, in 1834, the middle class had swept away the last economic refuge of the workers, the old Poor Law, and delivered them naked to the furies of competition.[4] Ten years turmoil and active emigration followed; and then the thin end of the wedge went in. The Income Tax was established; and the Factory Acts were made effective. The Income Tax (1842), which is on individualist principles an intolerable spoliative anomaly, is simply a forcible transfer of rent, interest, and even rent of ability, from private holders to the State without compensation. It excused itself to the Whigs on the ground that those who had most property for the State to protect should pay *ad valorem* for its protection. The Factory Acts swept the anarchic theory of the irresponsibility of private enterprise

The general impression that the old Poor Law had become an indefensible nuisance is a correct one. All attempts to mitigate Individualism by philanthropy instead of replacing it by Socialism are foredoomed to confusion.

out of practical politics; made employers accountable to the State for the well-being of their employees; and transferred a further instalment of profits directly to the worker by raising wages. Then came the gold discoveries in California (1847) and Australia (1851), and the period of leaps and bounds, supported by the economic rent of England's mineral fertility, which kindled Mr. Gladstone's retrogressive instincts to a vain hope of abolishing the Income Tax. These events relieved the pressure set up by the New Poor Law. The workers rapidly organized themselves in Trades Unions, which were denounced then for their tendency to sap the manly independence which had formerly characterized the British workman,[5] and which are to-day held up to him as the self-helpful perfection of that manly independence. Howbeit, self-help flourished, especially at Manchester and Sheffield; State help was voted grandmotherly; wages went up; and the Unions, like the fly on the wheel, thought that they had raised them. They were mistaken; but the value of Trade Unionism in awakening the social conscience of the skilled workers was immense, though to this there was a heavy set-off in its tendency to destroy their artistic conscience by making them aware that it was their duty to one another to discourage rapid and efficient workmanship by every means in their power. An extension of the Franchise, which was really an instalment of Democracy, and not, like the 1832 Reform Bill, only an advance towards it was gained in 1867; and immediately afterwards came another instalment of Socialism in the shape of a further transfer of rent and interest from private holders to the State for the purpose of educating the people. In the meantime, the extraordinary success of the post office, which, according to the teaching of the Manchester school, should have been a nest of incompetence and jobbery, had not only shewn the perfect efficiency of State enterprise when the officials are made responsible to the class interested in its success, but had also proved the enormous convenience and cheapness of socialistic or collectivist charges over those of private enterprise. For example, the Postmaster General charges a penny for sending a letter weighing an ounce from Kensington to Bayswater. Private enterprise would send half a pound the same distance for a farthing, and make a handsome profit on it. But the Postmaster General also sends an ounce letter from Land's End to John O' Groat's House for a penny. Private enterprise would probably demand at least a shilling, if not five, for such a service; and there are many places in which private enterprise could not on any terms maintain a post office. Therefore a citizen with ten letters to post saves considerably by the uniform socialistic charge, and quite recognizes the necessity for rigidly protecting the Postmaster's monopoly.

[. . .]

See Final Report of Royal Commission on Trade Unions, 1869. Vol. 1., p. xvii., sec, 46.

This, then, is the humdrum programme of the practical Social Democrat to-day. There is not one new item in it. All are applications of principles already admitted, and extensions of practices already in full activity. All have on them that stamp of the vestry which is so congenial to the British mind. None of them compel the use of the words Socialism or Revolution: at no point do they involve guillotining, declaring the Rights of Man, swearing on the altar of the country, or anything else that is supposed to be essentially un-English. And they are all sure to come – landmarks on our course already visible to far-sighted politicians even of the party which dreads them.

Let me, in conclusion, disavow all admiration for this inevitable, but sordid, slow, reluctant, cowardly path to justice. I venture to claim your respect for those enthusiasts who still refuse to believe that millions of their fellow creatures must be left to sweat and suffer in hopeless toil and degradation, while parliaments and vestries grudgingly muddle and grope towards paltry instalments of betterment. The right is so clear, the wrong so intolerable, the gospel so convincing, that it seems to them that it *must* be possible to enlist the whole body of workers – soldiers, policemen, and all – under the banner of brotherhood and equality; and at one great stroke to set Justice on her rightful throne. Unfortunately, such an army of light is no more to be gathered from the human product of nineteenth century civilization than grapes are to be gathered from thistles. But if we feel glad of that impossibility; if we feel relieved that the change is to be slow enough to avert personal risk to ourselves; if we feel anything less than acute disappointment and bitter humiliation at the discovery that there is yet between us and the promised land a wilderness in which many must perish miserably of want and despair: then I submit to you that our institutions have corrupted us to the most dastardly degree of selfishness. The Socialists need not be ashamed of beginning as they did by proposing militant organization of the working classes and general insurrection. The proposal proved impracticable; and it has now been abandoned – not without some outspoken regrets – by English Socialists. But it still remains as the only finally possible alternative to the Social Democratic programme . . . .

*

Shaw's more than twenty plays written between 1885 and 1920 cover a wide variety of topics. In addition to rack renting (*Widowers' Houses*), these include eugenics and his idiosyncratic concept of evolution (*Man and Superman*), colonialism (*John Bull's Other Island*), religion and arms-manufacture (*Major Barbara*), and medical ethics (*The Doctor's Dilemma*). However, the most consistent issue, which is also subsumed in plays where the major focus is on a different subject, relates to the position and status of women. The figure of the "New Woman" recurs in several plays, particularly *The Philanderer* (1893), *Man and Superman* (1903), *Misalliance* (1910) – while part of *The Quintessence of Ibsenism* is an attack on the "Womanly

Woman", the conventional ideal of feminine behavior "that a vocation for domestic management and the care of children is natural to women":

> If we have come to think that the nursery and the kitchen are the natural sphere of a woman, we have done so exactly as English children come to think that a cage is the natural sphere of a parrot – because they have never seen one anywhere else. No doubt there are Philistine parrots who agree with their owners that it is better to be in a cage than out, so long as there is plenty of hempseed and indian corn there. There may even be idealist parrots who persuade themselves that the mission of a parrot is to minister to the happiness of a private family by whistling and saying "Pretty Polly," and that it is in the sacrifice of its liberty to this altruistic pursuit that a true parrot finds the supreme satisfaction of its soul . . . Still, the only parrot a free-souled person can sympathize with is the one that insists on its being let out as the first condition of making itself agreeable . . .
>
> The sum of the matter is that unless Woman repudiates her womanliness, her duty to her husband, to her children, to society, to the law and to everyone but herself, she cannot emancipate herself.

Candida (1894) is a conscious variation on *A Doll's House*; *Getting Married* is a "disquisition" on laws governing marriage. But the point where the case against patriarchy and the battle for women's rights finds its sharpest form is in prostitution, the major theme of *Mrs Warren's Profession*.

Prostitution had been a recurrent issue of public concern in England during the latter part of the nineteenth century; and in the 1880s legislation, which previously had largely been concerned with control of communicable disease, was passed summarily banning brothels and criminalizing both prostitutes and their male customers. The catalyst for this triumph of moral puritanism was a campaign by the Quaker activist Alfred Dyer, who began investigating "white slavery" in Brussels in 1879. As publisher of a newspaper, *The Sentinel*, he was able to broadcast his findings. He also issued a pamphlet on "the foreign slave traffic in English girls" that focussed on "the system of slavery, which this traffic exists to supply with victims" (*The European Slave Trade in English Girls*, 1880), and was one of the principal signatories to a memorial presented to the Foreign Secretary in August 1880.

As a direct result, a Select Committee of Parliament was set up "to inquire into the state of the law relative to the protection of young girls". The scale of the problem in Britain, and the perceived need for legal regulation are well illustrated by the evidence given to this Committee by Howard Vincent, Director of the Criminal Investigation Department for the Metropolitan Police. The outcome of the inquiry was a series of provisions culminating in The Criminal Law Amendment Act of 1885, "An Act to make further provision for the protection of women and girls, the suppression of brothels, and other purposes" that set the tone of repressive morality, for which Victorian society became known. A

"National Vigilance Association of men and women for the enforcement and improvement of the laws for the repression of vice and public immorality" was founded, bringing together the Society for the Suppression of Vice, the Minors' Protection Society, the Belgian Traffic Committee and the Central Vigilance Society. This organization attracted a huge demonstration in Hyde Park of between 100,000 and a quarter million people in August 1885, and set up local volunteer Vigilance Associations with the aim of initiating prosecutions for

(1) the corruption and prostitution of girls under sixteen; (2) the abduction of girls under eighteen; (3) the procuration of the seduction of girls under twenty-one; (4) the fraudulent seduction of women of any age; (5) the entrapping or enveigling of girls or women into brothels; (6) the procuring of women for foreign brothels; and (7) the detention of women in houses of ill-fame.

(*The Sentinel*, February 1886)

Further legislation was passed over the remaining years of Queen Victoria's reign, such as the 1898 Act to Amend the Vagrancy Act, specifically aimed at male pimps.

Prostitution continued of course, and with an average of 1,200 prosecutions of "bawdy houses" a year between 1885 and 1914 – as against an average of 86 before the Act – prostitutes were driven into the streets of slums like Whitechapel (where they became the prey of the Jack the Ripper murders in 1888). The attitude of proponents of women's rights to this moral reform was ambiguous. However, the connection between prostitution and slavery was not missed by the suffragette movement, who adopted it as an emblem of women's subjugation to men. Its extension and parallel to women's status in marriage has become a cliché of contemporary feminism – as Germaine Greer put it in the programme essay for a modern revival of *Mrs Warren's Profession*, "Marriage itself is legalized prostitution, for legitimate sex is as frequently deployed for advantage as any other sort. The wife who is trained as laboriously as any Geisha in the arts of keeping her husband, and keeping him contented and successful, is a sanctified whore" ("A Whore in Every Home" National Theatre, 1985). But the same point was already being made by the American political activist, Emma Goldman, in 1917. Her pamphlet, *The Traffic in Women*, also makes the connection between prostitution and Capitalism, and cites Shaw's play as support for her argument.

6.1.2 The European Slave Trade in English girls – Memorial to the Foreign Secretary, 1880

Alfred S. Dyer and others

The following Memorial (with Declarations in corroboration) has been laid before Earl Granville by the London Committee [. . .],

197

To the Right Honourable the Earl Granville, KG, Her Majesty's
Principal Secretary of State for Foreign Affairs.

The memorial of the undersigned members of a Committee, formed in
London for the purpose of exposing and suppressing the existing traffic in
English, Scotch, and Irish Girls, for the Purpose of Foreign Prostitution,

Respectfully sheweth:

That there exists a system of systematic abduction, to Brussels and elsewhere on the Continent, of girls who are British subjects, for purposes of
prostitution, and that the girls so abducted, being sold to the keepers of
licensed houses of infamy, are generally confined and detained against their
will in such houses.

Many of the girls so abducted are induced by men of respectable exterior
to go abroad under promise of marriage or of obtaining employment or
situations; and, on arrival there are taken to the office of the *Police des Moeurs*
[Vice Police] for registration as prostitutes.

In most cases, the girls know nothing of the language or customs of the
country, and are entirely ignorant of the system of registration of prostitutes which exists on the Continent, and of what is being transacted at the
office aforesaid; and, before being taken there, they are often made to
believe that the place is the Custom House, and that they are going there to
comply with formalities required from travellers who arrive there from
another country, and they are generally registered for reasons that are here-
inafter stated, in false names.

According to the letter of the Belgian law, a woman may not be registered
as a prostitute under the age of twenty-one years, but this legal rule is easily
and most frequently evaded, for the purpose of securing young victims, by
the following means: Any certificate of birth can be obtained in England, by
any person whomsoever, on payment of a few shillings. The abductor, therefore, produces a true certificate of the birth of some female who has
attained twenty-one years, and presents such certificate to the *Police des
Moeurs* as that of the girl's who is under age, and whom he wishes to
register [. . .]

After a girl has been registered (with or without her knowledge or consent),
and immured in a licensed house of prostitution, it is, in most cases, impossible for her to regain her freedom [. . .] The houses are constructed so as to
prevent egress without the concurrence of the keepers thereof. Terrorism is
also exercised over these girls, if any wish or attempt to escape is manifest;
they are subjected to violence, and are intimidated by threats of the
imprisonment to which they have become liable through being registered in a
false name. They are also invariably kept in debt to the keepers of the toler-
ated houses, and these persons frequently sell the miserable girls from one
house to another, that traces of them may be lost or rendered difficult [. . .]

A female British subject, who has been entrapped into, and is kept
against her will in a *maison tolerée* in Brussels, is seldom allowed to go out of

the house – never unless accompanied by a person in charge; and it has been found almost impossible for friends desiring to assist her, to obtain any help, either from the Belgian Police or the English Diplomatic or Consular authorities. Her condition is that of a slave to the lust of all who will pay the brothel-keeper's charge for permission to violate and outrage her, until disease renders her unprofitable, or death shall afford release.

Your Memorialists have made themselves acquainted with the cases of English, Scotch and Irish girls who have been decoyed into or detained in this horrible slavery; and some of your Memorialists have personally visited Brussels for that purpose, and have failed in releasing others [. . .]

Your Memorialists submit to your Lordship that such changes ought to be made in the English and Belgian law as shall make it impossible for any woman, who is a subject of Her Majesty the Queen to be deprived of her liberty by fraud or force, and to be kept in that country, in bondage for the vilest of purposes [. . .]

6.1.3 Child Prostitution in London

Minutes of "Select Committee to inquire into the state of the law relative to the protection of young girls," evidence of Howard Vincent, Director of Criminal Investigation Department, Metropolitan Police, 1881

There are houses in London, in many parts of London, where there are people who will procure children for the purposes of immorality and prostitution, without any difficulty whatsoever above the age of 13, children without number at 14, 15 and 16 years of age. Superintendent Dunlap will tell you that juvenile prostitution is rampant at this moment, and that in the streets about the Haymarket, Waterloo Place, and Piccadilly, from nightfall there are children of 14, 15 and 16 years of age, going about openly soliciting prostitution [. . .] this prostitution actually takes place with the knowledge and connivance of the mother and to the profit of the household. I am speaking of some facts within my own knowledge, from hearsay, of course, but I have no reason whatever to doubt them. These procuresses [. . .] have an understanding with the mother of the girl that she shall come to that house at a certain hour, and the mother perfectly well knows for what purpose she goes there, and it is with her knowledge and connivance, and with her consent that the girl goes [. . .]

591. (Chairman) Do you know whether the police are able to trace these children as they get older, and to know what becomes of them?

I am afraid not. The police are absolutely powerless as regards prostitution in London.

592. With regard to children of this age, or any age, who are soliciting prostitution in the streets, have the police no power at all?

No power whatever.

593. (Lord Aberdare.) Only to keep order?

Only to keep order; and the consequence is that the state of affairs which exists in this capital is such that from four o'clock, or one may say from three o'clock in the afternoon, it is impossible for any respectable woman to walk from the top of the Haymarket to Wellington Street, Strand. From three or four o'clock in the afternoon, Villiers Street and Charing Cross Station, and the Strand, are crowded with prostitutes, who are there openly soliciting prostitution in broad daylight. At half past twelve at night, a calculation was made a short time ago that there was 500 prostitutes between Piccadilly Circus and the bottom of Waterloo-place.

6.1.4 Emma Goldman, *The Traffic in Women*, 1917

What is really the cause of trade in women? Not merely white women, but yellow and black women as well. Exploitation, of course; the merciless Moloch of capitalism that fattens on underpaid labor, thus driving thousands of women and girls into prostitution. With Mrs. Warren these girls feel, "Why waste your life working for a few shillings a week in a scullery, eighteen hours a day?"

Naturally our reformers say nothing about this cause. They know it well enough, but it doesn't pay to say anything about it. It is much more profitable to play the Pharisee, to pretend an outraged morality, than to go to the bottom of things.

However, there is one commendable exception among the young writers: Reginald Wright Kauffman, whose work *The House of Bondage* is the first earnest attempt to treat the social evil – not from a sentimental Philistine viewpoint. A journalist of wide experience, Mr. Kauffman proves that our industrial system leaves most women no alternative except prostitution. The women portrayed in *The House of Bondage* belong to the working class. Had the author portrayed the life of women in other spheres, he would have been confronted with the same state of affairs.

Nowhere is woman treated according to the merit of her work, but rather as a sex. It is therefore almost inevitable that she should pay for her right to exist, to keep a position in whatever line, with sex favors. Thus it is merely a question of degree whether she sells herself to one man, in or out of marriage, or to many men. Whether our reformers admit it or not, the economic and social inferiority of woman is responsible for prostitution.

Just at present our good people are shocked by the disclosures that in New York City alone one out of every ten women works in a factory, that the average wage received by women is six dollars per week for forty-eight to sixty hours of work, and that the majority of female wage workers face many months of idleness which leaves the average wage about $280 a year.

In view of these economic horrors, is it to be wondered at that prostitution and the white slave trade have become such dominant factors?

[. . .]

Dr. Alfred Blaschko, in *Prostitution in the Nineteenth Century*, is even more emphatic in characterizing economic conditions as one of the most vital factors of prostitution.

"Although prostitution has existed in all ages, it was left to the nineteenth century to develop it into a gigantic social institution. The development of industry with vast masses of people in the competitive market, the growth and congestion of large cities, the insecurity and uncertainty of employment, has given prostitution an impetus never dreamed of at any period in human history."

And again Havelock Ellis, while not so absolute in dealing with the economic cause, is nevertheless compelled to admit that it is indirectly and directly the main cause. Thus he finds that a large percentage of prostitutes is recruited from the servant class, although the latter have less care and greater security. On the other hand, Mr. Ellis does not deny that the daily routine, the drudgery, the monotony of the servant girl's lot, and especially the fact that she may never partake of the companionship and joy of a home, is no mean factor in forcing her to seek recreation and forgetfulness in the gaiety and glimmer of prostitution. In other words, the servant girl, being treated as a drudge, never having the right to herself, and worn out by the caprices of her mistress, can find an outlet, like the factory or shopgirl, only in prostitution.

[. . .]

It would be one-sided and extremely superficial to maintain that the economic factor is the only cause of prostitution. There are others no less important and vital. That, too, our reformers know, but dare discuss even less than the institution that saps the very life out of both men and women. I refer to the sex question, the very mention of which causes most people moral spasms.

It is a conceded fact that woman is being reared as a sex commodity, and yet she is kept in absolute ignorance of the meaning and importance of sex. Everything dealing with that subject is suppressed, and persons who attempt to bring light into this terrible darkness are persecuted and thrown into prison. Yet it is nevertheless true that so long as a girl is not to know how to take care of herself, not to know the function of the most important part of her life, we need not be surprised if she becomes an easy prey to prostitution, or to any other form of a relationship which degrades her to the position of an object for mere sex gratification.

It is due to this ignorance that the entire life and nature of the girl is thwarted and crippled. We have long ago taken it as a self-evident fact that the boy may follow the call of the wild; that is to say, that the boy may, as soon as his sex nature asserts itself, satisfy that nature; but our moralists are scandalized at the very thought that the nature of a girl should assert itself. To the moralist prostitution does not consist so much in the fact that the woman sells her body, but rather that she sells it out of wedlock. That this is no mere statement is proved by the fact that marriage for monetary considerations is perfectly legitimate, sanctified by law and public opinion, while any other union is condemned and repudiated. Yet a prostitute, if properly defined, means nothing else than "any person for whom sexual relationships are subordinated to gain."

[. . .]

"The wife who married for money, compared with the prostitute," says Havelock Ellis, "is the true scab. She is paid less, gives much more in return in labor and care, and is absolutely bound to her master. The prostitute never signs away the right over her own person, she retains her freedom and personal rights, nor is she always compelled to submit to man's embrace."

Nor does the better-than-thou woman realize the apologist claim of Lecky that "though she may be the supreme type of vice, she is also the most efficient guardian of virtue. But for her, happy homes would be polluted, unnatural and harmful practice would abound."

Moralists are ever ready to sacrifice one-half of the human race for the sake of some miserable institution which they cannot outgrow. As a matter of fact, prostitution is no more a safeguard for the purity of the home than rigid laws are a safeguard against prostitution. Fully fifty per cent of married men are patrons of brothels. It is through this virtuous element that the married women – nay, even the children – are infected with venereal diseases. Yet society has not a word of condemnation for the man, while no law is too monstrous to be set in motion against the helpless victim. She is not only preyed upon by those who use her, but she is also absolutely at the mercy of every policeman and miserable detective on the beat, the officials at the station house, the authorities in every prison.

*

Although Ibsen had observed both the European revolutions of 1848 and at rather closer hand (during his exile in Germany) the Franco-Prussian war, while Chekhov presaged the Russian Revolution in his plays, only Shaw experienced a major conflict. The death toll and devastation of the First World War in 1914–18 was more extreme than anything that had come before, although the American Civil War had provided a foretaste of the bloodshed that modern weapons could produce. The social structure of European nations was destabilized, with revolutions followed by civil war in Germany as well as Russia, while even the victors were demoralized. The First World War became a watershed in Shaw's writing, marking the end of his commitment to Naturalism. However, as a citizen of the dominant imperial power Shaw lived in a nation almost continuously at war, and as an Irishman he was acutely aware of military colonialism.

Even before the First World War, Shaw had already commented obliquely on warfare and militarism in various plays. Most of these – *Arms and the Man* (1894), *The Man of Destiny* (1895), *The Devil's Disciple* (1896) – focus on the popular vision of war promoted by nineteenth-century military melodramas, as being the most egregious example of the "policy of forcing individuals to act upon the assumption that all ideals are real, and to recognize and accept such action as standard moral conduct, absolutely valid under all circumstances, contrary conduct or any advocacy of it being discountenanced and punished as immoral . . ." (*The Quintessence of Ibsenism*, 1891). He had also already written widely on the subject in the press, his fundamental position being that all war is "an orgy of crime based on the determination of the soldier to stick at nothing to bring it to an end and get out of the daily danger of being shot" (*The Humane Review*, January 1901). Between 1899 and 1902, in direct response to the Boer war, Shaw drafted *Fabianism and the Empire* (a manifesto for the general election of 1900), wrote a number of major essays for periodicals as well as many public letters to newspapers, and delivered several major lectures. In these he proposed a trade union for rank and file soldiers, with full civil rights and pensions, pointed out that there was nothing to choose between the two sides – "the piety of the Boer and the pugnacity of the Briton lead equally to the battlefield" (*The Clarion*, 26 May 1900) – and attacked jingoistic militarism. In the decade before the First World War Shaw published several essays on disarmament, arguing for an international agreement to outlaw war by force, under which any aggressor nation would be immediately attacked by all other states. And following the Russo-Japanese war, in *Major Barbara* (1905) he defended armament manufacture – and the international arms trade – as promoting class equality and Socialism.

Unlike almost all other naturalistic playwrights, Shaw intervened publicly in political debate. It is therefore logical to present some of his own writings as a primary context for his drama. All the main points made in his previous essays were summed up in his pamphlet "Common Sense About the War" published as a supplement to the *New Statesman* on November 14, 1914. However, in the context of national emergency and patriotic fervor, these arguments now aroused intense passions and controversy. The only comparable piece from a naturalistic writer is Emile Zola's pamphlet on the Dreyfus affair, *J'Accuse!* (1898). Shaw was vilified in the British press, although his ideas influenced President Wilson and eventually contributed to the founding of the League of Nations (the precursor to the UN). The extract selected deals with Shaw's analysis of the causes of the war, and gives a sense of the rhetoric – implying that the British were intellectually lazy, blinded by prejudice, blundering, and militaristic – that caused his unpopularity.

After the war, compelled to justify his position, Shaw republished the essay, with commentary, as *What I Really Wrote About the War* (1931). This emphasizes one of the themes in "Common Sense About the War" encapsulated in the image of "an engagement between two pirate fleets . . . All the ensigns were Jolly Rogers; but mine was clearly the one with the Union Jack at the corner" – and he went on to claim "that there are only two real flags in the world henceforth: the red flag of Democratic Socialism and the black flag of Capitalism, the flag of God and the flag of Mammon". Despite this polemic proclamation of the eventual triumph of International Socialism, Shaw's estimate of the effect of the war in the preface to *Heartbreak House* is more modest. Reverting to his theme of idealistic illusions, he outlines two opportunities:

> first, by the fact that many of us have been torn from the fool's paradise in which the theatre formerly traded, and thrust upon the sternest realities and necessities until we have lost faith in and patience with the theatrical pretenses that had not root either in reality or necessity; second, by the startling change made by the war in the distribution of income.

His attitude after the defeat of Germany and the personal cost of the war are illustrated by a letter Shaw wrote to the German translator of his plays, Siegfried Trebitsch, in 1920, the years after he finished *Heartbreak House*.

6.1.5 Bernard Shaw, "The Causes of the First World War"

Commonsense About the War, 1914

We must get rid of the monstrous situation that produced the present war. France made an alliance with Russia as a defence against Germany. Germany made an alliance with Austria as a defence against Russia. England joined the Franco-Russian alliance as a defence against Germany and Austria. The result was that Germany became involved in a quarrel between Austria and Russia. Having no quarrel with France, and only a second-hand quarrel with Russia, she was, nevertheless, forced to attack France in order to disable her before she could strike Germany from behind when Germany was fighting France's ally, Russia. And this attack on France forced England to come to the rescue of England's ally, France. Not one of the three nations (as distinguished from their tiny Junker–Militarist cliques) wanted to fight; for England had nothing to gain and Germany had everything to lose; whilst France had given up hope of her Alsace-Lorraine *revanche*, and would certainly not have hazarded a war for it. Yet because Russia, who has a great deal to gain by victory and nothing except military prestige to lose by defeat, had a quarrel with Austria over Servia, she has been able to set all three western friends and neighbors shedding "rivers of blood" from one another's throats: an outrageous absurdity.

[. . .]

The evidence of how the Junker diplomatists of our Foreign Office let us in for the war is in the White Paper, Miscellaneous No. 6 (1914), containing correspondence respecting the European crisis, and since reissued, with a later White Paper and some extra matter, as a penny bluebook in miniature. In these much-cited and little-read documents we see the Junkers of all the nations, the men who have been saying for years "It's bound to come," and clamoring in England for compulsory military service and expeditionary forces, momentarily staggered and not a little frightened by the sudden realization that it has come at last. They rush round from foreign office to embassy, and from embassy to palace, twittering "This is awful. Cant you stop it? Wont you be reasonable? Think of the consequences," etc., etc. One man among them keeps his head and looks the facts in the face. That man is Sazonoff, the Russian Secretary for Foreign Affairs. He keeps steadily trying to make Sir Edward Grey face the inevitable. He says and reiterates, in effect, "You know very well that you cannot keep out of a European war. You know you are pledged to fight Germany if Germany attacks France. You know that your arrangements for the fight are actually made; that already the British army is commanded by a Franco-British Council of War; that there is no possible honorable retreat for you. You know that this old man in Austria, who would have been superannuated years ago if he had been an exciseman, is resolved to make war on Servia, and sent that silly forty-eight hours ultimatum when we were all out of town so that he could begin fighting before we could get back to sit on his head. You know that he has the Jingo mob of Vienna behind him. You know that if he makes war, Russia must mobilize. You know that France is bound to come in with us as you are with France. You know that the moment we mobilize, Germany, the old man's ally, will have only one desperate chance of victory, and that is to overwhelm our ally, France, with one superb rush of her millions, and then sweep back and meet us on the Vistula. You know that nothing can stop this except Germany remonstrating with Austria, and insisting on the Servian case being dealt with by an international tribunal and not by war. You know that Germany dares not do this, because her alliance with Austria is her defence against the Franco-Russian alliance, and that she does not want to do it in any case, because the Kaiser naturally has a strong class prejudice against the blowing up of Royal personages by irresponsible revolutionists, and thinks nothing too bad for Servia after the assassination of the Archduke. There is just one chance of avoiding Armageddon: a slender one, but worth trying. You averted war in the Algeciras crisis, and again in the Agadir crisis, by saying you would fight. Try it again. The Kaiser is stiffnecked because he does not believe you are going to fight this time. Well, convince him that you are. The odds against him will then be so terrible that he may not dare to support the Austrian ultimatum to Servia at such a price. And if Austria is thus forced to proceed judicially against Servia, we Russians will be satisfied; and there will be no war."

Sir Edward could not see it. [. . .] Instead, he persuaded us all that he was under no obligation whatever to fight. He persuaded Germany that he had not the slightest serious intention of fighting. Sir Owen Seaman wrote in *Punch* an amusing and witty No-Intervention poem. Sporting Liberals offered any odds that there would be no war for England. And Germany, confident that with Austria's help she could break France with one hand and Russia with the other if England held aloof, let Austria throw the match into the magazine.

[. . .]

Nobody cared twopence about treaties: indeed, it was not for us, who had seen the treaty of Berlin torn up by the brazen seizure of Bosnia and Herzegovina by Austria in 1909, and taken that lying down, as Russia did, to talk about the sacredness of treaties, even if the waste-paper baskets of the Foreign Offices were not full of torn up "scraps of paper" [. . .] The man in the street understood little or nothing about Servia or Russia or any of the cards with which the diplomatists were playing their perpetual game of Beggar my Neighbor. We were rasped beyond endurance by Prussian Militarism and its contempt for us and for human happiness and common sense; and we just rose at it and went for it. We have set out to smash the Kaiser exactly as we set out to smash the Mahdi. Mr Wells never mentioned a treaty. He said, in effect "There stands the monster all freedom-loving men hate; and at last we are going to fight it." And the public, bored by the diplomatists, said: "Now you're talking!"

[. . .]

[L]et us have no more nonsense about the Prussian Wolf and the British Lamb, the Prussian Machiavelli and the English Evangelist. We cannot shout for years that we are boys of the bulldog breed, and then suddenly pose as gazelles. No. When Europe and America come to settle the treaty that will end this business (for America is concerned in it as much as we are) they will not deal with us as the lovable and innocent victims of a treacherous tyrant and a savage soldiery. They will have to consider how these two incorrigibly pugnacious and inveterately snobbish peoples, who have snarled at one another for forty years with bristling hair and grinning fangs, and are now rolling over with their teeth in one another's throats, are to be tamed into trusty watchdogs of the peace of the world. I am sorry to spoil the saintly image with a halo which the British Jingo journalist sees just now when he looks in the glass; but it must be done if we are to behave reasonably in the imminent day of reckoning.

6.1.6 Bernard Shaw, Letter to Siegfried Trebitsch

15 September 1920

Haus Herzenstock should be Haus Herzzereissen. Heartbreak is a chronic complaint, not a sudden shock. But I doubt whether there exists any German equivalent for heartbreak. A disappointment in love is called a broken heart. Carlyle said that Free Trade was "heartbreaking nonsense"; and there are lots of gradations between these extremes; but usually the word implies deep pathos in the affliction it describes [. . .]

Concerning my sister . . . what killed her was the war: her tuberculosis had stopped. But there was an aircraft gun quite close to her house on the southern heights, and during the air raids this gun shook and shattered everything near it. All the other guns were going too, varied by the crash of the bombs. I don't know whether you had this experience in Vienna; but London had a great deal of it; and it was very unpleasant, and got worse as it went on. At first people were excited and curious; but when that passed, and they saw what the bombs could do to them, there was nothing but sheer funk. I was not a bit frightened at Ypres or Arras; but in London, though I was too lazy to get out of bed and take refuge in an underground shelter, and dropped off to sleep between each burst of firing, my heart tightened in the most disagreeable manner in spite of all arguments as to the uselessness of bothering about it. Well, Lucy had to leave London; but it was too late: she could not eat and died of slow starvation. And – here is a dramatic contrast which I exploited in the funeral oration – whilst the German aces were doing their best to kill her she was kept alive by the devotion of her German nurse.

2 SHAW'S NATURALISTIC DRAMA

Shaw's dramatic output was eclectic from the first. It included a number of plays inverting or parodying theatrical stereotypes – such as military melodrama (*Arms and the Man*), romantic melodrama (*The Devil's Disciple*) and historical romance (*Caesar and Cleopatra*) – which retained elements of the conventional forms they targeted. A long dream sequence forms the centre of *Man and Superman*. Even some of his plays reflecting contemporary English life verged on farce, such as *The Philanderer; A Topical Comedy of the Early Eighteen-Nineties* (1898). But his first play, *Widowers' Houses*, was clearly recognized as naturalistic when it was performed in 1892, however idiosyncratic the technique. Shaw would have argued that his attacks on melodrama were also thematically realistic, and that his "Discussion Plays" in the first decade of the twentieth century were following Ibsen's substitution of discussion for the climax of the Well Made Play.

Commenting on the action of *Widowers' Houses*, one reviewer notes the uniquely Shavian quality of its naturalistic social critique: "Mr. Shaw has pulled out all his stops and shows modern middle-class society working as he conceives it in full blast. Now to reverse the process and to wind up the tune with an ironic note which is all his own ...." This early and remarkably sympathetic review of *Widowers' Houses* illustrates something of the interest Shaw's work inspired.

6.2.1 *The Illustrated London News*, 17 December 1892

The production of Mr. Bernard Shaw's play, "Widowers' Houses," is a dramatic event of very considerable significance. The vital quality of the play is its freshness of type. It is neither tragedy nor melodrama, nor comedy nor burlesque. Mr. Shaw chooses to call it a didactic play, and it is this and something more. It is a study of modern life, purely ironical in conception, and almost completely realistic in workmanship. What Mr. Shaw has endeavoured to do has been to set society before us not merely in its surface aspect of love-making, intriguing, dinner-giving and eating, but in what he conceives to be the more vital light of the "cash nexus." He exhibits the modern lover, the modern father, the modern friend, the modern young lady as he believes them to be conditioned by the way in which they make their money and spend it. He gives us love-making without romance, friendship without sincerity, landlordism without pity, life as it is lived in the upper middle-class without charm. Now, it is quite allowable for his hearers to quarrel with this conception, to say it is unnatural, overstrained, false to the facts. But I cannot conceive how it can be regarded as improper material for a play. All Mr. Shaw is bound to do is to make his characters plausible, to give validity to their motives and consistency to his conception of their mutual relations. In a word, Mr. Shaw has put before us the Socialist criticism of life, and that may be quite as interesting, even supposing it is not quite as true, as the individualist or the merely conventional view. The English stage can be none the worse for a sincere attempt to exhibit life as the dramatist really believes it is being lived in London to-day [. . .]

This is Mr. Shaw's play. Its moral is obvious, its didactic purpose is revealed from the raising of the curtain to its fall, its irony is at times a trifle too fine for its purpose and the shafts fly over the heads of the audience. But the reproach of slovenly construction or essentially uninteresting character does not lie against it. It reverses the conventional ending, the conventional set of characters, the conventional stage types; nevertheless it has a convincing method of its own. Its characters are drawn with perfect clearness, and in the case of the girl with specially minute, if a trifle malicious, art. And it gives the experiment of the Independent Theatre a new basis of original effort which one may very well hope to see developed.

However, like almost all Shaw's early plays with the exception of *Arms and the Man*, it had been several years between the writing of *Widowers' Houses* and the play's first public production – at Manchester in 1907. That was a private performance, staged at a theatre club, the Independent Theatre Society, which was exempt from censorship. This was the case for four out of the twelve plays Shaw wrote up to 1904. For seven of Shaw's other early plays there was a single copyright performance – the only method of protecting the authorship of a play – and there was an average of almost six years between the club or copyright performances and the first public productions. Shaw was forced to rely on publication of the script to gain an audience for his plays, the most extreme example being *Mrs Warren's Profession*. Written in 1893–4, even its first club performance was delayed by the "immoral" subject matter until 1902; and although it was produced (and banned) at public theatres in America in 1905, it was not until 1925 that it could be staged publicly in England.

The challenge to accepted conventions and ideals, which initially barred Shaw's plays from public performance, also affected other naturalistic dramatists. As Shaw pointed out in introducing the translation of Eugène Brieux to English readers, it was partly the rejection of standard theatrical formulas that explains "the refusal of the critics of all nations to accept great original dramatists like Ibsen and Brieux as real dramatists, or their plays as real plays". Shaw was closer to Brieux's explicitly didactic work than to Ibsen, whom he claimed as his model. He subtitled *Widowers' Houses* a "Didactic Realist Play", and his preface to *Three Plays by Brieux* provides essential insights into his own approach:

6.2.2 Shaw: *Three Plays by Brieux*, 1911

The man you see stepping into a chemist's shop to buy the means of committing murder or suicide, may, for all you know, want nothing but a liver pill or a toothbrush. The statesman who has no other object than to make you vote for his party at the next election, may be starting you on an incline at the foot of which lies war, or revolution, or a smallpox epidemic or five years off your lifetime. The horrible murder of a whole family by the father who finishes by killing himself, or the driving of a young girl on to the streets, may be the result of your discharging an employee in a fit of temper a month before. To attempt to understand life from merely looking on at it as it happens in the streets is as hopeless as trying to understand public questions by studying snapshots of public demonstrations. [. . .] Life as it occurs is senseless: a policeman may watch it and work in it for thirty years in the streets and courts of Paris without learning as much of it or from it as a child or a nun may learn from a single play by Brieux. For it is the business of Brieux to pick out the significant incidents from the chaos of daily happenings, and arrange them so that their relation to one another becomes significant, thus changing us from bewildered spectators of a monstrous confusion to men intelligently conscious of the world and its destinies. [. . .]

Now if the critics are wrong in supposing that the formula of the well made play is not only an indispensable factor in playwriting, but is actually the essence of the play itself—if their delusion is rebuked and confuted by the practice of every great dramatist, even when he is only amusing himself by story telling, what must happen to their poor formula when it impertinently offers its services to a playwright who has taken on his supreme function as the Interpreter of Life? Not only has he no use for it, but he must attack and destroy it; for one of the very first lessons he has to teach to a play-ridden public is that the romantic conventions on which the formula proceeds are all false, and are doing incalculable harm in these days when everybody reads romances and goes to the theatre. Just as the historian can teach no real history until he has cured his readers of the romantic delusion that the greatness of a queen consists in her being a pretty woman and having her head cut off, so the playwright of the first order can do nothing with his audiences until he has cured them of looking at the stage through the keyhole, and sniffing round the theatre as prurient people sniff round the divorce court. The cure is not a popular one. [. . .] But the hatred provoked by deliberately inflicted pain, the frantic denials as of a prisoner at the bar accused of a disgraceful crime, the clamor for vengeance thinly disguised as artistic justice, the suspicion that the dramatist is using private information and making a personal attack: all these are to be found only when the playwright is no mere *marchand de plaisir*, but, like Brieux, a ruthless revealer of hidden truth and a mighty destroyer of idols.

*

Just after he had completed *Mrs Warren's Profession*, when he himself was still active as a drama reviewer, Shaw mounted an attack on dramatic criticism which helps to position his plays in the naturalistic movement. Again – his consistent theme – Shaw distinguishes between life and its theatrical simacrulum; and the article defines Shaw's view of his dramatic mission at this period in his career. It also emphasizes the orientation to a more hopeful (optimistic) future that underlies even Chekhov's depictions of a decaying society.

6.2.3 *The New Review*, July 1894

I am, among other things, a dramatist; but I am not an original one, and so have to take all my dramatic material either from real life at first hand, or from authentic documents. The more usual course is to take it out of other dramas, in which case, on tracing it back from one drama to another, you finally come to its origin in the inventive imagination of some original dramatist. Now a fact as invented by a dramatist differs widely from the fact of the same name as it exists or occurs objectively in real life. Not only stage pumps and tubs, but (much more) stage morality and stage human nature differ from the realities of these things. Consequently to a man who derives all his knowledge of life from witnessing plays, nothing appears more unreal than objective life. A dramatic critic is generally such a man; and the more exactly I reproduce objective life for him on the stage, the more certain he is to call my play an extravaganza.

[. . .]

We have, then, two sorts of life to deal with: one subjective or stagey, the other objective or real. What are the comparative advantages of the two for the purposes of the dramatist? Stage life is artificially simple and well understood by the masses; but it is very stale; its feeling is conventional; it is totally unsuggestive of thought because all its conclusions are foregone; and it is constantly in conflict with the real knowledge which the separate members of the audience derive from their own daily occupations. For instance, a naval or military melodrama only goes down with civilians. Real life, on the other hand, is so ill understood, even by its clearest observers, that no sort of consistency is discoverable in it; there is no "natural justice" corresponding to that simple and pleasant concept, "poetic justice"; and, as a whole, it is unthinkable. But, on the other hand, it is credible, stimulating, suggestive, various, free from creeds and systems – in short, it is real.

This rough contrast will suffice to show that the two sorts of life, each presenting dramatic potentialities to the author, will, when reproduced on the stage, affect different men differently. The stage world is for the people who cannot bear to look facts in the face, because they dare not be pessimists, and yet cannot see real life otherwise than as the pessimist sees it. It might be supposed that those who conceive all the operations of our bodies as repulsive, and of our minds as sinful, would take refuge in the sects which abstain from playgoing on principle. But this is by no means what happens. If such a man has an artistic or romantic turn, he takes refuge, not in the conventicle, but in the theatre, where, in the contemplation of the idealised, or stage life, he finds some relief from his haunting conviction of omnipresent foulness and baseness. Confront him with anything like reality, and his chronic pain is aggravated instead of relieved: he raises a terrible outcry against the spectacle of cowardice, selfishness, faithlessness, sensuality – in short, everything that he went to the theatre to escape from. This is not the effect on those pessimists who dare face facts and profess their own faith. They are great admirers of the realist playwright, whom they embarrass greatly by their applause. Their cry is "Quite right: strip off the whitewash from the sepulchre; expose human nature in all its tragi-comic baseness; tear the mask of respectability from the smug bourgeois, and show the liar, the thief, the coward, the libertine beneath."

Now to me, as a realist playwright, the applause of the conscious, hardy pessimist is more exasperating than the abuse of the unconscious, fearful one. I am not a pessimist at all. It does not concern me that, according to certain ethical systems, all human beings fall into classes labelled liar, coward, thief, and so on. [. . .] As a realist dramatist, [. . .] it is my business to get outside these systems.

The belief in a socialist alternative and in the real possibility of moral reform implied in Shaw's definition of a "realist dramatist", together with the stress on interpreting life expressed in his preface to Brieux's plays, lead Shaw developing what has been called "the Drama of Ideas" within the naturalistic frame. As Bertolt Brecht, a dramatist who rejected Naturalism, recognized: "the reason why

Shaw's dramatic works dwarf those of his contemporaries is that they so unhesitat-
ingly appealed to reason. His world is one that arises from opinions. The opinions
of his characters constitute their fates" (*Berliner Börsen-Courier*, 25 July 1926).

These "Discussion Plays" still clearly conform to naturalistic principles. However, the effect of the First World War is directly measured in Shaw's work. His
approach changed radically, as indicated by subtitles for his later plays such as "A
Political Extravaganza", "A Johnsonian Comedy", "A Vision of Judgement". It
was the critic and translator of Ibsen, William Archer, who lamented the change. It
was Archer, the most effective promoter of naturalistic drama in England, who
had first induced Shaw to write for the theatre; and indeed *Widowers' Houses* had
begun as a collaboration between Shaw and Archer. Now, responding to the
"Metabiological Pentateuch" – as Shaw subtitled *Back to Methuselah*, the first play
written after the war, which Shaw had begun in 1918 – Archer complained:

> If this Bible of yours is ever going to have any effect, it will be 100 or 1,000
> years hence; and it's tomorrow that needs salvation . . .
>
> I doubt if there is any case of a man so widely read, heard, seen and known
> as yourself, who has produced so little result on his generation. I am strongly
> under the impression (I may be wrong) that you have less of a following to-day
> than you had twenty years ago . . . It isn't as if any newer prophet had arisen to
> oust you. You have no serious competitor; but your public (small blame to
> them) declines to take you seriously. Can't you fix your will upon the high
> growing frondage of Practical Influence . . .
>
> [Letter to Bernard Shaw, 22 June 1921]

The question of social effectiveness, raised by Archer's letter, was a basic rationale
for all naturalistic drama. The underlying aim in analyzing contemporary society
was to produce reform, the need for which was demonstrated by the objectivity of
the presentation.

3 MRS WARREN'S PROFESSION

The play

When Shaw began to write *Mrs Warren's Profession* in 1885 prostitution was at the
forefront of the news in England. The campaign for criminalization of the sex
trade and closure of the brothels had been brought to a pitch of public fervor by
inflammatory articles published in the *Pall Mall Gazette* by W. T. Stead. The first of
these, titled "The Maiden Tribute of Ancient Babylon", gives a good illustration
of tone and moral attitudes of the debate.

> In ancient times, if we may believe the myths of Hellas, Athens was compelled
> by her conqueror to send once every nine years a tribute to Crete of seven
> youths and seven maidens . . . This very night in London, and every night, year
> in and year out, not seven maidens only, but many times seven . . . Maidens
> they will be when this morning dawned, but tonight their ruin will be accom-

plished, and to-morrow they will find themselves within the portals of the maze of London brotheldom . . . this vast tribute of maidens, unwitting and unwilling, which is nightly levied in London by the vices of the rich upon the necessities of the poor. London's lust annually uses up many thousands of women, who are literally killed and made away with – living sacrifices slain in the service of vice. That may be inevitable . . . But I do ask that those doomed to the house of evil fame shall not be trapped into it unwillingly, and that none shall be beguiled into the chamber of death before they are of an age to read the inscription above the portal – 'abandon hope all ye who enter here'.

(6 July 1885)

To illustrate the crimes of the "sale and purchase and violation of children" and the "procuration of virgins", Stead included the story of a girl from Derbyshire, sold by her own mother to a procuress, who had her examined by a midwife to certify virginity and sold her on to a brothel keeper. "Notwithstanding her extreme youth" the girl is chloroformed and a man led to her room – "then there rose a wild and piteous cry . . ." Questions in Parliament about the possibility of prosecuting the *Pall Mall Gazette* (for supposedly corrupting the public by revealing such facts) led to threats by Stead of naming the clients of high-class London brothels, including royalty, from the witness box. Following mass demonstrations, in July a petition with 393,000 signatures was presented to Parliament by the Salvation Army.

Shaw was clearly responding to the demonization of brothel-keepers in his characterization of Mrs. Warren; and in his "Author's Apology" to the Stage Society edition of the play he emphasizes that "my characters behave like human beings, instead of conforming to the romantic logic of the stage" (1902). His ex-prostitute turned sexual capitalist is presented as ordinary, humane, energetic, and "truly not one wee bit doubtful – or – ashamed" in sharp contrast to both Stead's picture of brothel-keepers as "the most ruthless and abominable" criminals, and to the theatrical stereotype of the "fallen woman" driven to suicide by shame (like Pinero's *Second Mrs. Tanqueray*, 1893). From a modern perspective Shaw's picture of successful and self-assured prostitution is itself romanticized. As the programme to a National Theatre production asked: "Can Shaw's play be written by a man who had ever known a prostitute? What would he have made of Bengali Rose and Jane the Urdu who relieve the total sexual deprivation of whole households of Pakistanis in a hour, for a pound a head?" In addition, the refusal of Shaw's characters to name Mrs. Warren's profession, which is only written on scraps of paper and torn up or passed round silently, leads to the accusation that "What is bad about Mrs. Warren's Profession is as efficiently repressed as its unspeakable name. Shaw refrains from making his spectators desire his heroine, but the whole structure of the play relies on prurience for its interest" (Germaine Greer, "A Whore in Every Home", 1985).

At the time Shaw wrote the play, however, even describing prostitution in print might be cause for criminal prosecution, as the Parliamentary reaction to Stead's articles indicates; and the theatre was considerably more restrictive. When Shaw

213

arranged for a copyright performance in 1898, the Lord Chamberlain's office completely refused a licence for it to be staged, even when Shaw offered extensive cuts – including omitting the whole of the second act. When the Stage Society did perform it in 1902, even J. T. Grein, the founder of the Independent Theatre Club which had produced *Widowers' Houses*, asserted that "the representation [of such a subject on the stage] was unnecessary and painful" (*Sunday Special*, 2 January 1902). Over a decade later mentioning the subject in middle-class society was still considered impossible, as Emma Goldman, the woman's rights and socialist activist states in one of the earliest essays on the play:

> it is not respectable to talk about these things, because respectability cannot face the truth . . . Indeed, no lady or gentleman would discuss the profession of *Mrs. Warren* and her confrères. But they partake of the dividends. When the evil becomes too crying, they engage in vice crusades, and call down the wrath of the Lord and the brutality of the police upon the Mrs. Warrens and her victims. While the [male] victimizers [. . .] and the other patrons of *Mrs. Warren's* houses parade as the protectors of woman, the home and the family.
> (*The Social Significance of Modern Drama*, 1914)

Emma Goldman approaches *Mrs Warren's Profession* as a naturalistic play – her discussion follows essays on Ibsen and Brieux – giving a completely realistic treatment of the issues. And in fact, although the subject of several conversations in *Mrs Warren's Profession*, prostitution is not itself a target, but an example of Capitalism in action, and a metaphor for the whole capitalist system. As Shaw argues in the preface, "rich men without conviction are more dangerous in modern society than poor women without chastity". This is the last and most effective of *Plays Unpleasant* (and the moral outrage caused by the way Shaw presents prostitution was perhaps a displaced refusal to recognize the wider attack on the system), but even a strong supporter of the play, such as William Archer, criticized the secondary theme of incest as diverting from the social commentary. Shaw's letters to Archer on the subject, written after the furore that greeted the staging of *Mrs Warren's Profession* in America, offer insights into the composition of the play and Shaw's aims in writing it.

6.3.2 Letter to William Archer, 7 November 1905

Apart from the emergency created by the trial in America, I am glad to have the opportunity of making you reconsider your old explanation – that I cannot touch pitch without wallowing in it &c &c. The incestuous part of Mrs Warren is a genuine part of the original plan because it is what you call an anecdote, or rather two anecdotes. I knew of a case of a young man who, on being initiated by a modern Madame de Warens (observe the name), was rather taken aback by her reproaching him for being "not half the man his father was." I also watched the case of a man who was a friend of my mother in her young days. When my sister grew up he became infatuated about her and wanted to marry her. And there was, of course, the famous ——[6] case, where a young married woman was seduced (in the street from which Mrs W's name was taken) by a man who had formerly seduced her mother. A certain inevitability about these cases had struck me as being dramatic long before I wrote Mrs Warren, also a certain squalid comicality consisting partly, I think, in the fact that there was such an utter absence of any tragic consequences when there was no exposure. These and many confirmatory observations made the solid mass of "Mrs W's P"—there is really no side issue.

Mrs Warren's Profession: chronology of major early performances

March 1898, Lord Chamberlain refuses permission to perform the play for copyright purposes		
5 January 1902 (repeated 6 January 1902) London	The Stage Society New Lyric Club Private performance produced by Bernard Shaw	Mrs. Warren: Fanny Brough Frank: Harley Granville Barker Vivie: Madge McIntosh
1903 Stage edition is published based on The Stage Society production and includes photographs of the actors		
October 1905 New Haven	Hyperion Theater Producer: Arnold Daly	Mrs. Warren: Mary Shaw Frank: Arnold Daly Vivie: Chrystal Herne
October 1905 New York	Garrick Theater Producer: Arnold Daly	Mrs. Warren: Mary Shaw Frank: Arnold Daly Vivie: Chrystal Herne
December 1907 Prague	National Theatre	
March 1918 New York	Washington Square Players Comedy Theater	Mrs. Warren: Mary Shaw Frank: Saxon Kling Vivie: Diantha Pattison
July 1925 Birmingham	Macdona Players Prince of Wales Theatre Producer: Esmé Percy	Mrs. Warren: Florence Jackson Frank: George Bancroft Vivie: Valerie Richards
September 1925 London	Macdona Players Regent Theatre	Mrs. Warren: Florence Jackson Frank: George Bancroft Vivie: Valerie Richards
February 1928 London	Macdona Players Little Theatre Producer: Esmé Percy	Mrs. Warren: Leah Bateman Frank: George Bancroft Vivie: Dora Macdona

[6] The dash is Shaw's.

Performance and reception

Shaw was a founding member of the Stage Society, which produced *Mrs Warren's Profession* (for two performances) in 1902, and became its major dramatist. When the Stage Society took on its own theatre for the Granville Barker-Vedrenne seasons of 1904–7 at the Court, out of a total of 988 performances 701 were of plays by Shaw. Following practices that had become associated with naturalistic drama, the company was run as an ensemble, rejecting both the standard actor-manager structure and the star system. It also became known for a radical political programme. Many of the performers were active in the Actresses' Franchise

Figure 6.1 Mrs Warren's Profession, The Stage Society, London: 1902 (directed by Bernard Shaw, performed without scenery).
In rehearsal: Bernard Shaw with Vivie (Madge McIntosh) and Mrs Warren (Fanny Brough)

League, the theatrical wing of the woman's suffrage movement; and Lillah McCarthy, who became a leading interpreter of Shaw's female roles, described the Court Theatre as a "mission hall" in which Shaw was "the General Booth of this Salvation Army" (*Myself and Friends*, 1933).

Shaw was responsible for directing many of his own plays in the first decade of the century – even when the director of record was Granville Barker – and viewing the whole range of his surviving prompt books gives a fairly good picture of his theatrical principles. Unlike Stanislavsky, Shaw had no need to visualize character, motivation or relationships in advance, and these prompt books contain none of the novelistic description found in the director's notes for the Moscow Art Theatre productions of *The Seagull* or *The Cherry Orchard*. Although Shaw prepared equally meticulously before the rehearsal period, his focus was almost entirely on moves and blocking. Actors' positions, stage business and the location of furniture and props was worked out on a chessboard, then noted in color-coded ink on the margins of the text, providing an exact structure for the action that seems to have been followed precisely in performance. Shaw's primary aim as a director was to create focal points for the spectators at each moment in the play; and there are few notations on characters' emotion or state of mind. However, since so many of his early plays were printed before they could be performed and Shaw had to rely on published texts to reach an audience his stage directions already give an unusual amount of information about the characters, which also served as guidance for the actors.

Critics have frequently concluded that Shaw was not naturalistic, because of his insistence on technical acting skills, encouragement of theatricality or bravura performance, and emphasis on music (casting his plays according to the "voice" of the actor – tenor, bass or soprano for specific roles). In addition, as Shaw pointed out,

> my plays require a special technique of acting, and in particular, great virtuosity in sudden transitions of mood that seem to the ordinary actor to be transitions from one 'line' of character to another. But, after all, this is only fully accomplished acting; for there is no other sort of acting except bad acting, acting that is the indulgence of imagination instead of the exercise of skill.
>
> (*The New York Times*, 12 June 1927)

Linked with his characteristic technique of reversals in the dramatic action to disturb stock responses and make spectators question their conventional beliefs, this has led to suggestions that Shaw was moving towards a prototype of the "alienation" developed by Bertolt Brecht in his anti-naturalistic "epic" theatre. However these are also traditional comic techniques, and less evident in his social "problem" plays, while Shaw always maintained that his aim was to "make the audience believe that real things are happening to real people" ("The Art of

Rehearsal", 1922). The misinterpretation of Shaw is largely due to a limiting of focus, in which naturalistic drama had become identified solely with the type of pyschological naturalism developed by Antoine and associated – despite the evidence of the Moscow Art Theatre stagings of Chekhov (see above: Laurence Kitchin) – with Stanislavsky's theories. The problems Shaw's characters face are mainly social rather than internalized, requiring a more presentational performance; and both styles of acting were within the range of the Stage Society company. This can be seen in a comparison of Granville Barker's direction of a play by Galsworthy (another of the major Court Theatre dramatists) to *Misalliance*, both performed in the same season. As a reviewer commented, the actors in Shaw's play presented "a new convention of acting, rather formal, and tending a little towards caricature – the very opposite of the acting in *Justice*" (*The Spectator*, 26 February 1910).

In addition to the prompt books, Shaw kept detailed notebooks on rehearsals, and wrote daily comments to the cast – all evidence of the way Lillah McCarthy described his direction as "serious, painstaking, concentrated and relentless in the pursuit of perfection" (*New York American*, 18 September 1927). Most of these rehearsal notes concern intonation and vocal stress, or for the kind of interaction by other actors that would focus attention on particular points in a speaker's words. As well as illustrating such detail, one of Shaw's letters to Granville Barker (who had played Eugene Marchbanks in *Candida* and whose own play, *The Marrying of Ann Leete*, had been performed in January that year) during the rehearsals for *Mrs Warren's Profession* provides insights into the characters and tone of the play.

6.3.3 Shaw's staging for *Mrs Warren's Profession*

Bernard Dukore, *Bernard Shaw, Director*, Allen & Unwin, 1971

In the margins of the prompt-script, Shaw the director blocked the action – transforming explicit movements in the text into pictorial patterns or reduced cues, elaborating and refining implicit movements, and inventing new movements that Shaw the author did not indicate. For the introduction scene at the end of the first act of *Mrs Warren's Profession*, for example, the author provided few directions. In preparing the play for production, Shaw had to devise blocking that would accomplish several goals: as Reverend Samuel Gardner is introduced to the other characters, he must see and be seen by each person to whom he is introduced; Mrs Warren should have an unobstructed view of him; she should have time to observe him before crying out her recognition; and her movement should build to that recognition. As the dialogue begins, Mrs Warren and Crofts are upstage, Vivie and Frank stage-centre, Praed downstage right and Gardner downstage left. Vivie and Frank are designated by the initials of their first names, the others by the initials of their last names. Shaw blocked the scene in six movements:

	FRANK. . . . Let me introduce – my father: Miss
(1) G to LC	Warren. (1)
	Vivie (*going to the clergyman and shaking his hand*) (2) Very
(2) V to C	glad to see you here, Mr Gardner. (3) Let me introduce
(3) F to L	everybody. (4) Mr Gardner – Mr Frank Gardner – Mr
(4) W down to RC	Praed – Sir George Crofts, and – (5) (*As the men are raising their hats to one another; Vivie is interrupted by an*
(5) V a step up	*exclamation from her mother, who swoops down on the Reverend Samuel*).
(6) W to G	MRS WARREN. (6) Why, it's Sam Gardner, gone into the church!

These movements comprise a shifting picture which begins with Mrs Warren, in a crowded centre area, almost hidden by Frank and Vivie. The centre area becomes less congested when Frank moves to stage left. Mrs Warren gradually gains more prominence: she moves toward Gardner, Vivie then clears the way for her, and finally she goes directly to centre-stage to greet him. The gradual shifts can be seen in a series of plans (only the first of which Shaw drew in the margin of his script). At the beginning of the dialogue, when Vivie asks Frank to introduce her to his father, the focus is on her and Frank; Mrs Warren is almost hidden.

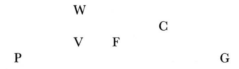

When Gardner and Vivie meet each other – (1) and (2) – the focus is on them, but Vivie's movement provides Mrs Warren with space: she becomes more prominent and we can observe her.

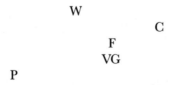

After Vivie introduces herself to Gardner, Frank moves to the left (3), in sufficient time to clear the space so that his father and Crofts can see each other when they are introduced. The central area is now less crowded; Mrs Warren is set off by more space.

```
        W
                    C
                F
                VG
        P
```

219

During these introductions, as Gardner turns from downstage right to upstage left, Mrs Warren begins to move toward him (4): she can now do so without being observed by him. Gardner first looks downstage right, at Praed.

```
                       C
        W                          F
              VG
   P
```

Vivie then moves upstage a step (5), giving the focus to her mother and Gardner, who is at this point looking upstage left, at Crofts.

```
                    C
                              F
           WV
             G
      P
```

Mrs Warren steps forward to Gardner, calling his name and making him turn in a sweeping movement from upstage left to stage right.

```
                    C
                              F
             V
            WG
      P
```

Mrs Warren has moved from upstage to stage centre as Vivie and Frank relinquish the centre area and Gardner turns more than 180 degrees to focus on her. Shaw the director has fulfilled the requirements of the scene, and the entire process occurs so quickly and smoothly that the stages are unobtrusive.

The movements in this scene derive from a basic situation in the text (one character is introduced to other characters) as well as from two explicit stage directions (Vivie going to Gardner and Mrs Warren swooping down upon him). Early in the first act, when Vivie and Praed discuss Mrs Warren, Shaw the director – in order to delineate character and help generate atmosphere – suggests movement where the stage directions indicate only that Praed rises.

PRAED rises – down to float [footlights] – back to audience.

PRAED. . . . Of course you and your mother will get on capitally. (*He rises, and looks abroad at the view*). What a charming little place you have here!

VIVIE (*unmoved*) If you think you are doing anything but confirming my worst suspicions by changing the subject like that, you must take me for a much greater fool than I hope I am.

220

Pup to VIVIE – intimately.	PRAED. Your worst suspicions! Oh, pray dont say that. Now dont.
	VIVIE. Why wont my mother's life bear being talked about?
	PRAED. Pray think, Miss Vivie. It is natural that I should have a certain delicacy in talking to my old friend's daughter about her
(1) Away a little R from V.	behind her back. (1) You will have plenty of opportunity of talking to her about it when
(2) Up, fidgetting.	she comes. (*Anxiously*) (2) I wonder what is keeping her.
	VIVIE. No: she wont talk about it either. (*Rising*) However, I wont press you. (3) Only, mind
(3) P down again to her, protesting.	this, Mr Praed. I strongly suspect there will be a battle royal when my mother hears of my Chancery Lane project.
(4) P stock still.	PRAED (4) (*ruefully*) I'm afraid there will.

All of the movements in this scene are stimulated by Praed's attitude to Vivie, which is based on who she is and what she does not know. Although the text indicates urbane replies to Vivie's questions and charges, the subtext implies nervousness, for Praed fears she will learn the truth. Shaw creates movement from this subtext. As Vivie dominates the situation by remaining strongly anchored in the same stage area, Praed nervously moves about – going downstage, moving to and then away from Vivie, walking upstage as he fidgets, returning to her. The tension between text and subtext is enhanced by the movement devised by the director.[7]

6.3.4 Letter to Harley Granville Barker, 31 December 1901

You are losing sight in the last act of the new attitude of Vivie, hard as nails, and fiercely intolerant of any approach to poetry. Being of a poetic turn yourself, you have a constant tendency to modulate into E flat minor (which is short for Eugene [from *Candida*] flat minor) which is steadily lowering the tone of Frank, until he seems fairly likely to end as Hamlet. Instead of being incorrigibly good-for-nothing, you are incorrigibly the other thing. I have serious thoughts of having you to dinner on Sunday and making you very drunk; only I fear that you would become pious in your cups instead of gay. Instead of getting boundless amusement out of everything disastrous, you become the man of sorrows at every exhibition of human frailty, and seem

British Museum, Add. 50600. The copy used was *Plays: Unpleasant* (London: Grant Richards, 1900). The prompt-book contains no indication of a date of production, though the play was first presented in London by the Stage Society at the New Lyric Club in 1902. In revising the play for the 1931 Standard Edition, Shaw rewrote this scene.

Figure 6.2 The capitalist and the Lovers, Act III: Granville Barker and Madge McIntosh
with Charles Goodheart,. The Stage Society 1902

to be bitterly reproaching me all through for the flippancy of my dialogue.
Two rehearsals more, and you will draw tears even in the third act.

There is one passage which is particularly dreadful because it has absolutely
no sense unless its mood is perfectly conveyed. "What do YOU say, govnor,
eh?" You express neither curiosity nor amusement here; and far from singing
"good Old Crofts" like a lark in the heavens, you convey the impression that
you know the man well and habitually talk of him and to him in that way.

In short, you need not be afraid of overdoing the part: the real danger is underdoing it. You have a frightful air of a youth in love – with Ann Leete probably.

It is a question of feeding, perhaps: you must come to lunch oftener.

When I was unable today to conceal the shock with which I saw you suddenly hit on the idea of playing that scene with Vivie exactly like the scene with Prossy in *Candida*, you sank into despair like a man whose loftiest inspiration has been quenched and whose noblest motives brutally misunderstood.

IT was really the fault of your cold, not mine. You nearly made Miss Brough cry.

It only wants lifting the least bit in the world. You should soar not gravitate. If you let the part weigh on your mind much more, you will find yourself breaking into the Seven Ages of Man on the night . . .

We begin tomorrow with the fourth act – Vivie and Frank.

Figure 6.3 The confrontation in Act IV: Chrystal Herne and Mary Shaw, New York 1905

The first public performance of *Mrs Warren's Profession* was staged by the American producer Arnold Daly, one of the earliest champions of Shaw in the United States, who had already mounted successful productions and tours of *Candida* and *The Man of Destiny* in 1903. Shaw wrote *How She Lied to Her Husband* specifically for Daly to perform in his 1904–5 New York season, together with three other plays by Shaw, the last of which was to be *Mrs Warren's Profession*. Shaw had inserted a special clause in his contract with Daly, specifying that "the Manager shall endeavour as far as may be practicable to apprise the public of the fact that the Play is suitable for representation before serious adult audiences only" – but the unexpected failure of *John Bull's Other Island* meant that *Mrs Warren's Profession* was put hurriedly into rehearsal. There was no attempt to educate the public about the social value of the play, so publicity consisted of an exchange of letters with Anthony Comstock, the Secretary of the Society for the Suppression of Vice. Threatened by legal prosecution if he persisted in his "intention to put upon the stage one of Bernard Shaw's filthy products, entitled *Mrs. Warren's Profession*" Daly responded that the play was "a strong sermon and a great moral lesson" (*The New York Times*, 25 October 1905); and Shaw commented:

> Let him imprison Daly by all means . . . the scandal of his imprisonment would completely defeat Comstock's attempt to hide the fact that Mrs. Warren's "profession" exists because libertines pay women well to be evil, and often show them affection and respect, whilst pious people pay them infamously and drudge their bodies and souls to death at honest labor.
>
> Because I have been striving all my life to awaken public conscience to this, while Comstock has been examining and destroying ninety-three tons of indecent postcards, it is concluded that I am a corrupt blackguard and Comstock's mind is in such a condition of crystal purity that any American who reads, sees, writes, or says anything of which he disapproves or which he is "dogonned it he understands" must be put in prison.
>
> (*The New York Times*, 27 October 1905)

The play tried out in New Haven, and achieved front page headlines: BARRED IN NEW HAVEN – "MRS. WARREN'S PROFESSION" SHOWN ONCE THEN STOPPED – TOWN IN AN UPROAR. When the production reopened three days later in New York, the sensation crested crowds at the box-office and scalpers selling tickets at up to three times the regular price, while one of the New York newspapers (*The World*) distributed voting-slips to the audience:

In your opinion is "Mrs. Warren's Profession" a play fit to be presented on the American stage?

FIT

Erase one

UNFIT

This card will be collected as you leave the theatre.

Approximately 60 percent of the audience responded, with just over half voting the play to be "fit" – although this was certainly not the official view.

The police attended the first performance, and warrants were issued for Daly and the management of the Garrick Theatre, charging a violation of the Penal Code relating to "offending public decency". Although no charges were actually laid, the play was closed, and a notice posted on the theatre doors: "Further Performance of *Mrs. Warren's Profession* will be abandoned, owing to the universal condemnation of the press."

6.3.4 Banning the play in America
The New York Times, 29 October 1905

The first night's performance was all New Haven could stand of Arnold Daly's production of "Mrs. Warren's Profession," by Bernard Shaw. There was an uproar here to-day over any further presentation of the piece from all quarters – the newspapers, the police, those who had seen the perform-ance last night, and the public generally. Because of this Mayor John P. Studley at noon directed Chief of Police Wrinn to revoke the license of the Hyperion Theatre as long as Daly was in town. The police then sent word to Mr. Daly that he could not present the play at the scheduled matinée this afternoon and to-night on the ground that "Mrs. Warren's Profession" was "grossly indecent and not fit for public presentation".

Mr. Daly, his manager, his press agent, and a squad of attorneys made every effort to get Mayor Studley to change his mind, but he was obdur-ate. Mr. Daly left New Haven in high dudgeon late this afternoon, saying before he went: "New York will stand for the play if New Haven will not."

[. . .]

New Haven papers this evening are severe in their condemnation of "Mrs. Warren's Profession."

The New Haven Leader says it is "the most shockingly immoral dialogue ever publicly repeated" and that "the words, suggestions – the whole rotten mess of immoral suggestions – have no place on a public platform."

The New Haven Register says to-night: "The play itself is fit for publication only as a document for the sociologist and reformer, and even the most ardent of Mr. Shaw's admirers cannot plead that as a justification for putting it in dramatic form. Acted, it is incredibly worse. The full force of the utterance and gestures only add to its vulgarity and the necessity of acting up to the parts makes it equally repulsive, one would imagine, both to those who live without and to those who live within the world it describes. On these facts alone its pretended value of moral purpose must rest: To ask a hearing for it on the time-worn plea of artistic realism would be simply grotesque. The play drew last night, in a large part, the type of audience that it was seeking to reprove, and their behaviour indicated that they went away more pleased and amused than rebuked. The fatuous sophistry, by which Mrs. Warren defended her conduct to her daughter, was greedily observed and approved of by an element that clearly wished to believe in it. A spectator at last night's performance who failed to note and be impressed by this quality of the audience, must have been densely ignorant of human nature.

[. . .]

Distinction may have to be drawn sharply as to plays that are to be read and plays that are to be acted, but such a play as 'Mrs. Warren's Profession' cannot under any circumstances be given before a mixed audience.

The New York Times, 1 November 1905

SHAW'S PLAY STOPPED; THE MANAGER ARRESTED

McAdoo Calls the Piece Revolting and Indecent.

WARRANTS FOR THE PLAYERS

Tickets Still on Sale Late in the Day, Notwithstanding Condemnation by the Press.

Police Commissioner McAdoo took steps yesterday which stopped the further presentation at the Garrick Theatre of "Mrs. Warren's Profession," George Bernard Shaw's play. Mr. McAdoo saw the performance on Monday night, and the first thing he did when he reached his office yesterday morning was to report to Mayor McClellan that the production was "revolting, indecent, and nauseating where it was not boring."

After talking with the Mayor Mr. McAdoo wrote to Arnold Daly, ex-Senator Reynolds, who is said to be the owner of the theatre, and Samuel

W. Gumperts, its manager, telling them that he would prevent a second performance and arrest those participating therein. Later a warrant was issued by Magistrate Whitman calling for the arrest of Mr. Reynolds, Mr. Gumperts, Mr. Daly, and the other actors and actresses in the cast, which was served by Inspector Brooks in person.

[. . .]

The warrant charged a violation of that section of the Penal Code which relates to "offending public decency."

[. . .]

Attached to the papers in the case were affidavits signed by Inspector Brooks and Detective Sergeant Cohen. There was also a typewritten report made by Commissioner McAdoo. The report, which was addressed to Magistrate Whitman, read:

"Last night I attended in person, accompanied by Inspector Nicholas Brooks and one or two other police officials, the play known as 'Mrs. Warren's Profession' by George Bernard Shaw, at the Garrick Theatre. The play is in four acts. I saw three of them. There are six characters in the play. The leading characters profess to have led and are leading immoral lives, and defend their position with all the cleverness and ability of the author; they are and they continue prosperously immoral to the end of the play.

"The daughter and son condone the immorality of their parents, for both of whom otherwise they express contempt and hatred, and hold them up to ridicule in public. The clergyman is portrayed as a hypocrite, sneak, sniveling blackguard, and promiscuous adulterer. Mrs. Warren defends her profession successfully to the close of the play. Her daughter condones her mother's mode of living and accepts her own shame with indifference until her pride is stung by the fact that her mother has deceived her as to her present sources of income.

"Mrs. Warren and her titled partner conduct in European capitals highgrade disorderly houses, which in the play are called hotels, something like the disreputable Raines law hotels, I presume. The conduct of these houses is a cold business proposition in which they make a great deal of money and at the close of the play they both avowed that they would give more attention hereafter to their business for the profit that is in it.

"The whole play, to my personal view, is revolting, indecent, and nauseating where it is not boring. It tells working girls that it is much better to live a carefully calculated life of vice rather than of honest work. No character in the play, not even the clergyman, has one word for the cardinal virtues in man or woman. Played at the Academy of Music, in the east side, or at the Grand Opera House, on the west side, at popular prices, the effect on the public morals would be most pernicious. I doubt, however, if the

227

hard-working and plain-minded heads of families in those neighborhoods will permit it to be played.

"That the audience last night did not hiss the play off the stage or engage in mob demonstrations against it was due I think to the fact that the audience was not a representative one. Even in the galleries seats sold as high as $5, and in the afternoon $35 was asked for one seat in the orchestra. There was nothing during the evening that could really be called applause. Some young women present, from foolish bravado, applauded a little at certain points; but as the dialogue grew stronger and ranker, even this ceased. I think the play is distinctly against public morals, and decency, and utterly discreditable to the managers and those taking part in it. If artfully and cleverly acted, so much the worse."

A duplicate of the report had been sent to Mayor McClellan earlier in the day. The Mayor referred it to Corporation Counsel Delaney, and late yesterday afternoon the Commissioner received the following letter:

> My advice is to immediately notify the managers of the play that you consider it indecent and immoral, and that if they produce it tonight you will cause their arrest. This threat will undoubtedly cause them to procure an injunction against you, and by so doing you will be in a much better position than if you went to court yourself. If you apply for an injunction the court will be apt to say that if this play is indecent and immoral it is your duty and not the court's duty to suppress it.
>
> On the other hand, if you threaten to act and are stayed the responsibility lies not with you, but on the court.

It was said last night that ex-Senator Reynolds will apply for an injunction to prevent further interference with the play.

[. . .]

Until the posting of the notice announcing the discontinuance of the play ticket speculators fairly haunted the Garrick. Every passer-by was buttonholed and asked to buy seats for them.

The notice came so late and the assurances of those in the box office until its appearance had been so positive that many persons who bought tickets in the morning and early afternoon went to the theatre last night fully expecting to see a performance. As a rule ticket holders demanded the return of their money. It was given to them without a word. There were a few who had bought from speculators and who insisted that the whole amount of their outlay should be refunded, irrespective of box office prices.

"I paid $80 for my ticket," said one woman, "and you only give me $2 back."

"You're lucky to get that," said the man in the window.

The speculators, by the way, will lose nothing.

Inspector Schmittberger and Roundsman Brown of the Tenderloin Police Station were at the theatre by 7 o'clock with a large force of policemen, including the theatre squad commanded by Sergt. Fogarty. They had all they could do to preserve order.

[. . .]

At 9:30 o'clock the following statement was handed out by Winchell Smith [Daly's] personal representative, who said it was authorized:

"When Mr. Daly said on Saturday night that he would abide by the decision of the press with regard to the merits of 'Mrs. Warren's Profession,' he meant what he said. At that time the approaching production through no wish of ours had been surrounded by so much sensationalism we feared that the public would get an erroneous impression of the play and our purpose in presenting it. And the turn of events proved that this was true. On the opening night the theatre was besieged by a motley throng of curiosity seekers, who came expecting to see something that would appeal to their morbid tastes.

"This was exactly the portion of the public to which we did not wish to appeal, and, had it not been too late to withdraw, we would not have produced the play then. When, this morning, we saw how unanimous the papers were in condemnation of the drama, we then and there gave up all thought of continuing its presentation."

[. . .]

Anthony Comstock of the Society for the Suppression of Vice, was early advised of the position assumed by Commissioner McAdoo. He chuckled when the news reached him.

"I had full confidence that Mr. McAdoo would do his duty," he said. "And now I will do all in my power to help him see to it that Arnold Daly and those associated with him in the production get the limit of the law. I will forward to Mr. McAdoo a copy of the warning I sent to Mr. Daly. This warning will prevent any plea in extenuation of the outrageous offense against decency which was perpetrated last night.

"I did not witness last night's performance, nor did I have any agents there. I knew that Mr. McAdoo would be present. An example should certainly be made of the guilty persons."

Throughout his life Shaw conducted a campaign against censorship of the stage, which in Britain was imposed by the Lord Chamberlain's office through an official Examiner of Plays. Most European governments exercised some control over the theatre during the nineteenth century, although like Russia they were primarily concerned with political material. For instance, the 1832 riot caused by references to King Louis-Phillipe in Victor Hugo's *Le Roi S'Amuse* served as opportunity for the re-imposition of state censorship in France. Similarly the enthusiastic reception of Verdi's *Nabucco* in 1842 led Italian authorities to clamp down on anything that could be construed as nationalistic. By contrast, although censorship had also been originally imposed in Britain for political reasons (dating back to Elizabethan times, and extended in 1737 by the Prime Minister Robert Walpole in reaction to plays lampooning his government), by the mid-nineteenth century it had evolved into the control of moral standards – which was only finally abolished in 1968. This imposition of "public morality" particularly affected naturalistic plays, and led Shaw to a running battle with Redford, the Examiner of Plays for most of the period from the early 1890s to just before the First World War.

Shaw's basic argument was that the system of censorship allowed "vicious plays, and refuses to license serious and exemplary ones" by prohibiting the depiction of the unattractive (i.e., realistic) aspects of vice and its corrupting consequences:

> I have myself had a play [*Mrs Warren's Profession*] prohibited by Mr Redford. People imagine that he refused to license it because the heroine is a prosti- tute and a procuress. They are indeed wide of the mark. The licensed drama positively teems with prostitutes and procuresses. One of the most popular melodramas of our time is called *The Worst Woman in London* . . . You can also see in many a humble melodrama a brothel on stage, with its procuress in league with the villain and the bold, bad girl whom he has ruined, all set forth as attractively as possible under the protection of the Lord Chamberlain's certificate.
>
> But in my play the consequences of promiscuity are not shirked. I provide the feast (an acridly medicinal one); but I also present the reckoning. The daughter of my heroine meets the son of one of her father's clients, who falls in love with her. And the two have to face the question, Is he her half-brother? only to find it unanswerable. That is one of the inevitable dilemmas produced by "group marriage." To suppress it is to pack the cards in favour of such arrangements. My refusal to pack them brought me into conflict with the taboo against incest. That is why *Mrs Warren's Profession* is forbidden, whilst dozens of plays which present Mrs Warren as well-dressed, charming, luxuriating in "guilty splendour," and suffering nothing but some fictitious retribution at the end, in which nobody believes, because everybody knows it need not happen in real life, teach their cynical lesson to the poor girl in the gallery, and send the young man in the pit into the arms of the best imitation the streets can offer him of the guiltily splendid young lady he has been admiring inside.
>
> Letter to *The Nation*, 16 November 1907)

Associating his own play with Ibsen's *Ghosts* (banned for its inclusion of syphilis as well as the possibility of incest) and Brieux's *Damaged Goods*, Shaw concludes that censorship "buys off the licentious playwrights and managers by licensing their agreeable plays" which advertise the attractiveness of immorality, while suppress- ing "intellectually honest writers who insist on drawing the moral. The natural and inevitable result is that the British drama has become the impudent and shallow-hearted propaganda of gaiety in the policeman's sense of the word."

When *Mrs Warren's Profession* was finally licensed for performance at a public theatre in England – in 1925 – it was received with general equanimity. The critics still found the play "unpalatable" but tended to focus on its dramatic qualities. The production was so popular that the next year it was transferred from a repertory season at the Regent Theatre to the Strand Theatre, where it ran for 68 performances. However, having been written over 30 years earlier, there was a tendency to see the major theme as being less relevant. To counter this, Shaw wrote a programme note, updating the economics in the play.

6.3.5 Shaw, the continued relevance of Mrs Warren: 1926

This play, after being witheld from public performance in England by the Censorship for thirty years, has at last been released (Heaven knows why!) too late, I am sorry to say to save Parliament from the folly of passing an Act which has only secured a monopoly of Mrs. Warren's trade to her sex by flogging all her male competitors.

On the recent experimental performance by The Macdona Players, the Press assured us all that we might now enjoy the play as a striking early specimen of my well-known artistic virtuosity, as of course the state of things it dramatizes has long since passed away. I was irresistibly reminded of the cheerful village boy who, when they told him the tragedy of the Gospels, said 'Oh well, since it happened so long ago and it's all so dreadful, let's hope it ain't true.'

If this play no longer had any relation to life I should not trouble the public with it now that I have so many riper and more delicate specimens of my workmanship to offer instead. But the truth is that the economic situation so forcibly demonstrated by Mrs. Warren remains as true as ever in essentials to-day. The fact that we now call Mrs. Warren's sister's eighteen shillings thirty-six, does not increase its purchasing power by one crumb. When the war came the late Mary Macarthur found women 'doing their bit' for twelve hours a day at twopence-halfpenny an hour. Strongly countenanced by a much more highly placed lady, whose name must not be dragged into this discussion, she put a stop to that particular atrocity; but it convicted us, twenty years after the date of my play, of making the wages of virtue lower than the wages of sin at a moment when the nation needed all its virtue very urgently. To be precise, the twopence-halfpenny is now sixpence-halfpenny, shewing that we still do everything for the virtue of British womanhood except pay for it.

In short, Mrs. Warren's profession is a vested interest; and when a woman of bold character and commercial ability applies to herself the commercial principles that are ruthlessly applied to her in the labour market, the result is Kitty Warren, whom I accordingly present to you. You will hear her justify

231

herself completely on those principles. Whether you and I, as citizens and voters, will be able to justify ourselves, in higher principles than those of commerce, for having made her justification not only possible but unanswerable, is another matter.

I cannot pretend to feel easy about it. Can you?

4 *HEARTBREAK HOUSE*

The play

Shaw later commented that the composition of *Heartbreak House* "began with an atmosphere" and – as he remarked in reaction to a presentation at the Oxford Playhouse in 1923, which distorted the play into "a farcical comedy" (Letter to H.K. Ayliff, 31 October 1923) – was conceived as "a quiet, thoughtful, semi-tragic play after the manner of Chekhov" (cited, Reginald Denham, *Stars in My Hair*, 1958). The Oxford director's presentation of *Heartbreak House* as a comedy, and Shaw's response, are strikingly similar to the disagreement between Stanislavsky and Chekhov over *The Cherry Orchard*, a play that had long impressed Shaw. He had urged its production in England as early as 1905, scornfully attacking the negative response of the audience when the Stage Society finally performed it in 1911. The elegiac mood of Chekhov's play was appropriate to Shaw's theme, since *Heartbreak House* was both a direct response to the First World War, and (as the Preface indicates) looked back to the world of "cultured, leisured Europe before the war" that was widely seen as bringing the end of European civilization.

Shaw began *Heartbreak House* in 1916, the year of the Battle of the Somme in which the death-toll reached unsurpassed heights. But the central figure as well as the setting was specifically rooted in pre-war experience, echoing a story Shaw was told by the actress Lena Ashwell in 1913. His initial title for the play was "Lena's Father" – a naval commander, who had retired to live on a sailing ship moored in the river Tyne that he had remodeled to include a drawing room and conservatory, and when dying refused to accept extreme unction unless cheese was put on the consecrated communion bread. The various titles for *Heartbreak House*, which changed during its composition more than any of his other plays, signal the difficulty Shaw had in dealing with the material. But each of the titles also provides insights into essential aspects of the theme.

While writing the script Shaw referred to it as "the Hushabye play" ("hush-abye" being a traditional refrain when rocking a baby to sleep), which relates to the willful ignorance of the characters who have shut their eyes to approaching disaster. It also explains the emphasis on sleep with one visitor (Ellie) dozing off, and another (Mangan) being put to sleep in a hypnotic trance. "The Soldier" – a poem by Rupert Brooke that had been read out in St. Paul's Cathedral after his death in 1915 – speaks of the war having "wakened us from sleeping" and Shaw's play can be seen as a response to that metaphor. Brooke, a leading member of the Cambridge Fabian Club before the war, now adopted as the voice of patriotic sacrifice, had come to represent the idealism that was Shaw's primary target in his earlier plays. This perhaps explains some of the underlying tone of despair in *Heartbreak House*, as well as being reflected in the apocalyptic hope of renewal expressed at the end of the play. If Fabian gradualism cannot survive such a war environment, then the only possibility of reform is through destruction of the social order (symbolized by the house).

The title for the first draft became *The House in the Clouds*, later *The Studio in the Clouds*, which encapsulates the sense of dreamlike unreality and disconnection that infects the inhabitants of this country house, and its connection with the artistic Bloomsbury group. Shaw started drafting the play while staying in a house-party at Sussex manor with the Woolfs and his fellow Fabians, the Webbs; and there are echoes of Virginia Woolf and her sister Vanessa Bell in the Shotover daughters, as well as the fantastically dressed Lady Ottoline Morrell in Hesione Hushabye. As Shaw subsequently wrote to Virginia Woolf, the concept of *Heartbreak House* was shaped by that weekend in June 1916 (Letter, 10 May 1940). Indeed the garden – from which they could hear the guns of the Somme offensive across the English Channel – which had a lamp post on the terrace (which Virginia Woolf described as casting a circle of light like the moon) as well as a quarry beyond the gardener's cottage, forms the setting for the last act of the play.

Shaw had been a leading contributor to the *New Statesman*, a newspaper founded by the Fabian Society, as well as a member of its board; at the time he was writing *Heartbreak House* he felt himself forced to resign. This may have been partly to protect the newspaper from the fallout after the publication of his *Commonsense About the War*, but it was also (Shaw's publicly stated position – due perhaps to a new sharpening of focus from working on the play) because he found himself identified with opinions about the war which he rejected, printed in its pages. A letter explaining his resignation to his co-Fabians, the Webbs, indicates the connections between some of the symbols in *Heartbreak House* and the political scene of the time, as well as providing insights into the ending of the play through Shaw's analysis of his own response to a Zeppelin bombing raid.

6.4.1 Letter to Beatrice and Sidney Webb, 5 October 1916

I have [. . .] written formally to the secretary to convey my resignation to the next meeting and regard me in the future as a simple shareholder. My withdrawal will be a great relief to everybody, probably;

[. . .]

As far as policy and tactics go, the paper is suburban-Tory-cum-Webb-Limited. It is now clear that it will never attack any minister who is not already the lower middle class butt of Blackheath and West Kensington. Lloyd George, as a little Radical Welsh attorney, or John Burns, as an upstart, will be mercilessly handled; but no blow will be struck at the towering crests, and this not because of conscious snobbery, but from a genuine awestruck inability to escape from the social prestige of the country house and the plutocrat-professionals. [. . .]

What I wanted, and still want, is a paper which will not only put in your articles and mine (which plenty of more widely circulated ones are only too anxious to do) but will fight for our policy; disable and discredit our opponents when it cannot convert them; use the events of every week to drive home our morals; and, above all, attack the big national idols, and do it with sufficient tact, generosity and gallantry to compel the tolerance and applause of the political world and the ideal old English spirit. [. . .] I do not expect it to believe in me, because after spending thirty years in keeping Englishmen from quarrelling, and steering them to their own ends without shipwreck on squabbles, and telling them the truth as far as human judgment is capable of the truth, I find that they remain invincibly persuaded that I am a mischief maker, a liar, and a wrecker

[. . .]

I foresee that the development of the war will sooner and later compel you to make your plans so topical that Sharp will find them inconsistent with his vision of a disarmed Germany and a Cecil-Chestertonic Last Judgment On The Huns. And then I shall observe with amusement your course.

The oddest thing about the whole business is that no Englishman seems to have any real concern for the future of England provided his immediate passions are gratified. It seems to me plain enough that Germany is going to be smashed to the extent of completely eliminating from European diplomacy that dread of her which has dominated the continent for years and produced and held together the Alliance. Nothing is more plainly printed across the skies than that the removal of that dread will operate on the Alliance like the removal of the string from a faggot; and that Germany, forced to relinquish her dream of a Pax Germanica and to seek alliances like other human species, will seek them either in the east with Russia or in the west with America. Also that the dread of Germany will be succeeded by the no less formidable bogey of the British Empire. Our position will then be an extremely critical one.

[. . .]

The Potters Bar Zeppelin manoeuvred over the Welwyn valley for about half an hour before it came round and passed Londonwards with the nicest precision over our house straight along our ridge tiles. It made a magnificent noise the whole time; and not a searchlight touched it, as it was the night-out of the Essenden and Luton lights. And not a shot was fired at it. I was amazed at its impunity and audacity. It sailed straight for London and must have got past Hatfield before they woke up and brought it down. The commander was such a splendid personage that the divisional surgeon and an officer who saw him grieved as for an only son. At two o'clock another

Zeppelin passed over Ayot; but we have no telephone, and nobody bothered. I went to see the wreck on my motor bicycle. The police were in great feather, as there is a strict cordon, which means that you cant get in without paying. The charges are not excessive, as I guess; for I created a ducal impression by a shilling. Corpses are extra, no doubt; but I did not intrude on the last sleep of the brave. What is hardly credible, but true, is that the sound of the Zepp's engines was so fine, and its voyage through the stars so enchanting, that I positively caught myself hoping next night that there would be another raid. I grieve to add that after seeing the Zepp fall like a burning newspaper, with its human contents roasting for some minutes (it was frightfully slow) I went to bed and was comfortably asleep in ten minutes. One is so pleased at having seen the show that the destruction of a dozen people or so in hideous terror and torment does not count. "I didnt half cheer, I tell you" said a damsel at the wreck. Pretty lot of animals we are!

[. . .]

ever

G.B.S

The play operates on various levels. There is a through-line relating to Shakespeare and Wagner, with Ellie reading *Othello*, and the moonlight reminding Hesione of *Tristan and Isolde*. The Othello image is picked up in Hesione's husband. However there are several other Shakespearean tragedies underlying the play. Shaw referred to *Heartbreak House* as his *King Lear*, and to the Shotover daughters as Goneril and Regan, while Ellie – who corresponds to Cordelia – is also conceived as Lady Macbeth (Letters to Lillah McCarthy, 10 August 1917, and to St John Ervine, 23 October 1921). Similarly the weaving together of recurrent motifs in the dialogue, as well as (in a different sense) the ending are Wagnerian, while Shaw described the pre-war sleep-world in which the characters are trapped as "a palace of enchantment, as in the second act of Parsifal" (Letter to J.C. Squire, 14 October 1919). However, the play is also essentially realistic, as even details like the age of various characters indicate.

The youngest male in the play "has an engaging air of being young and unmarried, but on close inspection is found to be at least over forty" as the stage directions specify. Although most of the action takes place before the war, the ending is designed to bring an audience face to face with the grim actualities of 1917 (the date Shaw completed the play) when all the men in their twenties and thirties were absent – either away at the Front, or increasingly missing in action, and dead. This also included the actors, since those who might have played younger parts were in uniform too; and as Shaw commented, "The hero is 88, and all the other men 50 or more, which of course suits the war conditions" (Letter to Lillah McCarthy, 10 August 1917). In addition, Shaw's explanation of the play to his Swedish translator, Hugo Valentin, emphasizes that the characters have real-life analogues and their social context is intended as an accurate depiction of actual conditions.

6.4.2 Bernard Shaw, Letter to Hugo Valentin, 27 October 1917

10 Adelphi Terrace WC2
27th October 1917

... I am still perplexed about Heartbreak House. It is a horrible symptom of old age in me that I am beginning to write quantities of stuff without being able to make up my mind to regard them as finished and publish them. [. . .] You say you do not understand it; but there is nothing to understand beneath the surface: it is a picture of a certain sort of life that our civilization tends to produce among people of exceptional vitality and sensibility, with such visitors as Lord Devonport (Mangan), the Foreign Office toff, the man who is poor because he is honest and has no push, meaning no greed or vulgar ambition, and the burglar who uses our obsolete and savage criminal system as an instrument of blackmail. The only part of society which is not a quicksand is the life of the equestrian country house class and the frankly autocratic Crown-Colony-Governing-Class extolled by the daughter of the house who happens to be born conventional. The old Captain is your prophet Jeremiah bawling the judgment of God on all this insanity. And you have the undercurrent of sex continually reproducing quicksand as fast as the welter tries to consolidate itself. That is the best account I can give you of it. I think what makes it puzzling is that the people seem to be so interesting and attractive and novel at first sight that one is led to expect great things from them; and when they are all reduced to absurdity, and even the solution of blowing them to bits misses fire, the spectator feels baffled and disappointed, as if something very promising had been wantonly spoilt.

[. . .]

ever
G.B.S

Heartbreak House: chronology of major early performances

November 1920 New York	The New York Theatre Guild Garrick Theatre Producer: Dudley Digges Designer: Lee Simsonson	Ellie Dunn: Elizabeth Risdon Captain Shotover: Albert Perry Hesione Hushabye: Effie Shannon Boss Mangan: Dudley Digges
October 1921 London	The Court Theatre Producers: Bernard Shaw and James B. Fagan Designers: James B. Fagan	Ellie Dunn: Ellen O'Malley Captain Shotover: Brember Wills Lady Utterwood: Edith Evans Hesione Hushabye: Mary Grey Boss Mangan: Alfred Clark

April 1932 London	Queen's Theatre Producer: H.K. Ayliff Designer: Paul Shelving	Ellie Dunn: Eileen Beldon Captain Shotover: Cedric Hardwicke Lady Utterwood: Edith Evans Hesione Hushabye: Margaret Chatwin Boss Mangan: Wilfrid Lawson
March 1937 London	Westminster Theatre Producer: Michael MacOwan	Ellie Dunn: Margaret Hood Captain Shotover: Cecil Trouncer Lady Utterwood: Agnes Lauchlan Hesione Hushabye: Mary Grey Boss Mangan: Mark Dignam
April 1938 New York	The Mercury Theatre Director: Orson Welles Designer: John Koenig	Ellie Dunn: Geraldine Fitzgerald Captain Shotover: Orson Welles Lady Utterword: Phyllis Joyce Hesione Hushabye: Mady Christians Boss Mangan: George Coulouris

Performance and reception

Lillah McCarthy, Granville Barker's wife who had acted leading roles in several of Shaw's plays including *Man and Superman* and *The Doctor's Dilemma*, had approached Shaw for permission to stage *Heartbreak House* in 1917. However, Shaw refused to have the play performed during the war; and the negative reaction to the text, published in 1919, continued his reluctance to allow a production. Ironically, the criticism was very much the same as the English reaction had been to *The Cherry Orchard*, which dismissed Chekhov's characters as incredible in an English context. Despite Shaw's insistence on the English focus in the subtitle – "A Fantasia in the Russian Manner upon English Themes" – J.C. Squire's comment was typical:

> his recent plays should be classified as 'Dramas of My Dotage.' A worse volume than his new collection (*Heartbreak House, Great Catherine*, and *Playlets of the War*, Constable, 6s. net) has never appeared under the name of a man of reputation . . . The characters in [*Heartbreak House*] are the most extraordinary collection of figments that ever failed to be produced on an English stage . . . It is no use Mr. Shaw saying that he meant to show them as to the last degree grotesque, for they represent nobody and satirize nobody. Until Mr. Shaw invented them such people – or such *simulacra* – never existed

on this earth, unless Shaw has found them in some monstrous half-world of inhuman cranks to which he alone has access . . . Had the play a vestige of reality it would be very nasty.

(*Land and Water*, 9 October 1919)

The reason for such vehemence was the perception that Shaw was indulging in "unseemly jeers" against "the dead or the bereaved" – and Shaw replied to this review, asserting "you think the war is over; but the sense of proportion has not yet been regained. Shame, guilt disillusion have upset it even more" (Letter to J.C. Squire, 14 October 1919). Because none of the connections (Bloomsbury, or Lord Devonport) were recognized, even when the critics saw some of the qualities in the play, these were misunderstood. For instance, several critics followed J. Middleton Murry – a strong supporter of Shaw's earlier work – who commented "all the characters seem to be scurrying around like lunatics" but drew the conclusion that this made the play itself ludicrous, a "fantastic farce". The parallel to Chekhov also created misunderstanding, as is clear from Murry's review:

Mr. Shaw . . . says that '"Heartbreak House" is not merely the name of the play . . . it is cultured, leisured Europe before the war.' All that we can reply is that we do not recognize it . . .

The comparison with 'The Cherry Orchard,' of which Mr. Shaw deliberately reminds us on the first page of his preface, could not possibly be escaped. It would in any case have leapt to the eye . . . There is not, as the mathematical logicians would say, a one-to-one correspondence between the futility of the Russian *intelligentsia* and our own; therefore a formula by which the one is completely expressed cannot be used to express the other. The corresponding object has to be seen and studied for itself. Instead of this we suspect that Mr. Shaw has projected the Russian formula on to English society. The result is chaos and pandemonium.

(*The Atheneum*, 17 October 1919)

As a result of such criticism, Shaw discouraged producers – such as Esmé Percy, who had staged the first complete version of *Man and Superman* – from performing *Heartbreak House*.

The first production took place in America, staged by the Theatre Guild in 1920. Even from across the Atlantic, Shaw exercised considerable control over the way the play was performed. The contract, drawn up by Shaw, specified that

[t]he Manager shall not in any performance of the said play . . . wilfully make or allow any alterations transpositions interpolations or omissions in or from the text . . . nor shall the Manager wilfully do or allow the performers to do anything that would have the effect of misrepresenting the Author's meaning either for better or for worse.

When the director (Emmanuel Reichler, the former managing director of the Berlin Volksbühne) requested cuts, Shaw threatened to cancel the contract, and asserted "the alternative to attracting audiences by pleasing them for two hours is to put the utmost strain on their serious attention for three, and sending them home exhausted but indelibly impressed" (Letter to Theresa Helburn, 21 October 1920). Reichler was replaced by Dudley Digges, who also played Mangan, and the script was performed in full. Shaw also sent sketches, stage plans and specifications for the scenery – which formed the basis for the setting designed by Lee Simonson, a founding member of the Theatre Guild who went on to design over half their productions and promote a style of simplified realism. His letter to Simonson provides a very exact visualization for both the physical setting and mood of *Heartbreak House*.

Further productions followed over the next year – in Vienna, followed by Sweden and England – and Shaw's correspondence, dealing particularly with the casting of the female roles, gives essential insights into the characters, and the balance between them. His letter to Tor Hedberg, the managing director of Kungliga Dramatiska Theatern in Stockholm, (though actually addressing his brother Karl Hedberg, who was staging the play) also helps to define the mood of the play. When Nigel Playfair – who had taken over the Lyric Theatre, where he was shortly to establish a brilliant reputation with a highly influential revival of John Gay's eighteenth-century *Beggar's Opera* – disagreed with Shaw's suggestion for casting Ellie, he withdrew the play. As he commented, Playfair "had made up his mind that Ellie must be a sweet little sexual attraction and that Hesione (Mrs. Hushabye) was the heavy part" (Letter to St. John Ervine, 23 October 1921).

Heartbreak House was taken over by James Fagan (whose wife played Hesione), with Shaw himself directing. His choice for Ellie was an Irish actress, Ellen O'Malley, whom he already had in mind for the part having seen her "playing Shakespeare with Barker at the Court" (*As You Like It* in 1904) as he explained to Arnold Bennett: "I gave her Ellie . . . because Ellie is technically the heavy lead in the play, just as I should give her Lady Macbeth" (20 October 1921). Shaw's reference to stock nineteenth-century acting roles – the "heavy", the "ingenue" – is a way of underlining that the character of Ellie does not correspond to a type; and his response to a reviewer who found Ellen O'Malley's Irish accent misplaced, provides further detail on the pivotal significance of her part:

Why the devil should Ellie Dunn seem in her element in Heartbreak House? I took the greatest care that she should not be – that she should be in the sharpest contrast to all the heartbreakers, and when she is lured into it she should walk over Hector and Hesione straight to the Captain, the positive efficient man on whose shoulders the whole structure is carried. The contrast is forced almost to discordance by having Ellie played by an Irish actress . . . I can only say that Ellen O'Malley presents Ellie Dunn precisely as I planned

Figure 6.4 Ellie Dunn and Captain Shotover, Act I, New York 1920

Figure 6.5 Waiting for the bombs in Act III, London 1921

her: the strong respectable woman of the play, virginal by contrast with the demon daughters, and yet audaciously passionate and imaginative.

(Letter to St. John Ervine, 28 October 1921)

There were problems with the production, partly due to a shortness of rehearsal time, which led to difficulties with pacing, as well as to technical delays (which were particularly obvious on the first night) due to faulty stage machinery. Shaw even suggested cuts to Fagan, and the actors were encouraged to speed up the delivery of their speeches. His letter to Ellen O'Malley (addressed to "Ellie-Ellen") focusses on this – but it also indicates the way her character is intended to develop and the type of balance Shaw considered necessary for the play's performance.

6.4.3 Bernard Shaw, Letter to Lee Simonson, 23 August 1920

To Lee Simonson

Parknasilla, Kenmare. Cork

23rd August

The XVII century Dutch marine pictures shew us lovely windows in brown woodwork with magnificent gilt framing, tall, handsome, with a balcony or stern gallery, gold in the framing, gold in the water, gold in the brown paint. They are set like this mostly except that they stand much higher above the water line, and are *very* ornamental. Now I know no picture which shews what they are like from the inside; so I have (or rather *you* have) to imagine what Captain Whatshisname would have imagined about them when he designed his house. As the captain is 150 years old or thereabouts his notions of naval architecture would not be more modern than those of the Flying Dutchman. Unfortunately I cannot draw; so I cannot help you out with a sketch; but I enclose a plan of the stage, and a rough view. The perspective and construction are impossible; but you can adapt them to 3-dimensional space. The mountains are like slate crags instead of Sussex hills; but that is what the inside of my envelopes gives me.

The difficulty of the arc light has bothered me all along. Here we use for street lighting (or used to) a white globe; and my first notion was to make it a very soft moon throwing a circle of light on the stage, so that the characters could, as directed, disappear into the surrounding darkness and emerge into the radiance. But, as you say, if you put even a candle in a dark scene the audience can see nothing else. I think you will have to shade the light (it need not be an arc) – drape it ornamentally or put a prosaic green tin to conceal the actual glare (there must be something that can be visibly extinguished) and do the real lighting off the stage.

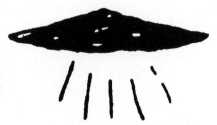

The observatory is a cupola. The top of the dome sticks up behind the first profile, and helps to suggest the ravine supposed to be between it and the back cloth.

The flagstaff is only an excuse for something characteristic to attach the cable which feeds the arc light. All these things are suggestions and makeshifts. So long as you do not alter or mask the positions of my people on the stage, or cut out an essential effect like the cutting off of the light and leaving the group in the dark, you may do your job in your own way. The more of your own you put in, the richer the play will be. You know, I take it, that comedy dialogue is impossible unless the faces of the speakers are seen quite distinctly. That is all you have to look out for as far as the author is concerned. For the rest, let yourself rip. Artist and author are co-equal and co-eternal – see the Athanasian creed.

[. . .]

PS Thanks for the pictures. They are VERY reassuring.

6.4.4 Bernard Shaw, Letter to Tor Hedberg, 27 September 1921

Miss Ebba Bystrom tells me that you are in some doubt as to how to handle Heartbreak House, and, in particular, that you want me to change the title.

I am quite aware that the play is a very puzzling one. In America a noted German producer who was engaged to direct the rehearsals said that nothing could make it presentable but drastic cutting. I immediately withdrew it. The managers thereupon dismissed the producer and pledged themselves to perform the play word for word exactly as it was written, whatever the consequences might be. The result was that it ran in New York for about 125 performances, drawing roughly Kr 3625 at each performance.

In Vienna the play was produced at the Burgtheater. It was not cut: but my instructions were disregarded; the atmosphere of the piece was missed; the sexually attractive parts were given to elderly actresses without charm and the virginal heroine given to the siren of the company. Result: the play was dropped after five performances.

I cannot sufficiently urge you not to attempt the play if you are not prepared to take it as it is, without the slightest modification to suit the taste of the public or the conventions of the theatre. I have not neglected these things in writing it: there is not a line that will not make its effect if it is properly delivered, and if the atmosphere which makes the play a picture of a house, an enchanted, amazing sort of house, is created. That is why the title is so important: if you take the title away and substitute the name of one of the characters, you will lose your way at once.

The casting is extremely important. The two sisters must be the most fascinating women you can find on the stage. Ariadne must be a brilliant comedian: Hesione must be irresistible. In contrast the girl Ellie must be perfectly virginal: her spiritual marriage with the old captain must be like the marriage by which a nun is made the bride of Christ. If you get the women right you will have no trouble with the men: their parts are easy and obvious. Even the old captain's part, though it is effective enough for a great actor, is not really difficult.

I am rehearsing the play in London just now myself, and can therefore speak from experience as to what can be done with it. I am a practical producer, and always handle the original productions of my plays in London myself. I do not write merely as a theatre poet whose work has to be handed to a *regisseur* to be adapted to the stage: my plays are written for the stage, and the stage business is as much a part of the play as the dialogue. If you will take the play as it is written and go through it with the company on the stage every day for a fortnight I think you will find that it will cease to be puzzling and that even the most unpromising parts of it will prove amusing and indispensible to the effect of the whole.

The successful American production, which ran for 125 performances over five months in 1920, established the Theatre Guild as one of New York's leading companies. It began the Theatre Guild's long association with Shaw, during which they staged almost all Shaw's plays up to *My Fair Lady*, the musical version of *Pygmalion* which they also commissioned, in 1952. By contrast, the reception of *Heartbreak House* when it finally reached the stage in London in October 1921 was extremely negative. In addition to the faults of the production, public opinion had already been set by the printed text. Around 20,000 copies had been published on both sides of the Atlantic in 1919. In addition to miscomprehension of the play itself in the reviews of the book, outrage had been caused by the preface. Even Lena Ashwell, the actress who had told Shaw the story of her father that became the inspiration for *Heartbreak House*, wrote an angry article accusing Shaw of traducing those who had sacrificed their lives in battle as well as ordinary people who had aided the war effort. Shaw's attitude to the criticisms – indicated by his reply to Lena Ashwell: "you said that I had attacked the soldiers. I did exactly the opposite: I shewed that the soldiers saved the situation while a noisy gang of civilians were disgracing us" (Letter, 31 October 1919) – was hardly designed to win public support. The two-year gap between publication and staging meant that many of the English audience would have already read and discussed the play before seeing it. Quite apart from the way the criticism of the published version might have conditioned the spectators' response, as one critic (*The Westminster Gazette*) remarked, there was little unexpected that could hold attention.

The abusive tone of the reviews is well represented by *The Sunday Times*:

It really was not Mr. Shaw's fault that we slept. He made all his characters shout and roar, bluster and scream. His piece is a series of interminable harangues, discussions, interjections, ejaculations, observations and verbal explosions dealing in a confused jumble with life, politics, ethics, manners and sex slavery. As a contribution to drama it is negligible. He finishes it with a bomb. If he had not, probably one of the audience would have done the job for him. The piece did not seem concludable otherwise. The noise of the bomb exploding might have awakened the seven sleepers of Ephesus, but it did not awaken one old gentleman to whom Mr. Shaw had administered a sleeping draught compared to which doses of poppy and mandragora were as the blackest coffee . . .

Some people may label all these crazy folk, these garrulous, inconsequential maunderers, drivellers and shouters of epigram, philosophy and balderdash as allegorical, but what possible parable can there be in such a mountain of rubbish.

(23 October 1921)

Even sympathetic reviewers – such as James Agate in the *Saturday Review* – missed Shaw's point, interpreting the play as a purely spiritual statement. However, the general tone was so clearly unfair that the editor of the *Sunday Express* published an appeal for the critics to re-evaluate the play, and a special matinée was scheduled for them to attend a month after the opening, at which another journalistic supporter (on the *Daily Express*) had arranged for Shaw to appear and debate the critics. This certainly revised opinions: the *Sunday Times* now described it as "an agreeable entertainment for the rabidly intellectual and a witty, shrewd – if over long – exposition of Shavian doctrines upon things in general and the English people in particular" (27 November 1921).

6.4.5 Reviews – New York versus London: *The New York Times*, 11 November 1920

With the first production on any stage of the new Shaw play called "Heartbreak House," the Theatre Guild recorded last evening its most ambitious effort and, all things considered, its most creditable achievement. At the Garrick this brilliant comedy is superbly mounted and, with one fairly insignificant exception, wisely and richly cast. An admirable play has been added to the season's rather scanty list and overnight that list has quite doubled in cerebral values.

"Heartbreak House," despite the doldrums of tedium into which its second act flounders toward the end, is quite the larkiest and most amusing one that Shaw has written in many a year, and in its graver moments the more familiar mood of Shavian exasperation gives way to accents akin to Cassandra's. Of course that second act seems the more wearing because of our habit and disposition to a lunch-counter tempo, even in the theatre, but inasmuch as the Theatre Guild is not permitted to tamper with the sacred text, it is too bad that its company should feel so oppressed by it.

A good many of last evening's blurred impressions can be traced to players so uneasily conscious of the play's unwonted length that they rattled nervously through their pieces. It will all go better when the conclusion is forced upon them that a mumbled scene may save time, but is the last device in the world to ward off boredom.

Heartbreak House is Shaw's Bunyanesque name for cultured, leisured England (or Europe, for that matter) before the war – as distinguished from that part of leisure England called Horseback Hall, wherein the stables are the real centre of the household, and wherein, if any visitor wants to play the piano, he must upset the whole room, there are so many things piled on it.

The play is his picture of the idly charming but viciously inert and detached people who dwell in Heartbreak House, using their hard-earned (by someone else) leisure to no purpose. They are loitering at the halfway station on the road to sophistication. They have been stripped of their illusions and pretense, but instead of using this freedom to some end they sit around naked and doing nothing, except, perhaps, catching moral colds.

The moral of the piece is spoken by Captain Shotover. It is always possible to find the clear, honest eyes of Bernard Shaw peering out from behind the thin disguise of one of his characters, and it is tempting in this comedy to identify him at times with this disconcerting and slightly mad old mariner whom the natives suspect of an ability to explode dynamite by looking at it. Captain Shotover is sick of a languid reliance on an overruling Providence. One of the casual ways of Providence with drunken skippers is to run them on the rocks. Not that anything happens, he hastily explains. Nothing but the smash of the drunken skipper's ship on the rocks, the splintering of her rotten timbers, the tearing of her rusty plates, the drowning of the crew like rats in a trap.

"And this ship that we are all in?" asks the heroic Hector. "This soul's prison we call England?"

"The Captain is in his bunk," retorts Captain Shotover, "drinking bottled ditch-water, and the crew is gambling in the forecastle. She will strike and sink, and split. Do you think the laws of God will be suspended in favor of England because you were born in it?"

No wonder the agitated Hector asks what he should do about it.

"Learn your business, as an Englishman," replies the Captain, tartly.

"And what may my business as an Englishman be, pray?"

"Navigation – Learn it and live, or leave it and be damned."

But just then the war visits Heartbreak House in the guise of an air raid that sounds from a distance like Beethoven. It enraptures some, alarms others, and a business man who had hidden too near the Captain's store of dynamite, destroys the rectory and passes on, leaving Heartbreak House not greatly changed, and with no firmer foundations than it had had before.

[. . .]

The air raid which jounces "Heartbreak House" out of its purely conversational vein is capitally managed at the Garrick and both the settings, by

Lee Simonson, are rich and beautiful. Indeed, they are almost too handsome. Somehow, a lovely investiture of a Shaw play seems a little incongruous – like perfuming the board room in a bank. The austerity of his text seems to chafe against the Simonson opulence as Shaw himself might rebel disgustedly at any *étalage de luxe*.

Saturday Review, 21 October 1921

Four hours of persistent button-holing at the Court Theatre convinced the dramatic critics that as a simple entertainment *Heartbreak House* was a failure. But what else it might be they did not try to find out.

[. . .]

When Whitman writes: 'I have said that the soul is not more than the body, And I have said that the body is not more than the soul, And nothing, not God, is greater to one than oneself is', we must either assent or dissent. Simply to cry out 'Whitmanesque!' is no way out. When Ibsen writes a play to prove that building happy homes for happy human beings is not the highest peak of human endeavour, leaving us to find out what higher summit there may be, he intends us to use our brains. It is beside the point to cry out 'How like Ibsen!' *Heartbreak House* is a re-statement of these two themes. You have to get Ibsen thoroughly in mind if you are not to find the Zeppelin at the end of Shaw's play merely monstrous. It has already destroyed the people who achieve; it is to come again to lighten the talkers' darkness, and at the peril of all the happy homes in the neighbourhood. You will do well to keep Whitman in mind when you hear the old sea-captain bellowing with a thousand different intonations and qualities of emphasis: 'Be yourself, do not sleep.' I do not mean, of course, that Shaw had these two themes actually in mind when he set about this maundering, Tchehovian rhapsody. But they have long been part of his mental make-up, and he cannot escape them or their implications. The difficulty seems to be in the implications. Is a man to persist in being himself if that self run counter to God, or the interests of parish, nation, the community at large? The characters in this play are nearer to apes and goats than to men and women. Shall they nevertheless persist in being themselves, or shall they pray to be Zeppelin-destroyed and born again? The tragedy of the women is the very ordinary one of having married the wrong man. But all these men – liars and humbugs, ineffectual, hysterical, neurasthenic – are wrong men. The play, in so far as it has a material plot, is an affair of grotesque and horrid accouplements. It is monstrous for the young girl to mate in any natural sense with a, superficially considered, rather disgusting old man. Shall she take him in the spirit as a spiritual mate? Shaw holds that she shall, and that in the theatre even spiritual truth shall prevail over formal prettiness. [. . .]

As this world goes [the old sea-captain] is mad. With him we are to climb Solness's steeple [in Ibsen's *Masterbuilder*] all over again, to catch at 'harps in the air'. To ears not ghostly attuned he talks a jargon nigh to nonsense; yet through him booms the voice of that restless Force which is Shaw's conception of God. [. . .]

The play stands or falls exactly as we get or miss this spiritual hang. As an entertainment pure and simple it is dull and incoherent – even for Shaw. It has all the author's prolixities and perversities. It has the old fault of combining thinking on a high level with joking on a low one. There is the old confusion of planes. There is the plane upon which the old man and the young girl, spiritual adventurers both, after the manner of Solness and Hilda Wangel, are fitting spiritual mates; but there is also the plane upon which the girl says: 'I am his white wife; he has a black one already.' The play is full of the 'tormented unreticence of the very pure'. Spirituality chambers with lewdness revealed: beauty beds with nastiness which any but the nicest mind had instinctively avoided. On all planes but the highest these people induce nausea. Throughout the evening Stevenson's 'I say, Archer – my God, what women!' came to mind over and over again. 'What a captain!' one said in ecstasy, but in the next breath, 'What a crew!' This, however, was merely the expression of a predilection. Shaw is concerned with the salvation of all his characters. Nowhere in this play do I find him with his tongue in his cheek. I refuse to believe that his Zeppelin is an irrelevant joke, a device for waking the audience up. If I did not take the author to be perfectly serious I should dismiss the play as a senile impertinence. I found it quite definitely exhilarating and deeply moving, and it therefore ranks for me among the great testaments. When I saw it at the Court Theatre it was admirably acted. The old captain of Mr. Brember Wills was magnificently distraught – Ibsen and Shaw, Whitman and General Booth rolled into one.

*

Lawrence Langner, himself a playwright, co-founder of the Washington Square Players that had introduced Chekhov and Eugene O'Neill to the New York stage, and (with Theresa Helburn) one of the main producers of the Theatre Guild, had a vision of the play's relevance to the post-war world of 1920. This carried over into the successful American production of *Heartbreak House* by bringing a new note of seriousness to the ending through projecting Shaw's message into the future.

The play's last scene with giant bombers droning over London [sic] was prophetic enough to make many of us feel uncomfortable, and even more of us scared to death, notwithstanding the fact that we had just won a war 'to make the world safe for democracy,' as the high-sounding slogan of Woodrow Wilson succinctly put it . . . Shaw sounded a warning blast against the possible world destruction which would ensue if mankind continued to fail to find a remedy other than war for disputes among nations.

(*G.B.S. and the Lunatic*, 1963)

The play as such specifically deals with Edwardian society and their moral responsibility for the First World War, which provided the immediate context for the apocalypse foreseen in the ending. However, it is this prophetic interpretation that has made *Heartbreak House* one of the most produced of Shaw's plays since it was revived by Robert Donat in 1943, in the middle of yet another world war. In the aftermath of German air raids that had destroyed great areas of London and burnt the Houses of Parliament no updating was necessary for the ending to be immediately relevant. Langner commented in his memoirs that "Three times in my own life I have witnesses periods when this play was topical the last being now upon us" (1963). This was the "Cold War" threat of nuclear Armageddon, which was at its height in the early 1960s; there were modern productions that made this nuclear parallel explicit in the staging of the final scene. However, one of the more interesting productions – by Harold Clurman at the Billy Rose Theatre, New York, in 1959 – resisted obviously updating the play.

While Clurman's other writings show his awareness of the danger of nuclear annihilation, this only carried over into his production in what he defined as the "spine" of the play's action – "to get the hell out of this place" – which led him to exaggerate the zany behavior of the characters. In an oblique reference to the then current military doctrine of MAD (Mutual Assured Destruction – which provoked such films as the black farce of *Dr. Strangelove* depicting an America ruled by certifiable madmen) the world of Heartbreak House was presented as a lunatic asylum. As Clurman commented in his preparatory notes for the production, the inhabitants of Heartbreak House "are all aware that they are living in a loony world, which they are expected to take seriously – but can't. As they progress they become aware of the need to act mad in order to approximate reality. To achieve their liberation – their world must be destroyed."

SELECTED CRITICAL
BIBLIOGRAPHY

Henrik Ibsen

Clurman, Harold. *Ibsen*. New York: Macmillan, 1977.

Durbach, Errol. *Ibsen and the Theatre: The Dramatist in Production*. New York: New York University Press, 1980.

Haugen, Einar. *Ibsen's Drama: Author to Audience*. Minneapolis: University of Minneapolis Press, 1979.

McFarlane, James, ed. *The Cambridge Companion to Ibsen*. Cambridge: Cambridge University Press, 1994.

Marker, Frederick J. and Lise-Lone. *Ibsen's Lively Art*. New York: Cambridge University Press, 1989.

May, Keith M. *Ibsen and Shaw*. New York: St. Martin's Press, 1985.

Meyer, Michael. *Ibsen: A Biography*. Harmondsworth: Penguin, 1974.

Northam, John. *Ibsen: A Critical Study*. London: Cambridge University Press, 1973.

—— *Ibsen's Dramatic Method: A Study of the Prose Dramas*. Oslo: Universitetsforlaget, 1971.

Templeton, Joan. *Ibsen's Women*. Cambridge: Cambridge University Press, 1997.

Theoharis, Constantine. *Ibsen's Drama: Right Action and Tragic Joy*. New York: St. Martin's Press, 1996.

Anton Chekhov

Carlile, Cynthia and Sharon McKee, trans. *Anton Chekhov and His Times.* Andrei Turkov, ed. Fayetteville: University of Arkansas, 1995.

Gilles, Daniel. *Chekhov: Observer Without Illusion.* New York: Funk & Wagnalls, 1968.

Gillman, Richard. *Chekhov's Plays: An Opening into Eternity.* New Haven, CT: Yale University Press, 1995.

Koteliansky, S.S., trans. and ed. *Anton Chekhov: Literary and Theatrical Reminiscences.* New York: Blom, 1968.

Magarshack, David. *Chekhov the Dramatist.* London: Eyre Methuen, 1952.

Miles, Patrick, ed. *Chekhov on the British Stage.* Cambridge: Cambridge University Press, 1993.

Peace, Richard. *Chekhov: A Study of the Four Major Plays.* New Haven, CT: Yale University Press, 1983.

Rayfield, Donald. *Chekhov: The Evolution of His Art.* New York: Harper, 1975.

Senelick, Laurence. *The Chekhov Theatre: A Century of Plays in Performance.* Cambridge: Cambridge University Press, 1997.

Styan, J.L. *Chekhov in Performance.* Cambridge: Cambridge University Press, 1971.

Valency, Maurice. *The Breaking String: The Plays of Anton Chekhov.* New York: Schocken, 1983.

Bernard Shaw

Berst, Charles A. *Bernard Shaw and the Art of Drama*. Urbana: University of Illinois Press, 1973.

Dukore, Bernard F. *Bernard Shaw, Director*. Seattle: University of Washington Press, 1971.

Crompton, Louis. *Shaw the Dramatist*. Lincoln: University of Nebraska Press, 1969.

Gainor, J. Ellen. *Shaw's Daughters: Dramatic and Narrative Constructions of Gender*. Ann Arbor: University of Michigan Press, 1991.

Holroyd, Michael. *Bernard Shaw*. New York: Random House, 1988.

Innes, Christopher, ed. *The Cambridge Companion to George Bernard Shaw*. Cambridge: Cambridge University Press, 1998.

Lorichs, Sonja. *The Unwomanly Woman in Bernard Shaw's Drama and Her Social and Political Background*. Uppsala: University of Uppsala, 1973.

May, Keith M. *Ibsen and Shaw*. New York: St. Martin's Press, 1985.

Meisel, Martin. *Shaw and the Nineteenth-Century Theatre*. Princeton: Princeton University Press, 1969.

Peters, Margot. *Bernard Shaw and the Actresses*. Garden City, NY: Doubleday, 1980.

Peters, Sally. *Bernard Shaw: The Ascent of the Superman*. New Haven, CT: Yale University Press, 1996.

Weintraub, Stanley. *Journey to Heartbreak: The Crucible Years of Bernard Shaw, 1914–1918*. New York: Weybright and Talley, 1971.

Wisenthal, J. L. *The Marriage of Contraries: Bernard Shaw's Middle Plays*. Cambridge: Harvard University Press, 1974.

INDEX

Bold numbers indicate extracts